D1591563

2

Life

SECOND EDITION

NATIONAL GEOGRAPHIC
LEARNING

JOHN HUGHES
HELEN STEPHENSON
PAUL DUMMETT

Australia · Brazil · Mexico · Singapore · United Kingdom · United States

Contents

Listening	Reading	Critical thinking	Speaking	Writing
a photographer talking about a diver an interview with an explorer people starting college	an article about a family of explorers an article about world population	types of text	asking questions friends and family facts about countries	text type: a personal description writing skill: *and, but*
someone talking about a family's plastic possessions an interview with Andy Torbet	an article about four apartments in Seoul an article about a global product	reading closely	a room in your home your possessions where things are from	a description of a room in your home text type: ads writing skill: describing objects with adjectives
someone talking about a famous meeting place in Melbourne an interview with a student living in New York three people talking about their jobs	an article about car-free zones an article about languages spoken around the world	main ideas and supporting information	your life exchanging information about a photographer your languages	text type: a description of a place writing skill: capital letters
three people talking about their free-time activities an interview with Norbert Rosing	an article about identical twins an article about extreme sports volunteer work	fact or opinion	likes and dislikes saying how often you do things your abilities	text type: short emails writing skill: reference words
someone talking about street food in Oaxaca people describing famous dishes from their countries a conversation at a market	an article about food markets around the world an article about labels on food	ways of giving advice	famous dishes from your country planning a special meal buying food at a market advice about healthy eating	advice about healthy eating text type: instructions writing skill: punctuation
someone talking about photographs showing how lives have changed a documentary about a woman who lived in a cave three people describing their evening	an article about famous people from the past an article about lifelogging	for or against?	describing someone's life talking about what you did over the weekend a survey about lifelogging	a description of someone's life text type: thank you messages writing skill: formal and informal expressions

Listening	Reading	Critical thinking	Speaking	Writing
someone talking about the journey of a ladybug / a documentary about a journey to the deepest place on Earth	an article about animal journeys / an article about Colombia's cities	writing for the reader	your opinion / places you know	a paragraph about your town / text type: a travel blog post / writing skill: *so* and *because*
someone describing the Dinagyang festival / a description of two photos of a festival	an article about a fashion business / an article about boys' and girls' color choices	is it in the text?	festivals in your town/city / your life at the moment / people's appearance / opinion of an article	text type: short messages / writing skill: the KISS rules
someone talking about a photo / two people at a film festival / the future of TV / two people discussing a Broadway show	an article about the Tallgrass Film Festival / an article about nature in art	the writer's preferences	deciding which movies to see / your future plans / explaining your preferences	text type: reviews / writing skill: giving your opinion with sense verbs
someone talking about a place for learning / a news report about a memory champion / someone calling his office	an article about what scientists have learned / tips about memory techniques / an article about good learning habits	supporting the main idea	experiences with learning / explaining memory techniques / talking about learning / giving advice about good habits and routines	advice about good habits and routines / text type: a telephone message / writing skill: imperatives
a man talking about his experience in Jordan / a podcast from a travel program / two friends discussing a trip to South America	a tourist information brochure / a questionnaire from a travel magazine / a travel article	reasons for and against	rules / advice for a tourist / a tourist destination / what's important in a hotel	a description of a tourist destination / text type: a questionnaire / writing skill: closed and open questions
a documentary about a photographer / a radio show about unexplored places on Earth	an article and a map about climate change / an article about finding a new planet / an article about Earth Day	the writer's opinion	predictions about the future / places on Earth / life on another planet / places you'd like to visit	predictions about the future / text type: an announcement / writing skill: important words and information

Life around the world—in 12 videos

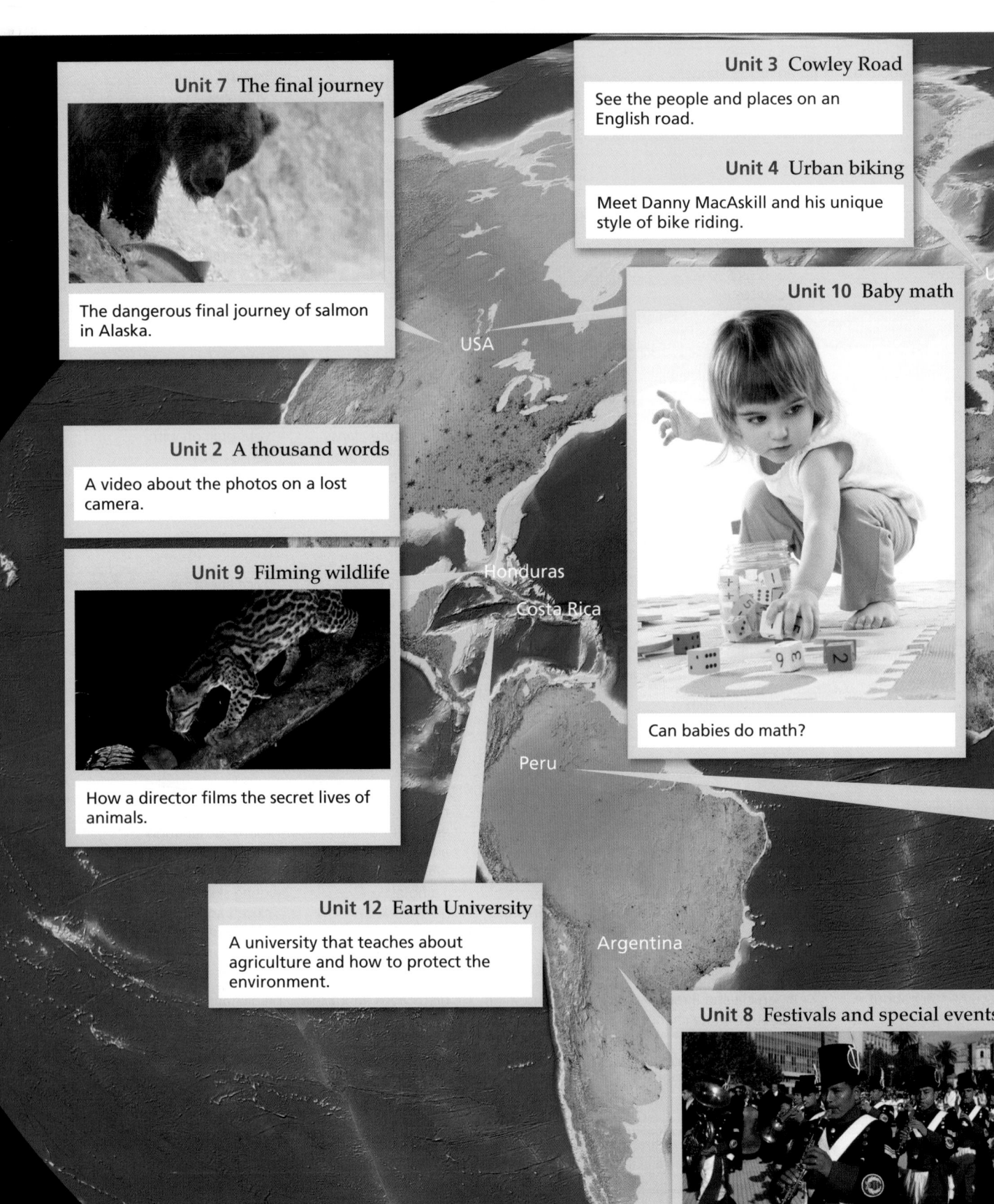

Unit 7 The final journey

The dangerous final journey of salmon in Alaska.

Unit 3 Cowley Road

See the people and places on an English road.

Unit 4 Urban biking

Meet Danny MacAskill and his unique style of bike riding.

Unit 10 Baby math

Can babies do math?

Unit 2 A thousand words

A video about the photos on a lost camera.

Unit 9 Filming wildlife

How a director films the secret lives of animals.

Unit 12 Earth University

A university that teaches about agriculture and how to protect the environment.

Unit 8 Festivals and special events

Visit some of the world's most colorful festivals.

UK

USA

Honduras

Costa Rica

Peru

Argentina

Unit 1 World party

How big is seven billion?

Unit 6 Objects from the past

A video about three different people's important objects from the past.

Russia

Japan

India

Unit 5 The world food quiz

A video quiz about foods around the world.

Unit 11 Tiger tourism

Can tourism help protect India's wildlife?

UNIT 1
PEOPLE

UNIT 2
POSSESSIONS

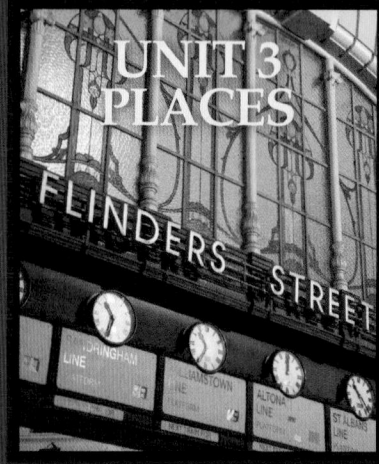

UNIT 3
PLACES

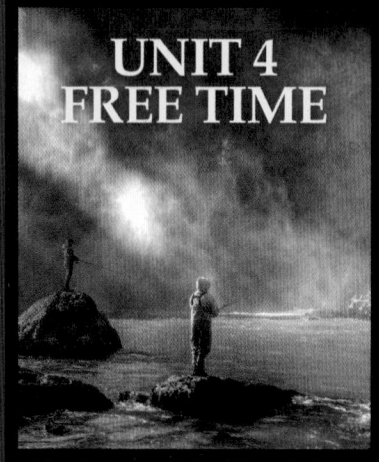

UNIT 4
FREE TIME

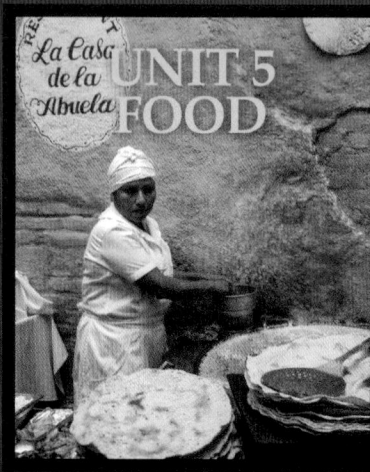

UNIT 5
FOOD

UNIT 6
PAST LIVES

UNIT 7
JOURNEYS

UNIT 8
APPEARANCE

UNIT 9
ENTERTAINMENT

UNIT 10
LEARNING

UNIT 11
TOURISM

UNIT 12
THE EARTH

Dinah Halstead is in Milne Bay, Papua New Guinea. She's a diver.

FEATURES

1 Look at the photo and the caption. Where is Dinah? What's her job?

2 ▶ 1 Match the answers with the questions. Then listen to an interview with the photographer. Check your answers.

1 What's your name? ○   ○ a   The US.
2 Where are you from? ○   ○ b   Her name's Dinah Halstead.
3 What's her name?   ○   ○ c   She's from Papua New Guinea.
4 Where's she from?   ○   ○ d   David Doubilet.

3 Work in pairs. Ask and answer these questions.

A: Hello. What's your name?
B: My name's …
A: Where are you from?
B: I'm from …

4 Work with another pair. Ask and answer these questions.

A: What's his/her name?
B: His/Her name's …
C: Where's he/she from?
D: He/She's from …

1a Explorers

Dereck and Beverley Joubert
in Botswana

Listening

1 Work in pairs. What can you see in the photo?

2 ▶ 2 Listen to an interview with Beverley Joubert. Circle the correct option.

1 Beverley Joubert is a *photographer / doctor*, explorer, and filmmaker.
2 Dereck Joubert is her *brother / husband*.
3 They are from *Africa / Australia*.

Vocabulary **personal information**

3 Complete this chart with information from Exercise 2 about Beverley and Dereck.

First name	Beverley	Dereck	You
Last name	1 _____	2 _____	_____
Job/Occupation	3 _____	explorer and filmmaker	_____
Place of birth	4 _____	5 _____	_____
Married or single?	6 _____	married	_____
Relationship	wife	7 _____	

4 Add information about you to the chart in Exercise 3.

Grammar *be* (*am/is/are*)

▶ *BE (AM/IS/ARE)*

Affirmative
I'm a photographer. ('m = am)
You/We/They're married. ('re = are)
He/She/It's from South Africa. ('s = is)

Negative
I'm not a journalist. ('m not = am not)
You/We/They aren't single. (aren't = are not)
He/She/It isn't from South America. (isn't = is not)

Questions and short answers
What's your name?
My name's Chiho.
Where are they from?
They're from Argentina.
How old is he?
He's 23.
Are you from Botswana?
Yes, I am. / No, I'm not.
Is she single?
Yes, she is. / No, she isn't.

For more information and practice, see page 158.

5 Look at the grammar box. Complete the information with the correct forms of the verb *be*.

   a affirmative: I _____ , you _____ , he _____
   b negative: I _____ , we _____ , she _____
   c questions: _____ you ...? _____ he ...?
   d short answers: Yes, I _____ . Yes, it _____ . No, you _____ . No, he _____ .

6 ▶3 Circle the correct options to complete the conversation. Then listen and check.

   A: Hello. What ¹ *are / 's* your name?
   B: My name's Mike Burney.
   A: ² *Are / Is* you married?
   B: Yes, ³ *I'm / I am*. My wife's name is Sally. She ⁴ *aren't / isn't* here today.
   A: What's her job?
   B: ⁵ *She're / She's* a teacher. ⁶ *I'm / I's* also a teacher.
   A: Are you both from the United States?
   B: No, we ⁷ *isn't / aren't*. I'm from the US, but Sally is from Canada.
   A: And how old ⁸ *are / 's* you?
   B: I'm thirty-six.
   A: Is Sally also thirty-six?
   B: No, she ⁹ *'m not / isn't*. She's thirty-five.

7 Pronunciation contractions

a ▶4 Listen to eight sentences. Circle the form you hear.

   1 'm   am
   2 're   are
   3 'm not   am not
   4 's   is
   5 aren't   are not
   6 're   are
   7 isn't   is not
   8 's   is

b ▶4 Listen again and repeat the sentences.

8 ▶5 Complete the conversation at an airport with the correct form of *be*. Use contractions where possible. Then listen and check.

   A: Good afternoon. ¹_____ you in New Zealand for work or a vacation?
   B: For work. I ²_____ a photographer.
   A: I see. What ³_____ your address in Auckland?
   B: We ⁴_____ at 106a Eglinton Road.
   A: We?
   B: Yes, I'm with my wife and two children. They ⁵_____ also here.
   A: ⁶_____ your wife also a photographer?
   B: Yes, she is, but she ⁷_____ in Auckland for work. She ⁸_____ here for a vacation.

Speaking myLife

9 Write questions with these words.

   1 what / first name?
      What's your first name?
   2 what / last name?
      _____
   3 are / student?
      _____
   4 what / job?
      _____
   5 where / from?
      _____
   6 how old / you?
      _____
   7 are / married?
      _____

10 Work in pairs. Ask and answer your questions from Exercise 9.

   A: *Are you a student?*
   B: *No, I'm not.*
   A: *What's your job?*
   B: *I'm a teacher.*

11 Introduce your partner to the class.

   Rosana's from Chile. She's a photographer.

1b A family in Kenya

Reading

1 Work in pairs. Is your family big or small? Where are all the people in your family?

2 Read about the Leakey family. Work in pairs. Answer the questions.

   1 Where does the Leakey family live?
   2 Are Louise and Meave explorers?
   3 What is Richard's job?
   4 What is Colin's job?
   5 Is Philip married?
   6 Is Katy an explorer?

3 Read the article again and complete the family tree.

A family in KENYA

▶ 6

The Leakey family lives in Kenya. Louise Leakey is an explorer, but for her family that's normal! Louise's mother, Meave, is also an explorer. Louise's father is Richard Leakey. Richard is a conservationist.[1] Richard's half-brother[2] is Colin Leakey. Colin isn't in Africa. He's retired[3] and he lives in England. Louise's grandparents (Louis and Mary) were also famous explorers. Louise's sister is Samira. Their uncle and aunt are Phillip Leakey and his wife Katy. They have an international company.

¹conservationist (n) /ˌkɒnsərˈveɪʃ(ə)nɪst/ someone who looks after nature
²half-brother (n) /ˌhɑːf ˈbrʌðər/ brother with one different parent
³retired (adj) /rɪˈtaɪərd/ no longer working

Louis Leakey
(1903–1972)

¹_____ Leakey
(1913–1996)

²_____ Leakey
(1933–)

³_____ Leakey
(1944–)

Meave Leakey
(1942–)

Phillip Leakey
(1949–)

⁴_____ Leakey

Louise Leakey
(1972–)

⁵_____ Leakey
(1974–)

Meave Leakey and her daughter Louise

12

Vocabulary family

4 Look at these family words. Which are men (M)? Which are women (W)? Which are both (B)?

aunt ____	cousin ____	grandparent ____
father ____	mother ____	half-brother ____
uncle ____	niece ____	mother-in-law ____
parent ____	nephew ____	stepbrother ____

5 Write the correct words from Exercise 4.

1 your father's brother and sister: _____ , _____

2 your brother's daughter and son: _____ , _____

3 your uncle and aunt's son or daughter: _____

4 a brother, but from one different parent: _____

5 your husband's or wife's mother: _____

6 your mother or father: _____

7 your parent's mother or father: _____

> ▶ **WORDBUILDING word roots**
>
> You can make more words from a root word.
> For example: *mother* → *grandmother, stepmother, mother-in-law*
>
> For more practice, see Workbook page 11.

6 Look at the wordbuilding box and the words in Exercise 5. Make six more words with the root words *sister* and *father*.

Grammar possessive 's and possessive adjectives

> ▶ **POSSESSIVE 'S AND POSSESSIVE ADJECTIVES**
>
> **Possessive 's**
> *Mike's wife is a teacher. Mike and Sally's home is in Canada.*
> Note: 's is also the contracted form of *is*.
>
> **Possessive adjectives**
>
> | subject pronoun | possessive adjective | subject pronoun | possessive adjective |
> |---|---|---|---|
> | I | my | we | our |
> | you | your | | |
> | he | his | they | their |
> | she | her | | |
> | it | its | | |
>
> *She's **my** sister. What's **your** name? **His** name is Charlie.*
>
> For more information and practice, see page 158.

7 Look at the grammar box. Then underline five examples of the possessive 's and three possessive adjectives in the article on page 12.

8 ▶7 Circle the correct word to complete the sentences. Then listen and check.

1 *I / My* parents are Spanish.
2 *I / My* am the only boy in my family.
3 What's *you / your* name?
4 Where are *you / your* from?
5 *She / Her* is a photographer.
6 *He / His* uncle is in the US.
7 *We / Our* family is from Asia.
8 *They / Their* cousins are both girls.

9 **Pronunciation the same or different sounds**

▶8 Listen to these pairs of words. Is the pronunciation the same (S) or different (D)?

1	they're / their	S	D
2	he's / his	S	D
3	its / it's	S	D
4	are / our	S	D
5	you're / your	S	D

10 ▶9 Complete the description of a person's family and friends with these words. Then listen and check.

her	her	his	my	their

> My family lives in Australia. ¹_____ mother is from Ireland and ²_____ three sisters (my aunts) live there. My father is from Australia and he's a businessman. My sister's name is Orla, and she's a teacher. She's married, and ³_____ husband is Tim. He's also a teacher. ⁴_____ children are Rory and Jack. My best friend is Peter. ⁵_____ father and my father have a company together.

Speaking my**Life**

11 Write the names of five friends or people in your family. Introduce them to your partner.

*Karina is **my** best friend. She's from Argentina. Stefan and Illona are **my** two cousins in Germany. They're **my** mother's nephew and niece.*

1c The face of seven billion people

Speaking

1 Pronunciation saying numbers and percentages

▶ **10** Listen and repeat these numbers and percentages.

1 billion	1.3 billion	3.5 billion	5.5 billion
7 billion	23%	38%	51%

Reading

2 Read the text about the people in the world and write the numbers in Exercise 1 next to the information (1–8).

1 the number of people in the world _____
2 the population of India _____
3 the number of speakers of English as a second language _____
4 the percentage of Muslims _____
5 the percentage of workers in agriculture _____
6 the percentage of people living in cities _____
7 the number of people with the internet _____
8 the number of people with a cell phone _____

Critical thinking types of text

3 Read the text again. What type of text is it? Circle the correct option (a–c).

a a text with facts
b a text with opinions
c a story

4 Which information in the text is new or surprising for you? Tell the class.

Vocabulary everyday verbs

5 Find these verbs in the text. Then complete the fact file about China with the verbs.

live	speaks	use	works

FACT FILE: China

- 1.4 billion people [1]_____ in China.
- 70% of the population [2]_____ Mandarin Chinese.
- 25% of the population [3]_____ in agriculture.
- 55% of Chinese people [4]_____ the internet.

Word focus *in*

6 Match the sentences (1–4) with the uses of *in* (a–c).

1 21 million people live in Mexico City. ____
2 There are 127 million people in Japan. ____
3 40% of the population works in the service industry. ____
4 49% live in the countryside. ____

a *in* + a country
b *in* + a city or region
c *in* + a type of work or industry

7 Write three sentences about people in your country using *in*.

Speaking *my*Life

8 Work in pairs.

Student A: Turn to page 154.

Student B: Turn to page 156.

Read the information in your chart. Then ask and answer questions to find out the missing information and complete your chart.

9 Work in pairs. How many people are in your:

- country?
- town or city?
- English class?
- family?
- school / place of work?

A: There are five people in my family.
B: There are sixty-five million people in my country.

14

THE FACE OF SEVEN BILLION PEOPLE

▶ 11

There are seven billion people in the world, and there are seven thousand people in this photo. Each person in the photo is equal to[1] one million people.

AGE
The average[2] age of all the people in the world is 28.

POPULATION
Twenty percent of the world's population lives in China. There are 1.3 billion people in India.

LANGUAGE
Fourteen percent of the world's population speaks Mandarin as their first language. Six percent speaks Spanish as their first language. Six percent speaks English as their first language, but English is a second language for one billion people.

RELIGION
There are many different religions in the world. For example, thirty-one percent of the world is Christian, twenty-three percent is Muslim, and fifteen percent is Hindu.

JOBS
Forty percent of people work in a service industry (hotels, banks, etc.), thirty-eight percent in agriculture, and twenty-two percent in manufacturing and production.

CITY AND COUNTRYSIDE
Fifty-one percent of the world's population lives in cities and forty-nine percent lives in the countryside.

INTERNET AND CELL PHONES
3.5 billion people in the world use the internet, and 5.5 billion people have a cell phone.

[1] **(is) equal (to)** /ˈiːkwəl/ the same as (e.g., two and two equals four)
[2] **average** (adj) /ˈævərɪdʒ/ usual, typical

1d The first day

Real life meeting people for the first time

3 ▶ 13 It's the first day for students at a college in the US. Listen to two conversations with Rita, Miguel, and Valérie. Answer these questions.

- Which two people are new students?
- Which person works at the college?

4 ▶ 13 Listen again. Choose the correct option to complete the sentences.

Conversation one
1   This is their *first / second* meeting.
2   Miguel's last name is *Ferreira / Pereira*.

Conversation two
3   Valérie's last name is *Moore / Moreau*.
4   *Valérie / Miguel* says goodbye to Rita.
5   Valérie is from *France / New Caledonia*.

5 ▶ 13 Look at the expressions for meeting people for the first time. Then listen again and circle the expressions you hear.

▶ MEETING PEOPLE	
Introducing yourself	**Introducing another person**
Hello ... / Hi ...	This is ...
My name's ... / I'm ...	He's / She's from ...
I'm from ...	**Saying goodbye**
Nice to meet you.	See you later.
Nice to meet you, too.	It was nice meeting you.
	Goodbye. / Bye.

6 Work in groups of three: A, B, and C. Practice the conversation. Then change roles and repeat the conversation two more times.

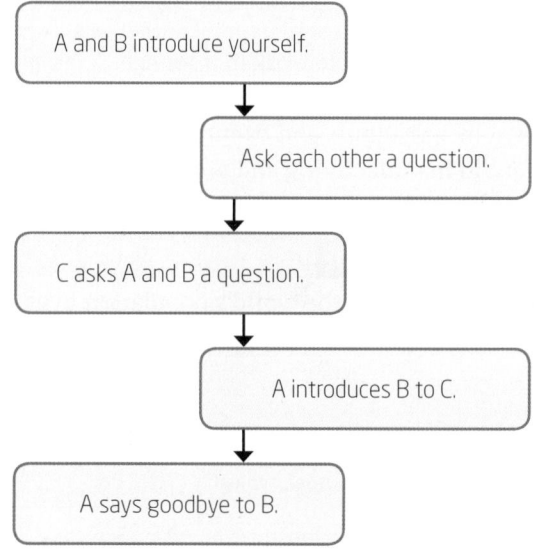

A and B introduce yourself.

↓

Ask each other a question.

↓

C asks A and B a question.

↓

A introduces B to C.

↓

A says goodbye to B.

Speaking

1 Pronunciation spelling

▶ 12 Listen and repeat the letters of the alphabet.

A B C D E F G H I J K L M N
O P Q R S T U V W X Y Z

2 Work in pairs. Ask your partner to spell these words. Listen and write the words. Check your partner's spelling.

- your first name
- your last name
- your country
- your job

A: Can you spell your first name?
B: It's Pablo. P-A-B-L-O.
A: Can you repeat that?
B: Sure. P-A-B-L-O.

1e Introduce yourself

Writing a personal description

1 Read the personal descriptions of Miguel and Valérie. Check (✓) the information they write.

	Miguel	Valérie
First name		
Last name		
Job/Occupation		
Home country/place		
Language		
Family		

MIGUEL FERREIRA

Hi! My name's Miguel Ferreira and I'm a student. I'm from Brazil, but I study at a university in the US. I'm single and I have two brothers.

VALÉRIE MOREAU

Hello. I'm Valérie Moreau and I'm from New Caledonia. It's a beautiful island in the Pacific Ocean. We speak French in New Caledonia, but I also speak English and Spanish.

2 Writing skill *and* and *but*

a Work in pairs. Look at the words *and* and *but* in the personal descriptions in Exercise 1. Which word is for extra information? Which word is for a difference?

b Rewrite the two sentences as one sentence. Use *and* or *but*.

1 I live in Spain. I'm from Argentina.
   I live in Spain, but I'm from Argentina.

2 I'm 21. My sister is 21.
   My sister and I are 21.

3 I'm Australian. I wasn't born in Australia.
   _____

4 He's from Germany. He speaks three languages.
   _____

5 My friend is 30. He's a teacher.
   _____

6 I have a sister. I don't have a brother.
   _____

7 She's a student. She's at Tokyo University.
   _____

8 My family lives in the countryside. I live in the city.
   _____

3 Write a personal description of yourself in the space in Exercise 1. Include all the information in the chart. Use *and* and *but*.

4 Work in pairs. Exchange your descriptions. Use these questions to check your partner's description.
   - Does the description include all the information from Exercise 1?
   - Does it use *and* and *but* correctly?

5 Display your descriptions around the classroom. Walk around and read about the other students in your English class.

九龙壁

Chinese New Year in Singapore

Before you watch

1 Work in pairs. Answer these questions.

1 When do you have parties in your country?
2 Where are the parties? (e.g., in your house, in the street, in a restaurant, at your college)

2 Key vocabulary

In the US, they use *feet* and *miles*, not *centimeters* and *kilometers*. Match the US measurements (1–5) with the metric measurements (a–e) that have the same meaning. Practice saying them.

1	1 foot	○	○	a	2,414 kilometers
2	3 square feet	○	○	b	805 kilometers
3	1 mile	○	○	c	30.5 centimeters
4	500 miles	○	○	d	1.6 kilometers
5	1,500 miles	○	○	e	0.28 square meters

While you watch

3 ▶ 1.1 Watch the video. Match the things in the video (1–8) with the numbers (a–h).

1 number of years to count from one to seven billion ____
2 number of stars you can see at night ____
3 number of times around the Earth with seven billion steps ____
4 number of text messages sent in the US every second ____
5 the area for one person to stand ____
6 the area for one person at a party ____
7 the area for seven billion people at a party ____
8 the area for seven billion people in a photo ____

a 3 square feet
b 6 square feet
c 133
d 200
e 500 square miles
f 1,000
g 1,500 square miles
h 65,000

---

a bit (n) /bɪt/ a small amount
compare (v) /kəmˈpeər/ to talk about the differences and similarities between one thing and another thing

---

4 ▶ 1.1 Watch the video again. Number these sentences from the video in the correct order (1–7).

<u> 1 </u> a There are seven billion stars.
____ b Or there's the state of Rhode Island.
____ c One person needs about three square feet.
____ d Smile!
____ e People send seven billion texts every 30 hours in the US.
____ f So everyone needs about six square feet.
____ g The Juneau Icefield in Alaska is the correct size. But it's a bit cold.

After you watch

5 Vocabulary in context

▶ 1.2 Watch the clips from the video. Choose the correct meaning of the words and phrases.

6 Interview other students in your class using the questionnaire.

How many people ...

are in your class? _____

are male? _____

are female? _____

are under 20? _____

are over 20? _____

are students? _____

have a job? _____

speak two or more languages? _____

are from this country (the country you are in now)? _____

have a cell phone? _____

---

7 Write a short report about your class.

Fifteen people are in my class. Eight are male and seven are female. Everyone is under 20 ...

UNIT 1 REVIEW AND MEMORY BOOSTER

Grammar

1 Write the words in order to make questions. Then work in pairs. Ask and answer the questions.

1 your / name? / 's / what

_____

2 from / are / the US? / you

_____

3 are / you / where / from?

_____

4 married? / you / are / single or

_____

2 Complete the conversation with 's, isn't, are, or aren't.
A: What ¹_____ his name?
B: His name ²_____ Felipe.
A: What ³_____ her name?
B: Camila.
A: ⁴_____ they from Mexico?
B: No, they ⁵_____ . They're from Brazil.
A: What ⁶_____ Felipe's job?
B: He ⁷_____ a conservationist.
A: Is Camila an explorer?
B: No, she ⁸_____ . She ⁹_____ a conservationist too!

3 >> MB Write a similar conversation about Beverley and Dereck Joubert. Use the language from Exercise 2.

4 Circle the correct options to complete the sentences.

1 What's *you / your* name?
2 *He / His* aunt is French.
3 *They / Their* are my cousins.
4 The *photographer's / photographer is* wife is *my / I* best friend.
5 *She / Her* mother is from Germany, but *her / she* is from Switzerland.

I CAN	
use the verb *be* in sentences	
use possessive 's and possessive adjectives	

Vocabulary

5 Match the words 1–5 with a–e.

1 last name   ○   ○ a 28
2 relationship ○   ○ b Stephenson
3 age   ○   ○ c brother
4 job   ○   ○ d China
5 country   ○   ○ e teacher

6 Complete the sentences with verbs.

1 Ninety percent of families h_____ a computer in their house.
2 Eighty percent of the population s_____ English.
3 A lot of people l_____ in apartments, not houses.
4 How many people w_____ in agriculture?

7 >> MB Write the opposite word.

1 single _____
2 brother _____
3 uncle   _____
4 niece   _____
5 hello   _____

8 >> MB Write three sentences (two true and one false) with information about you. Then work in pairs and read your sentences. Guess your partner's false sentence.

I CAN	
talk about personal information	
talk about families	
use everyday verbs	

Real life

9 Number the lines of the conversation in the correct order (1–5).

___ Sonia: Arnold is, but I'm not. I'm from Colombia.

___ Arnold: Nice to meet you, too, Rosa. I'm Arnold and this is my wife, Sonia.

___ Rosa: I'm from Italy, but I live in the US. Are you and Arnold from the US?

___ Rosa: Hi. My name's Rosa. Nice to meet you.

___ Sonia: Hello, Rosa. Where are you from?

10 >> MB Work in groups of three. Practice a similar conversation to Exercise 9 using your real information.

I CAN	
introduce myself and other people	

Unit 2 Possessions

The Stow family with their plastic possessions, in Ohio, USA

1 Work in pairs. Look at the photo. How many people can you see in the photo? What are all the things made of?

2 ▶ 14 Match the numbers with the words. Then listen to someone talking about the photo. Check your answers.

3 ○   ○ balls
7 ○   ○ shoes and boots
22 ○   ○ couch
1 ○   ○ people
50 ○   ○ TVs

3 Work in pairs. Find these objects in the photo, and point to them. What color are they?

balls	boots	a chair	roller skates	TVs
a couch	shelves	shoes	a toy car	

A: *The ball is yellow.*
B: *The balls are black and white.*

4 Find three plastic objects in the classroom. What color are they?

My chair is black and grey.

2a A place called home

Reading

1 Work in pairs. Look at the four photos below. What is the same in all the photos? What is different?

2 Read the article about the homes in the photos. Are these things (a–e) the same (S) or different (D) in the four homes?

a	the country	S	D
b	the apartments	S	D
c	the number of rooms	S	D
d	the furniture	S	D
e	the rugs	S	D

Vocabulary furniture

3 Look at the chart. The checkmarks (✓) show the furniture and other objects in apartment 1. Find the things in the photo.

4 Look at the photos of apartments 2, 3, and 4 and complete the chart. Then work in pairs.

Which furniture is in your living room at home? Tell your partner.

	1	2	3	4
couch	✓			
chair	✓			
television (TV)	✓			
desk	✓			
lamp	✓			
computer	✓			
pictures	✓			
blinds				
curtains	✓			
cabinets and drawers	✓			
rug				
plant				
carpet				

▶ 15 A PLACE CALLED HOME

These four families are from Seoul, South Korea. Their apartments are in Evergreen Tower. There are twenty-five floors, and every apartment is the same. There is a living room, a kitchen, a bathroom, and there are two bedrooms.

In all the photos, there are parents and children. There is always a couch on the right, and there are pictures on the walls. But there are some differences; for example, there isn't a rug in every apartment, and the color and style of the furniture is different.

Grammar *there is/are*

5 Work in pairs. Look at the grammar box.
Answer the questions (1–3).

  1 Is the noun singular or plural after *there is*?
  2 Is the noun singular or plural after
     there are?
  3 What word usually comes after *there aren't*
     and *are there*?

6 Complete the sentences about apartment 3
with the correct form of *be*.

  1 There *'s*_____ a couch.
  2 There _____ a rug in this apartment.
  3 There _____ five people in this apartment.
  4 There _____ any curtains.
  5 _____ there a television?
     Yes, there _____ .
  6 _____ there any chairs?
     Yes, there _____ one chair.
  7 How many pictures _____ there?
     There _____ two.
  8 _____ there any books?
     No, there _____ .

7 ▶ **16** Listen and check your answers from
Exercise 6. Then listen again and repeat.

8 Work in pairs. Play a guessing game about the
apartments in the article.

Student A: Choose one apartment, but don't
tell your partner. Answer your partner's
questions.

Student B: Ask your partner questions and
guess the apartment.

*A: **Is there** a TV?*   *B: Yes, **there is.***
*A: **Are there** any curtains?* *B: No, **there aren't.***
*A: **Is there** a carpet?*   *B: Yes, **there is.***
A: It's apartment 2.

Grammar **prepositions of place**

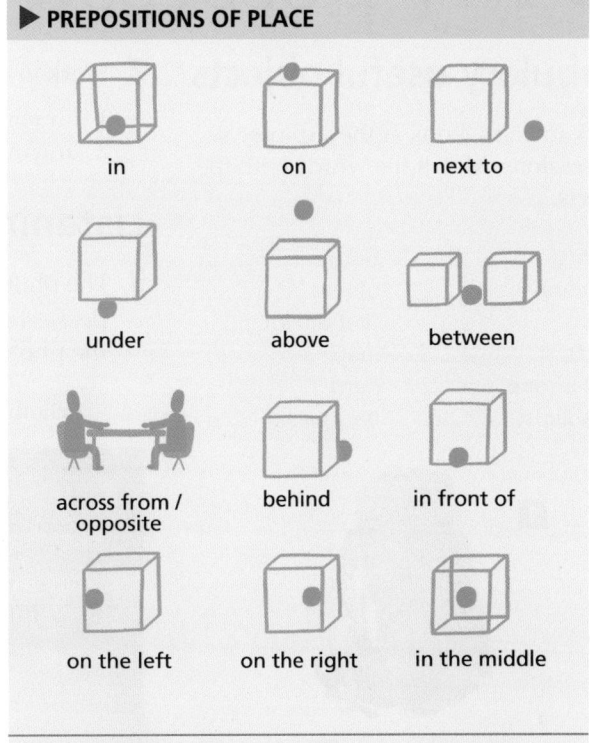

in   on   next to

under   above   between

across from / opposite   behind   in front of

on the left   on the right   in the middle

9 ▶ **17** Look at the grammar box. Then circle the
correct prepositions to complete the description of
apartment 4. Listen and check.

There are two pictures on the [1] *right / left* wall, and the
couch is [2] *under / next to* them. There's a TV [3] *opposite /
between* the couch, and there's a plant [4] *across from /
next to* the TV. There's a large rug [5] *on / under* the couch.
The family is [6] *in front of / behind* the window. The
parents are [7] *in front of / behind* the children.

10 Complete the description of apartment 1 with
prepositions of place.

The family is [1]_____ the room. They are
[2]_____ the TV and the couch. There isn't a rug
in this apartment. There's a picture [3]_____ the
wall on the right and the couch is [4]_____ it. The
computer is [5]_____ the desk and there's a lamp
[6]_____ the computer.

11 Work in pairs. Turn to page 154 and follow the
instructions.

Writing and speaking   `myLife`

12 Write a description of a room in your home. Then
work in pairs and read your description to your
partner. What is the same in both your rooms? What
is different?

2b My possessions

Vocabulary useful objects

1 Work in pairs. Look at the explorer's possessions. Match the words with the objects.

boots	____	bottle	____
camera	____	gloves	____
hat	____	first-aid kit	____
knife	____	map	____
cell phone	____	pens	____
flashlight	____	backpack	____

2 Work in pairs. Which objects in Exercise 1 are:
1 in your bag?
2 in your house?

Listening

3 The photos in Exercise 1 are of Andy Torbet's backpack and possessions. Look at Andy's website. Match these activities to the photos on the website.

1 climbing	2 diving	3 kayaking

4 ▶ 18 Listen to an interview with Andy. Circle the correct answers.

1 Andy and the interviewer are next to ____ .
   a a mountain   b the sea   c a forest
2 Where's Andy from?
   a England   c Northern Ireland
   b Wales   d Scotland
3 Which objects does he talk about? Circle them.

a camera	a first-aid kit	gloves
a hat	shoes	pens

Grammar plural nouns

> ▶ **PLURAL NOUNS SPELLING**

Singular nouns	Plural nouns
boot, glove	boots, gloves
beach, bus, class	beaches, buses, classes
country	countries
knife, shelf	knives, shelves
man, person, child	men, people, children

For more information and practice, see page 160.

5 Look at the grammar box. Complete the sentences about plural nouns.

1 We normally add __-s__ .
2 We add _____ to nouns ending in -ch, -s, and -ss.
3 We change nouns ending in -y after a consonant to _____ .
4 We change some nouns ending in -f or -fe to _____ .
5 Some nouns are irregular, e.g., the plural of *man* is _____ .

6 ▶ **19** Write the plural form of these nouns. Then listen and repeat.

1 map _____
2 bottle _____
3 hat _____
4 life _____
5 city _____
6 lunch _____
7 chair _____
8 woman _____

Grammar *this, that, these, those*

> ▶ **THIS, THAT, THESE, THOSE**

Singular nouns	Plural nouns
this	these ‖
that	those ‖‖

For more information and practice, see page 160.

7 Work in pairs. Look at the grammar box. Which two words are for objects near to you? Which are for objects away from you?

8 ▶ **20** Listen to part of the interview with Andy and circle the correct option.

I: I see. And what's ¹*this / that* here?
A: It's a first-aid kit. It's always in my backpack.
I: Mm. Good idea. And what's ²*this / that* in your hand?
A: It's my camera. I take it everywhere. And ³*these / those* are my climbing shoes.
I: Right. And over there. What are ⁴*these / those*?
A: My gloves.

9 Complete the questions with *this, that, these,* or *those*. Then complete the answers.

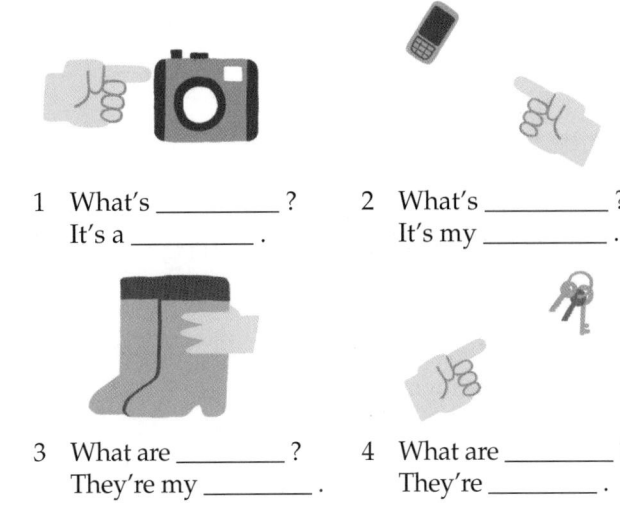

1 What's _____ ?
  It's a _____ .

2 What's _____ ?
  It's my _____ .

3 What are _____ ?
  They're my _____ .

4 What are _____ ?
  They're _____ .

10 Pronunciation /ɪ/ or /iː/

a ▶ **21** Listen to these vowel sounds: /ɪ/ and /iː/.

b ▶ **22** Listen to these words and circle /ɪ/ or /iː/. Then listen again and repeat.

1	this	/ɪ/	/iː/	5	pink	/ɪ/	/iː/
2	these	/ɪ/	/iː/	6	green	/ɪ/	/iː/
3	keys	/ɪ/	/iː/	7	big	/ɪ/	/iː/
4	it	/ɪ/	/iː/	8	read	/ɪ/	/iː/

11 Match the beginnings of the sentences (1–6) with the endings (a–f). Then work in pairs. Read the sentences. Be careful with /ɪ/ or /iː/.

1 What are ○
2 This ○
3 Those ○
4 Are ○
5 That's ○
6 These are ○

○ a those your boots?
○ b are their pens.
○ c Andy's gloves.
○ d these?
○ e bag is Sally's.
○ f my brother.

Speaking **myLife**

12 Work in pairs. Ask and answer questions about:

• objects in the classroom.
• possessions in your bag or pocket.

*What's **this/that**?*
*What are **these/those**?*

What color is it?
What color are they?

2c Global objects

Reading

1 Work in pairs. Look at the photo of the Mini on page 27. Is this car famous in your country? What are popular cars in your country?

2 Read the article about the Mini. Match the correct answer (a–c) for each question (1–3).

1 Which country is BMW from? ____
2 Where are the parts for a Mini from? ____
3 Where is the factory for the Mini? ____

a Germany
b Britain
c Many different countries

Critical thinking reading closely

3 Read sentences 1–8. Write the correct option for each sentence.

T = The sentence is **true**. The information is in the article.
F = The sentence is **false**. The information is different in the article.
NG = The information is **not given** in the article.

1 In the past, the Mini was a British car. ____
2 The Mini is cheaper to make than in the past. ____
3 The Mini is a global product. ____
4 The Mini is famous in Brazil. ____
5 The engines are from two different countries. ____
6 The seats are made in the US. ____
7 The windows are from a factory in Brazil. ____
8 The gas engine is made in the US. ____

Vocabulary countries and nationalities

> **▶ WORDBUILDING suffixes**
>
> Words for nationality often end with the suffixes -ish, -n, -an, -ian, or -ese:
> Poland—Polish, Australia—Australian, Vietnam—Vietnamese, Colombia—Colombian
>
> Some words for nationalities are irregular:
> France—French, the Netherlands—Dutch
>
> For more practice, see page 19 of the Workbook.

4 Look at the wordbuilding box. Complete the chart with the countries and nationalities in the article and Exercise 3.

Country	Nationality
1 The US	*American*
2 Germany	
3 Brazil	
4	Dutch
5 Canada	
6 Colombia	
7	Belgian
8	English
9 Spain	
10	French

5 Pronunciation word stress

a ▶ 24 Listen to the countries and nationalities in Exercise 4. Underline the main stress in each word.

The US, American

b ▶ 24 Listen again and repeat the words.

6 Work in pairs. Answer the questions about the regions and continents in the box.

Africa	Europe	the Middle East
Asia	North America	South America

1 Which two continents are in the article?
2 Name two countries for each region and continent in the box.

Speaking *my*Life

7 Work in pairs. Which country, region, or continent are these objects from?

• your shoes
• your bag
• your cell phone
• your car
• this book
• other objects in your bag or in the classroom

My bag is from China.
I think my phone is …
I don't know where my … is from.

GLOBAL OBJECTS

▶ 23

The Mini was a British car until 2000. Now BMW, a German company, is the producer of the Mini, but the car factory[1] is still in Oxford, England. There are 2,500 parts in the Mini, and they are from many different countries in Europe and North America. So, where is a car from a German company, with international parts, and from a factory in Britain really from? It's a global product.

Hood
This is from a factory in the Netherlands, but the company is Austrian.

Roof
Part of the roof is from England, but the company is Spanish.

Mirrors
These are from a factory in Germany, but the headquarters[2] is in Canada.

Car seats
An American company makes the car seats in a factory in Britain.

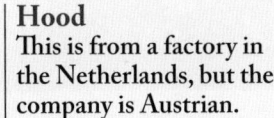

Front and back bumpers
These are from Britain, but the company is Canadian.

Engine
The Mini has one of two different engines. There's a gas engine and a diesel engine. The gas engine is from England and the diesel engine is from Austria.

Windows
The glass in the windows is from a company in France, but a factory in Belgium makes the frame around the windows.

Wheels
The wheels aren't from one country; they are from two! Italian and German factories produce them.

[1]**factory** (n) /ˈfæktəri/ the place where a company produces an object
[2]**headquarters** (n) /ˌhedˈkwɔːrtərz/ the main office of a company

2d At the store

Vocabulary prices and currencies

1 ▶ 25 Can you say these prices from a shop in the US? Listen and check.

| $1.00 | $2.50 | $31.35 | $90.99 | $111.11 |

2 Work in pairs. What are these currencies? Which countries use them?

1 $ 2 €   3 ¥   4 £

3 ▶ 26 Listen to three sentences and write the prices. Then work in pairs. Practice saying the prices.

1 _____ 2 _____ 3 _____

Real life shopping

4 ▶ 27 Listen to conversations in three stores. Write what the person buys and the price.

1: _____
2: _____
3: _____

5 ▶ 27 Look at the expressions for shopping. Who says them: the customer (C) or the sales clerk (S)? Listen again and check.

▶ **SHOPPING**

Can I help you? _S_	These ones are red. ____
I'd like a coffee, please. _C_	Those are nice! ____
Large or small? ____	How much are they? ____
A large one, please. ____	Are they all black and
These ones are large. ____	white? ____
Is there a medium size?	This one is red and blue.
____	____
Are there other colors?	OK, that one, please. ____
____	How much is it? ____

6 Work in pairs. Have a conversation between a sales clerk (S) and a customer (C). Then change roles and have a new conversation.

S: Hello. Can / help?
C: I'd / T-shirt
S: Large / Medium?
C: Medium. / other colors?
S: These / green and blue
C: How much / they?
S: $7.50

Word focus one/ones

7 Work in pairs. Underline *one* or *ones* in the expressions for shopping in Exercise 5. Then complete these sentences with *one* or *ones*.

1 I'd like two T-shirts. Small _____ , please.
2 This ball is nice, but that _____ is terrible!
3 These gloves are small, but those _____ are large.

8 **Pronunciation contrastive stress**

▶ 28 Listen to sentences 2 and 3 in Exercise 7. Notice the stress on *this, that, these,* and *those.* Listen again and repeat.

9 Work in pairs. Practice two conversations between a customer and a sales clerk in a tourist shop.

Student A: Turn to page 156.

Student B: Turn to page 153.

2e For sale

Writing ads

1 Look at the ads. Which ad:

1 has the price? ____   2 is for an old product? ____   3 is for something almost new? ____

A
COMPUTER DESK AND CHAIR

A useful, modern, white desk and chair. Cheap at only $5!

☎ Call **555-321-3278** today.

B
Car for sale

Red and blue British Mini from 1965 with fast new engine.

☎ Call **555-508-6296** today.

C
BACKPACK FOR SALE

Large, green backpack. Good for camping. Never used.
Email **l.taylor@hmail.net**

Vocabulary adjectives

2 Find the opposite of these adjectives in the ads in Exercise 1.

1 old   *modern / new*
2 bad   _____
3 useless   _____
4 slow   _____
5 small   _____
6 expensive _____

3 Writing skill describing objects with adjectives

We can describe objects with adjectives in two ways. Look at the example. Then rewrite sentences 1–3.

The desk is modern. = It's a modern desk.

1 The car is old.
  It _____ .
2 These laptops are slow.
  They _____ .
3 The couch is brown.
  It _____ .

4 Read the ads again and notice the order of the adjectives. Complete the chart with the adjectives.

Opinion	Size	Age	Color	Country	Noun
useful		*modern*	*white*		desk
					Mini
					engine
					backpack

5 Write the adjectives in the correct order to make sentences from ads. Use the chart in Exercise 4 to help you.

1 It's a (Japanese / new / fast) motorcycle.
  It's a fast, new, Japanese motorcycle.
2 They're (red / nice) gloves.
3 There are two (Italian / beautiful / old) chairs for sale.
4 A (gray / small) computer desk for sale.
5 For sale. A (large / modern / white) house.

6 Think of an object in your home. Write an ad for it.

7 Display your ads around the classroom. Read the ads. Which adjectives are there in the ads? Are they in the correct order?

2f A thousand words

A photographer takes a picture of his own
reflection in a door handle.

Before you watch

1 Work in pairs. What do you think the expression "A picture says a thousand words" means? Is there a similar expression in your language?

2 Work in pairs. Look at the picture below from the video. Try to predict the answers to these questions.

1 Where is the man in the photo?
2 Why is he there?
3 Who is holding the photo?

3 Key vocabulary

Match the phrases (1–3) with the uses (a–c).

1 I miss you. ____
2 Please forward. ____
3 Good luck! ____

a We say this to a person before they begin something new or difficult, e.g., a new course, a new job, an exam.
b We write this on an envelope so it goes from one address to another.
c We say this when we are sad because another person is not with us.

While you watch

4 ▢◀ **2.1** Watch the video. Are these objects the man's (M) or the woman's (W)?

Apartment 102 ____	a bed ____
a bicycle ____	a cake ____
a camera ____	a mailbox ____
a pen ____	a plant ____

5 Work in pairs. Number these parts of the video in the correct order from 1 to 8.

- _4_ a The woman is with two people and there is a cake.
- ____ b The man sends the camera to her old address in Los Angeles.
- ____ c The man and the woman are on the same train.
- ____ d The woman leaves the train with a box of possessions.
- ____ e The man finds her apartment, but it is empty.
- ____ f The man finds her camera and looks at the photographs.
- ____ g The man is in the photographs on the camera.
- ____ h The man photographs himself with a phone number.

6 ▢◀ **2.1** Watch the video again and check your answers to Exercise 5.

After you watch

7 Work in pairs and read the questions. Can you answer them? Compare your ideas.

1 Who are the two people with Nasim and the cake?
2 Nasim leaves Los Angeles and goes to Boston. Why does she go there?
3 How does the man feel when he sees his photo on her camera?
4 How does the man feel when he finds the apartment?
5 The man sends the camera to Nasim. Whose telephone number is on the photograph?

8 Work in pairs. Think about the next part of the story. Nasim receives her camera in the package and telephones the man. Write their conversation and practice it together.

Man: *Hello?*
Woman: ...

9 Work with another pair. Read your telephone conversations from Exercise 8. Are the conversations similar or different?

Grammar

1 Look at the photo. Choose the correct options to complete the sentences.

Concordia Hotel

1 There *is / isn't* a couch.
2 There *are some / aren't any* flowers.
3 There *is / isn't* a picture.
4 There *is a / aren't any* rugs.
5 The desk and chair are *in front of / between* the window.
6 The red shoes are *in / on* the floor.
7 The couch is *between / across from* the table and the bed.
8 The bed is *under / behind* the couch.

2 Write the singular form of these nouns.

1	classes	*class*	4 women	_____
2	shelves	_____	5 children	_____
3	families	_____	6 boots	_____

3 ▶▶ **MB** Write five singular nouns and read them to a partner. Your partner writes their plural form.

4 Complete the questions with *this*, *that*, *these*, or *those*.

1 Who's _____?

2 Is _____ your pen?

3 Are _____ your roller skates?

4 Are _____ your boots?

I CAN
talk about everyday objects and say where they are

Vocabulary

5 Cross out the incorrect word in each group.

1	**colors:**	red grey white ~~chair~~
2	**furniture:**	couch desk map chair
3	**country:**	Austria Dutch Belgium China
4	**on your feet:**	shoes roller skates hat boots
5	**on the floor:**	carpet blinds rug
6	**nationality:**	France British Brazilian Spanish
7	**adjectives:**	slow age useless large
8	**currencies:**	pounds euros dollars money

6 Complete the sentences with one word from each group in Exercise 5.

1 Stop the car at a ___*red*___ light.
2 The computer is on my _____ .
3 _____ is a country in Asia.
4 Are these _____ fast?
5 There's a _____ next to the bed.
6 _____ people speak Portuguese.
7 The opposite of "fast" is _____ .
8 You need _____ in the United States.

7 ▶▶ **MB** Choose eight more words from Exercise 5. Write a new sentence with each word.

I CAN
talk about furniture and objects in the house
say currencies, countries, and nationalities

Real life

8 Match the questions (1–5) with the correct responses (a–e).

1 Can I help you? ____
2 Large or small? ____
3 Is there a medium size? ____
4 Are there any other colors? ____
5 How much are they? ____

a A small one, please.
b Yes, please. I'd like a coffee.
c Three dollars and fifty cents.
d I'm sorry, but there isn't.
e Yes, there's also blue and gray.

9 ▶▶ **MB** Work in pairs. Practice a conversation in a store. Ask for the objects on page 21 or 24.

I CAN
ask about and buy objects in a shop

Unit 3 Places

Flinders Street Station in Melbourne, Australia

FEATURES

1 Work in pairs. Look at the photo and caption. What is the place in the photo? Where is it?

2 ▶ 29 Work in pairs. Listen to a description of the photo and answer the questions.

1 Why are there different times on the clocks?
2 Why is Flinders Street Station a good meeting place?

3 ▶ 30 Complete the times with these words. Then listen, check, and repeat.

half	minutes	o'clock	past	to	twelve

1 It's six _____ .
2 It's _____ past three.
3 It's twenty-five _____ nine.
4 It's quarter _____ four.
5 It's three _____ past two.
6 It's two minutes to _____ .

4 Work in pairs and answer the questions.

- What time is it now?
- What time is your English lesson?
- What times can you see in the photo?

3a Car-free zones

Reading

1 Read the article and complete the chart.

City	Which area is car-free?	Why do people go there?
London	*the parks*	*for a break*
Tokyo		
Bogotá		
Melbourne		

Vocabulary describing cities

2 Underline all the adjectives in the article.

Which adjective means:
1 doesn't cost money? _____
2 many people like it? _____
3 has lots of people? _____
4 has bad air? _____
5 very good? _____

Which adjective is the opposite of:
6 quiet? _____   9 dirty? _____
7 ugly? _____   10 cheap? _____
8 old? _____   11 big? _____

3 Work in pairs. Talk about your city or a city you know. Which places in the city are:
1 expensive or cheap?   4 modern and popular?
2 small and crowded?   5 beautiful and relaxing?
3 noisy and polluted?

Melbourne

▶ 31

CAR-FREE ZONES

Many people in cities have cars, so pollution is often a problem. Nowadays, some downtown areas of cities around the world don't allow cars. These car-free zones are areas for people, bicycles, and public transportation only.

LONDON

Eight million people live in the center of London, and another two million people go to work there every day. The city center is very noisy with hundreds of cars, buses, and taxis, but there are also a lot of beautiful parks with free music concerts. At lunchtime and after work, many people go there for a break.

TOKYO

In the Ginza area of Tokyo, there are no cars on weekends. This modern car-free zone is very popular. People like shopping there, so it's always crowded.

BOGOTÁ

In the past, Bogotá was polluted because there was lots of traffic. Now the downtown area is a car-free zone and the air is clean! Many people don't have a car, and half a million people go to work by bus every morning.

MELBOURNE

In some cities, people don't like shopping downtown. But in Melbourne, Bourke Street Mall is popular because there are lots of great shops and no cars. It's expensive, but lots of people eat lunch at the small cafés.

London

Tokyo

Bogotá

Grammar simple present (*I/you/we/they*)

4 Work in pairs. Look at the grammar box. What is the main verb in the sentences? How do you make the verb negative?

5 Choose the correct form to make these sentences true for you. Then tell your partner.

1 I *live / don't live* downtown.
2 I *have / don't have* a car.
3 I *go / don't go* to school/work by bus.
4 I *eat / don't eat* at a café at lunchtime.
5 I *meet / don't meet* friends downtown after school/work.
6 I *like / don't like* shopping downtown.

6 Are your sentences from Exercise 5 also true for most people in your town or city? Make more sentences about life in the city with these phrases.

eat lunch	go to work	have a car
like shopping	live	work

Most people in the downtown area **don't have** *a car.*
They **go** *to work by bus.*

Listening

7 ▶ 32 Listen to a reporter interviewing a student about living in New York City. Complete his notes with adjectives.

Manhattan Living

The stores are ¹_____.

There are lots of ²_____ places like art galleries and museums.

The city has ³_____ theaters.

The restaurant is ⁴_____ with tourists and is ⁵_____ at lunchtime every day.

Central Park is beautiful and ⁶_____.

8 ▶ 32 Match the reporter's questions (1–5) with the student's answers (a–e). Then listen again and check.

1 Do you have a car in New York City? __b__
2 Where do you live? ____
3 Do you like art? ____
4 What do you do? ____
5 What time do you finish work? ____

a I'm a college student, and I work in a restaurant at lunchtime.
b No, I don't. I ride my bike everywhere.
c At about three o'clock.
d Yes, I do. And I like the theater.
e In downtown Manhattan.

Grammar simple present questions (*I/you/we/they*)

9 Look at the questions (1–5) in Exercise 8. Then follow these instructions.

1 Underline the main verb in the questions.
2 Circle the auxiliary verb.
3 Put a check (✓) beside the questions with *yes/no* answers.

Example
(Do) you <u>have</u> a car in New York City? ✓

10 Look at the grammar box. Write questions with *do* and these words.

1 what / you / do?
   *What do you do?*_____

2 where / you / live?
   _____

3 you / like / shopping?
   _____

4 what time / you / finish / work?
   _____

5 you / have / a car?
   _____

6 you / eat out / at lunchtime?
   _____

Speaking my Life

11 Work in pairs. Ask and answer your questions from Exercise 10.

A: What do you do?
B: I'm a website designer.

3b Places of work

Vocabulary places of work

1 Work in pairs. Match these jobs with the places of work (1–7).

> a doctor _____   a pilot _____   a sailor _____
> a teacher _____   a waiter _____   a sales clerk _____
> an accountant _____

1 in an office
2 on a ship or a boat
3 on an airplane
4 in a hospital
5 in a restaurant
6 in a classroom
7 in a store

Listening

2 ▶ 33 Listen to a description of three people's jobs. Match the people with their place of work.

1 Beverly ○   ○ a downtown
2 Samuel ○   ○ b on a boat
3 James ○   ○ c in a store

3 ▶ 33 Listen again and circle the correct words.

1 Beverly Goodman is *an archaeologist / a teacher*.
2 She studies places *under the sea / on land*.
3 Samuel Diaz is *at school / in the army*.
4 He wants to travel around *his country / the world*.
5 He works *on weekends / on Mondays and Tuesdays*.
6 James is a *tour guide / tourist*.
7 He speaks *two / three* languages.
8 He works with tourists from *Mexico and Brazil / France and Japan*.

Dr. Beverly Goodman,
a marine archaeologist

Grammar simple present (*he/she/it*)

▶ **SIMPLE PRESENT (*HE/SHE/IT*)**

He **works** in a store.
She **studies** places under the sea.
He **has** exams soon.
It **is** his last year at school.
He **doesn't live** in London.

For more information and practice, see page 162.

4 Work in pairs. Look at the grammar box. Answer these questions.

1 In affirmative sentences, how does the verb change when used with the pronouns *he, she,* and *it*?
2 In negative sentences, what is the auxiliary verb?

5 Complete the text about Beverly Goodman with the correct form of the verbs.

Beverly Goodman is a marine archaeologist. She
¹ _____ (study) places under the sea and
objects from the past. She ² _____ (have)
an office, but she ³ _____ (not / work)
there very often. Normally, she ⁴ _____
(work) on her boat. She ⁵ _____ (get up)
just after five o'clock, and she ⁶ _____
(meet) her team for breakfast at seven o'clock. She
⁷ _____ (start) work after breakfast and
she ⁸ _____ (not / finish) work until the
evening.

6 Read about another archaeologist. Complete the text with the correct form of these verbs.

not / have	live	speak	study	travel

Dr. James E. Campbell ¹ _____ in
England. He's an archaeologist. He works from
home, so he ² _____ an office. He
³ _____ to different places around the
world and he ⁴ _____ ancient places.
James ⁵ _____ three languages: English,
French, and Arabic.

7 Pronunciation *-s* endings

▶ **34** Listen to the words. Do you hear the sound /s/, /z/, or /ɪz/? Circle the sound. Listen again and repeat the words.

1 works   /s/ /z/ /ɪz/
2 lives   /s/ /z/ /ɪz/
3 finishes /s/ /z/ /ɪz/
4 studies   /s/ /z/ /ɪz/
5 meets   /s/ /z/ /ɪz/
6 starts   /s/ /z/ /ɪz/
7 speaks   /s/ /z/ /ɪz/
8 teachers /s/ /z/ /ɪz/
9 goes   /s/ /z/ /ɪz/
10 travels /s/ /z/ /ɪz/

8 Work in pairs. Choose five verbs and use them in five questions to ask your partner. Write your partner's answers.

live	study	do	have	get up
meet	work	start	travel	speak

A: *Where do you live?*   B: *I live in Argentina.*

9 Work with a new partner. Talk about your partner from Exercise 8.

*Ania **lives** in Argentina.*

Grammar simple present questions (*he/she/it*)

▶ **SIMPLE PRESENT QUESTIONS (*HE/SHE/IT*)**

What **does** he **do**? He's a doctor.
Does she **have** children? Yes, she **does**. / No, she **doesn't**.

For more information and practice, see page 162.

10 Look at the grammar box. Put the words in order to make questions about Beverly. Then find the answers in Exercise 5.

1 does / do / Beverly / what / ?
 What does Beverly do? _____
2 what / does / study / she / ?
 _____
3 she / work / where / does / ?
 _____
4 get up / she / what time / does / ?
 _____
5 she / does / when / work / start / ?
 _____

11 Work in pairs. Look at the answers about James Campbell. Complete the questions.

1 A: Where _____ ?
 B: In England.
2 A: What _____ ?
 B: He's an archaeologist.
3 A: Does _____ ?
 B: No, he doesn't. He works from home.
4 A: Where _____ ?
 B: To different places around the world.
5 A: What languages _____ ?
 B: English, French, and Arabic.

Speaking [my Life]

12 Work in pairs. Exchange information to complete a fact file about photographer Joel Sartore.

Student A: Turn to page 154.

Student B: Turn to page 157.

3c Places and languages

Reading

1 Work in pairs. Which languages do people speak around the world? Which have the most speakers?

2 Read the article and check your answers to Exercise 1.

3 Work in pairs. Read the article again and answer these questions.

1 Where do most Spanish speakers live?
2 Do more people speak English as a first language or as a second language?
3 What do many people use English for?
4 How many people speak Amurdag?

Vocabulary ordinal and cardinal numbers

4 Work in pairs. Look at the words in **bold** in this sentence from the article. Which say the order (ordinal numbers)? Which say "how many" (cardinal numbers)?

Four hundred and eighteen million Spanish speakers live in Latin America. They all speak Spanish as their first language.

5 Circle the ordinal numbers and underline the cardinal numbers in the article. Can you say them?

6 Work in pairs. Complete the sequence of ordinal numbers.

1 _____ _____ 3rd _____ 5th 6th 7th
2 3rd 13th _____ _____ 43rd
3 21st 31st 41st 51st _____ _____ _____

7 Pronunciation ordinal numbers

▶ 36 Listen and repeat the ordinal numbers in Exercise 6.

Wordbuilding adjective + noun collocations

> ▶ **WORDBUILDING adjective + noun collocations**
>
> We often use some words together. These are called *collocations*.
> Many collocations are an adjective and a noun, e.g., *first language, official language*.

For more practice, see Workbook page 27.

8 Work in pairs. Find collocations in the article with the words *language* and *speaker*. Match the collocations with these definitions.

1 the language you learn after your first language
   _____
2 the main language that a person speaks
   _____
3 the language of the government
   _____
4 the language you first learn from your parents as a child
   _____
5 a person who speaks Spanish
   _____
6 a person who speaks the language from when they were a child _____

Critical thinking main ideas and supporting information

9 A paragraph often has a sentence with the main idea, and sentences with supporting information. Look at the example. Then find sentences 1–5 in the article and decide if they are main ideas (M) or supporting information (S).

M: *Chinese is the first language of more people than any other language.*
S: *Over one billion people in China speak Mandarin Chinese.*

1 English is a second language for over one billion other people. _M_
2 They speak English for business, reading the news, or studying science and medicine. _S_
3 It is also the language of education in many colleges and schools. ____
4 Many countries use lots of different languages. ____
5 For example, the country of Vanuatu ... has sixty-five different islands and one hundred and nine different languages. ____

10 Work in pairs. Read the last paragraph of the article. Which sentence gives the main idea of the paragraph? Which ones give supporting information? Compare your ideas with your partner and say why.

Speaking *my* Life

11 Work in groups. Discuss these questions.

1 What is your first language?
2 How many languages do you speak? Do you speak different languages in different places? (e.g., English at work, Hindi at home)
3 What languages do people normally learn at school in your country? Why these languages?

PLACES AND LANGUAGES

▶ 35 There are over one hundred and ninety countries in the world and about seven thousand languages. Chinese is the first language of more people than any other
5 language. Over one billion people in China speak Mandarin Chinese. Hindi, spoken in India, is in second place. Spanish is in third place. Spain isn't a big country, but there are over four hundred and seventy million
10 Spanish speakers in different countries around the world. Four hundred and eighteen million Spanish speakers live in Latin America. They all speak Spanish as their first language.

As a first language, English is the fourth
15 most common native language. About three hundred and eighty million people are native English speakers. But English is a second language for over one billion other people. They speak English for business, reading
20 the news, or studying science and medicine. In some countries, English is not the native language, but it is the official language of the government. It is also the language of education in many colleges and schools.

25 About eighty percent of the world's population speak the "big four" languages, and the other twenty percent speak around seven thousand languages between them. Many countries use lots of different languages. For example,
30 the country of Vanuatu in the South Pacific Ocean has sixty-five different islands and one hundred and nine different languages. That's one-and-a-half languages for every island.

Unfortunately, the world loses a language every
35 two weeks. This is because lots of younger people only speak one of the big four languages and they don't learn the languages of their parents and grandparents. For example, Charlie Muldunga lives in Australia and he speaks
40 English, but his native language is Amurdag. Charlie is the last speaker of this language. When he dies, the language dies, too.

Vocabulary places in a city

1 Work in pairs. When you are a tourist in a new city, what places do you normally visit?

2 Work in pairs. Look at the map of Atlanta, USA. Where do you do these things?

1	get tourist information	6	read a book
2	take classes	7	meet clients and
3	relax outside		colleagues
4	see a play or a musical	8	look at marine life
5	park your car	9	stay the night

Real life giving directions

3 ▶ **37** Listen to a conversation at the visitor center. What places on the map do they talk about?

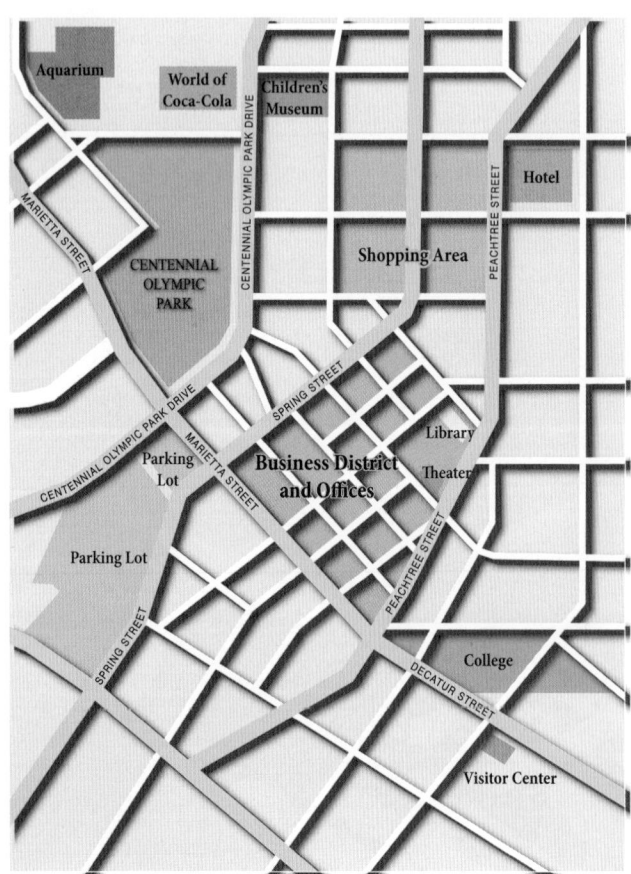

4 ▶ **37** Look at the expressions for giving directions. Complete the conversation at the visitor center. Then listen again and check.

T = Tourist, G = Guide

T: Hello. We'd like to go to the aquarium. Is it ¹_____ _____ ?

G: It's ²_____ fifteen minutes _____ , but you go past some interesting places on the way. So look at this map. Go ³_____ _____ Decatur Street and then up Marietta Street. ⁴_____ _____ Spring Street and take the first street ⁵_____ _____ _____ . Centennial Olympic Park is on the corner. It's very nice. Go past the park and turn left. On the right you can see the World of Coca-Cola.

T: Oh, that sounds interesting.

G: Yes, it is. ⁶_____ _____ it and the aquarium is on your right.

T: Great. Thanks a lot.

▶ **GIVING DIRECTIONS**

Asking for directions
Where is …?
I'd like to go to …
Is it near here?

Giving directions
It's near here. / It's about ten minutes away.

Go past the …

Go across …

Go straight up …

Take the first street on the left. /
Turn left.

Take the first street on the right. /
Turn right.

---

5 Work in pairs. Practice similar conversations at the visitor center. Ask for and give directions to different places on the map.

3e My favorite city

Writing a description of a place

1 Work in pairs. When you travel to a new place, where can you find information?

2 Bella Potachouck writes for a travel website. Read about her favorite city. Check (✓) the items she mentions.

- ☐ the name of her favorite city
- ☐ good places to visit
- ☐ her favorite time of the year
- ☐ activities she does with her friends
- ☐ her favorite cafés and restaurants
- ☐ good ways to travel around the city

WHY I LOVE MOSCOW

My favorite place in Russia is Red Square in Moscow because there are interesting museums and art galleries. I also like other parts of Moscow. For example, Krasnaya Presnya Park is great. On Saturdays in the summer, I meet friends there in the afternoon. We relax and play sports—and it's free! I also love the winter in Moscow. December is my favorite month because the snow is beautiful and we can go ice-skating.

3 Writing skill capital letters

a Read the description in Exercise 2 again. Which of these things have a capital letter?

- ☐ the word at the beginning of a sentence
- ☐ the pronoun *I*
- ☐ names of people, cities, or places
- ☐ countries, nationalities, or languages
- ☐ parts of the day
- ☐ days and months
- ☐ seasons
- ☐ streets, roads, parks, and squares

b Look at this description by a student. Which words need a capital letter? Look at the examples and circle all the incorrect letters.

ⓘ'm from ⓐustralia, and i love sydney! there are over four million people here, but it's never crowded. there's a harbor with the famous sydney opera house. there are also beautiful beaches. on saturdays, i go with my friends to narrabeen beach. it's quiet and relaxed. in the evening we go to the city center. there are over three thousand restaurants. my favorites are japanese and lebanese.

4 Write a description of your favorite town or city for a website.

5 Display the descriptions around the classroom. Walk around and read each other's descriptions. Check the capital letters.

3f Cowley Road

The city of Oxford, England

Before you watch

1 Work in groups. Look at the photo and read the caption. Use three adjectives to describe this city. Why do you think Oxford is a popular place for tourists?

2 Work in pairs. Imagine you are a visitor to Oxford. Write three questions to ask local people. Then compare your questions with the class.

3 Key vocabulary

Read the sentences (1–6). The words in **bold** are used in the video. Match the words with the definitions (a–f).

1 Can you go to the **post office** and buy a stamp?
2 I live in a city with lots of different **communities**.
3 There are parents with **pre-schoolers** in the park.
4 I feel sick. I need to go to the **medical center**.
5 To make a cake, you use different **ingredients**.
6 Stop when the **traffic light** is red.

a young children before they go to school _____
b nationalities and groups of people living in a city; Indian, Polish, Brazilian, etc. _____
c the different things you add together when you cook something, e.g., sugar, eggs _____
d a place to see a doctor _____
e lights on the road to control the traffic _____
f you send letters and packages from this place _____

While you watch

4 [3.1] Watch the video about a road in Oxford. Check (✓) the places you see.

☐ a university
☐ a school
☐ stores
☐ a bus stop
☐ a train station
☐ a post office
☐ a sports center
☐ restaurants
☐ a park
☐ a hospital
☐ supermarkets
☐ tourist information

5 [3.1] Work in pairs. Make questions with the words. Then watch the video again and check.

1 is / a post office / there / near here / ?

_____

2 is / to eat / good place / there / a / near here / ?

_____

3 around here / a park / is there / ?

_____

4 get to the supermarket / how do I / from here / ?

_____

6 [3.1] Watch the video again. Choose the correct answers to the questions.

1 Why is the city of Oxford famous?
 a because of the university
 b because of its history
 c both a and b
2 How does the first speaker describe Cowley Road?
 a busy b noisy c crowded
3 Where do you cross the road for the post office?
 a at the bus stop
 b at the traffic light
 c at the corner
4 Which types of restaurants do the two men talk about?
 ☐ British ☐ Portuguese
 ☐ Italian ☐ Greek
 ☐ Turkish ☐ American
5 Where are the two big supermarkets?
 a on Manzil Way
 b on the right
 c across from each other
6 Which small supermarkets does the woman talk about?
 ☐ Greek ☐ Russian
 ☐ Polish ☐ Colombian
 ☐ Lebanese ☐ Chinese

After you watch

7 Vocabulary in context

[3.2] Watch the clips from the video. Choose the correct meaning of the words and phrases.

8 Work in pairs. Tell your partner about your favorite place in your hometown or city.

1 Why do you like it?
2 Is it in the north, south, east, or west part of town?
3 Give your partner directions to the place from the center of town.

9 Work with a new partner.

Student A: Make a list of good places for tourists in your town or city. Think about these things.

places to visit	places to eat
places to shop	places to relax

Student B: You are a tourist in a new town. Write questions to find out about the things in the box.

When you are ready, practice a conversation. Then change roles and repeat.

UNIT 3 REVIEW AND MEMORY BOOSTER

Grammar

1 Complete the sentences with these verbs.

eat	have	like	live	goes

1 I _____ with my family in Dubai.
2 We _____ in a restaurant near my house on weekends.
3 I don't _____ shopping downtown because the stores are crowded.
4 She _____ to school by bus.
5 I don't _____ a car.

2 Complete the conversation with *do* or *don't*.

A: Where ¹_____ you live?
B: In New York.
A: ²_____ you like it?
B: Yes, it's great. There are lots of places to go.
A: ³_____ you have a car?
B: No, I ⁴_____ . And I ⁵_____ use public transportation because I have a bicycle.
A: Do you like shopping in New York?
B: No, I ⁶_____ . I shop online.

3 Circle the correct option to complete the sentences.

1 I *come / comes* from Egypt.
2 He *live / lives* in Singapore.
3 My friend *speak / speaks* four languages!
4 We *don't / doesn't* have much free time.

4 ▶▶ **MB** Work in pairs. What tense do you use in Exercises 1, 2, and 3? When do you add *-s* (or *-es*) to the verb?

5 ▶▶ **MB** Work in pairs. Say six things you do in a normal day, and what time you do them.

I get up at six o'clock.

I CAN	
use the simple present	
ask questions with the simple present	

Vocabulary

6 Match the words with the sentences.

parking lot	hospital	hotel
library	park	restaurant

1 There are waiters here. _____
2 People read books here. _____
3 Doctors work in this place. _____
4 Tourists spend the night in this building. _____

5 You can relax here at lunchtime. _____
6 You can leave your car here. _____

7 Complete the adjectives in the text about Bangkok.

Bangkok, in Thailand, is a ¹ b_g city with about ten million people. It's also a ² p_p_l_r city with tourists, so it's often very ³ cr_wd_d. The city is an interesting mix of ⁴ b_a_t_f_l old buildings and ⁵ m_d_rn office buildings. There's also a lot of traffic, so sometimes the air is ⁶ p_ll_t_d. For ⁷ c_e_n air and ⁸ q_i_t places, go to the parks and the river.

8 ▶▶ **MB** Work in pairs. Describe your town or city with words from Exercises 6 and 7.

I CAN	
say the time	
describe a town or city	
talk about places of work	

Real life

9 Complete the word in each sentence.

1 W_____ is the museum?
2 Is it n_____ here?
3 It's about ten minutes a_____ .
4 Go a_____ this street because it's on the other side of the road.
5 T_____ the first street on the right.
6 T_____ right and go straight up the road.

10 ▶▶ **MB** Work in pairs. Ask for and give directions from your English class to some of these places.

- a café
- a store
- a bank
- a movie theater
- your car or bicycle
- a bus stop

I CAN	
ask for and give directions	

Unit 4 Free time

Early morning at Snoqualmie Falls, Washington, USA

FEATURES

46 100% identical?

Identical twins look the same, but do they have the same interests?

48 Free time in the Arctic

How photographer Norbert Rosing spends his free time in the Arctic

50 Extreme sports

Meet four people who like dangerous sports

54 Urban biking

A video about a unique style of bike riding

1 ▶ 38 Look at the photo and listen to three people talking about their free-time activities. Which person (1, 2, or 3) is in the photo? ____

2 ▶ 38 Listen again and complete this chart.

	What?	When?	With who?	Why?
Person 1	go 1 _____	every Saturday	with 2 _____	It's fun!
Person 2	go to the 3 _____	three times a week	on my own	It's 4 _____
Person 3	go fishing	early in the 5 _____	with my brother	It's very 6 _____

3 Think about your favorite free-time activity. Write notes about these things.

- What?
- With who?
- When?
- Why?

4 Work in groups. Talk about your free-time activity.

I play video games on weekends with friends. It's fun!

4a 100% identical?

Reading

1 Work in pairs. Discuss these questions.

  1 Do you know any twins? Do they do the same job? Do they have the same hobbies and interests?
  2 Do you have any brothers or sisters? Do you spend your free time together?

2 Read the article about identical twins. Is the article about their work, their free time, or both?

3 Read the article again and complete the chart with information about the twins.

	The Mulgray twins	The Kitt twins	The Phelps twins
Job?	*writers*		
Free-time activities?			*golf,*

100% IDENTICAL?

▶ 39

Identical twins have the same eyes and the same hair, but do they like doing the same things? What do they do in their free time?

THE MULGRAY TWINS

Morna and Helen Mulgray are seventy-seven years old. They love books, and they write crime[1] books together. They live in the same house and they like the same free-time activities. They like gardening, and on weekends they go walking together.

THE KITT TWINS

Camille and Kennerly Kitt are musicians and actors. They both play the same musical instrument—the harp. They do taekwondo and they like swimming—together, of course.

THE PHELPS TWINS

James and Oliver Phelps are actors. They are famous as the identical twins in the *Harry Potter* movies. In their free time, they love playing golf and video games. They like soccer, but they don't like the same teams.

[1]crime (n) /kraɪm/ an act that is against the law

Wordbuilding verb + noun collocations

> **WORDBUILDING verb + noun collocations**
>
> We use certain verbs with certain nouns and -ing forms. These are verb + noun collocations.
> For example: *do yoga, go camping, go running, play video games, play soccer, play golf, read a magazine, watch TV*
>
> For more practice, see Workbook page 35.

4 Match the verbs (1–8) with the nouns (a–h) to make collocations.

1	go	○	○	a	video games
2	play	○	○	b	movies
3	do	○	○	c	friends
4	play	○	○	d	the gym
5	watch	○	○	e	swimming
6	play	○	○	f	taekwondo
7	go to	○	○	g	a musical instrument
8	meet	○	○	h	golf

5 Complete the questionnaire with five free-time activities.

*In your free time, do you **go swimming**?*

In your free time, do you ...

- _____ _____ ? ☐
- _____ _____ ? ☐
- _____ _____ ? ☐
- _____ _____ ? ☐
- _____ _____ ? ☐

6 Work in pairs. Interview your partner with your questionnaire.

A: In your free time, do you go swimming?
B: Yes, I do. / No, I don't.

Grammar *like/love* + noun or *-ing* form

> ▶ *LIKE/LOVE* + NOUN or *-ING* FORM
>
> They **love** books.
> They **don't like** the same soccer teams.
> **Does** he **like** soccer?
>
> She **likes** swimm**ing**.
> I **don't like** danc**ing**.
> **Do** they **like** do**ing** the same things?
>
> For more information and practice, see page 164.

7 Work in pairs. Look at the grammar box. Which three sentences have *like/love* + noun? Which three sentences have *like/love* + the *-ing* form of the verb?

8 Look at the article again. Underline the sentences with *like/love* + a noun or an *-ing* form.

9 Pronunciation /ŋ/

▶ **40** Listen and repeat these verbs in the *-ing* form.

playing	listening	singing	watching
going	doing	dancing	shopping

Speaking **myLife**

10 Write three sentences (two true and one false) about your free-time activities, interests, or hobbies. Use *love, like,* or *don't like.*

*I **love** play**ing** the guitar. (true)*
*I **like** watching soccer. (true)*
*I **don't like** going out for dinner. (false)*

11 Work in pairs. Read your three sentences to your partner. Guess which of your partner's sentences is false.

12 Now ask your partner questions about their free-time activities.

What kinds of music do you like playing?
What's your favorite soccer team?

4b Free time in the Arctic

Vocabulary everyday activities

1 Circle the activities you do every day.

do online shopping	go for a walk	have coffee
make phone calls	play online games	read a book
browse the internet	use social media	watch videos
text friends		

2 Write two activities you do every day and one activity you never do. Then work in pairs. Tell your partner your three activities. Guess which two activities your partner does every day.

Listening

3 Work in pairs. Look at the photos. What do you think Norbert Rosing photographs?

4 ▶ 41 Listen to part of a documentary about Norbert Rosing. Answer the questions with *yes* (Y), *no* (N), or *not given* (NG) if there is no information.

1 Are Norbert's photos in *National Geographic* magazine and on the website? ____
2 Does Norbert photograph people? ____
3 Does he go to the Arctic in the winter? ____
4 Are there roads in the Arctic? ____
5 Does he travel by snowmobile and by boat? ____
6 Does he travel with other people? ____
7 Does he photograph polar bears at night? ____
8 Does he sleep during the night? ____
9 Does he play video games? ____
10 Is Norbert often bored? ____

5 Do you think Norbert has a good job? Why or why not?

A: I think Norbert has a good job because he loves it.
B: I don't think it's a good job because the Arctic is cold!

One of Norbert Rosing's photos of a polar bear in the Arctic.

Grammar adverbs of frequency

6 ▶ **41** Listen again and complete the sentences with these adverbs of frequency.

always	never	rarely
often	sometimes	usually

1 Norbert's photos are _____ in *National Geographic* magazine.
2 He goes to the Arctic once a year and he _____ goes in the summer.
3 He's _____ there for a few weeks.
4 He _____ goes by snowmobile and by boat.
5 He _____ sleeps at night, so he sleeps for part of the day.
6 He's _____ bored.

7 Work in pairs. Look at the sentences in Exercise 6 and answer these questions.

1 Do adverbs of frequency come before or after the verb *to be*?
2 Do they come before or after other verbs?

8 Look at the grammar box. Complete the scale with *usually*, *often*, and *sometimes*.

▶ **ADVERBS OF FREQUENCY**

100% ◀━━━━━━━━━━━━━━━━━━━━━▶ 0%
always ¹_____ ²_____ ³_____ never

*I **sometimes** go swimming on the weekend.*
*I **often** watch TV.*
*I **usually** play video games in the evening.*

For more information and practice, see page 164.

9 Add an adverb of frequency to the sentences so they are true for you. Then work in pairs and tell your partner.

1 I work eight hours a day.

_____

2 I'm late for school.

_____

3 I have a long lunch break.

_____

4 I leave home early in the morning.

_____

5 I travel to other countries for my vacations.

_____

6 I play video games late at night.

_____

Grammar expressions of frequency

▶ **EXPRESSIONS OF FREQUENCY**

A: **How often** does Norbert go to the Arctic?
B: He goes **once a year**.
A: **How often** do you see polar bears in the Arctic?
B: Between August and November, you can see polar bears **every day**.

For more information and practice, see page 164.

10 Work in pairs. Look at the grammar box. Read the questions and answers, and answer these questions (1–2).

1 What two words start a question about frequency?
2 Where do expressions of frequency (e.g., *once a year*) usually go in a sentence?

11 Write *How often* questions and answers for the conversations. Use the information in the parentheses in your answers.

1 A: *How often do you go to the gym?* ?
   B: I go to the gym three times a week.

2 A: _____ ?
   B: My family goes on vacation once a year.

3 A: How often do you drink coffee? (every morning)
   B: _____ .

4 A: How often do you go to the movies? (twice a month)
   B: _____ .

5 A: _____ ?
   B: She has English class every week.

Speaking *myLife*

12 Choose one topic below and prepare five questions with *How often*.

- sports and exercise
- work and travel
- vacations and free time
- evenings and weekends

13 Work in groups. Take turns asking and answering your questions.

4c Extreme sports

Vocabulary sports

1 Work in pairs. Look at these sports and answer the questions.

baseball	basketball	boxing
ice hockey	running	sailing
surfing	swimming	tennis
cycling	soccer	skiing

1 Which sports do you play? Which sports do you like watching on TV?
2 Which sports:
   a need a ball?
   b are in water?
   c are on snow?
   d are between two teams?
   e use the verb *play*?
   f use the verb *go*?

Reading

2 Read the article. Match the sentences (1–4) with the sports (A–D) in the article. More than one answer is possible for some sentences.

1 This sport is in the air. _____
2 This sport is often or usually on a mountain. _____
3 This sport needs water. _____
4 This sport can take place over long distances. _____

3 Work in pairs. Find these adjectives in the article. Which sports in Exercise 1 do you think these adjectives also describe?

| exciting | popular | relaxing |

Critical thinking fact or opinion

4 Look at these sentences from the article and decide if they are a fact (F) or someone's opinion (O).

1 He can jump between twenty and thirty meters.   F   O
2 Cliff diving is a very exciting extreme sport.   F   O
3 In this photo, American Andy Lewis is walking above a canyon.   F   O
4 Highlining is a great adventure.   F   O
5 The landscape is perfect.   F   O
6 Extreme paragliders can fly over 3,000 meters high.   F   O

5 Work in pairs. What is the author's opinion of extreme sports? Do you think he likes them?

Grammar *can/can't*

> **▶ CAN/CAN'T (+ ADVERB)**
>
> a *He **can** jump between twenty and thirty meters.*
> b *He **can't** see **very well**.*
> c ***Can** you speak French?*
> d *I **can** speak French **very well / a little**.*
> e ***How well** can you swim?*

For more information and practice, see page 164.

6 Work in pairs. Look at the sentences in the grammar box. Answer the questions (1–5).

1 *Can* is a modal verb. Does it come before or after the main verb?
2 Do we add *-s* to *can* for *he/she/it* forms?
3 Do we need *don't* in a negative sentence?
4 What are the adverbs in sentences b and d? Where are they in the sentences?
5 How do you form the question in e?

7 Look at the grammar box again. Complete these sentences with *can* or *can't*. Which sentences contain adverbs?

1 I _____ swim well, but I can't dive.
2 How well _____ you play tennis?
3 A: _____ you cycle up a mountain?
   B: No, I _____ .
4 I'm just a beginner. I _____ play the guitar well.
5 How many languages _____ you speak?
6 I _____ speak French, but I _____ speak Chinese a little.

8 Pronunciation *can* and *can't*

a ▶ 43 Listen to the different pronunciations of *can* and *can't*.

/kən/	/kæ:nt/
I can swim.	*I can't play tennis.*
/kæn/	/kən/
Can you play the guitar?	*How well can you play?*

b ▶ 44 Listen and repeat the sentences from Exercise 7.

Speaking my Life

9 Write down a sport, a musical instrument, and a language. Then work in pairs. Ask your partner *Can you …?* questions with your ideas.

Can you play the violin?

▶ 42

EXTREME SPORTS

Lots of people play sports in their free time, but these people do extreme sports!

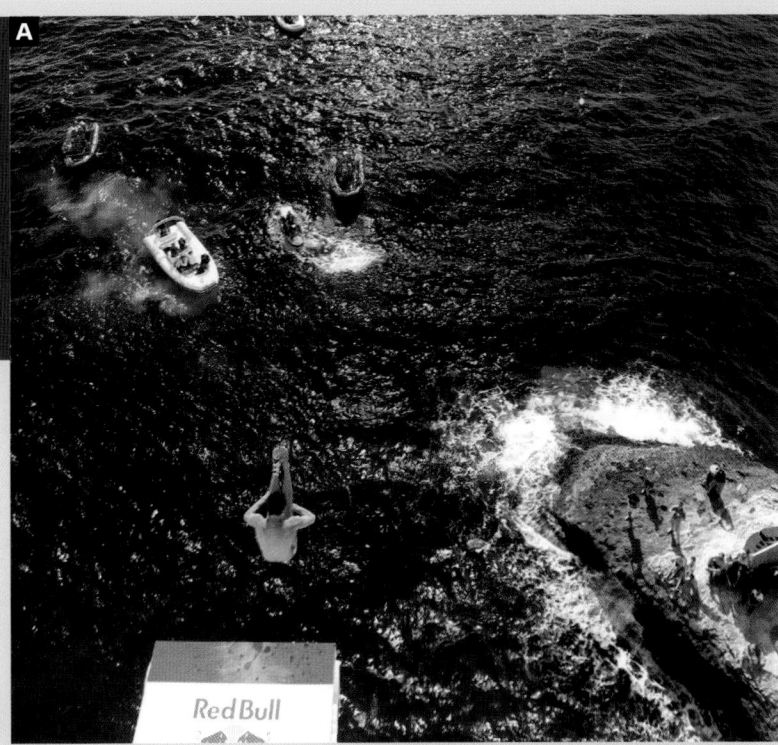

A CLIFF DIVING

Cliff diving is a very exciting extreme sport. Cyrille Oumedjkane is an expert cliff diver. In this photo, he is in Kragerø, Norway, at
5 the cliff diving world series. He can jump between twenty and thirty meters into the water feet first. Normal divers jump from ten meters or less, and they jump into the water head first. He can jump from any
10 high place. "I cliff dive because I don't like soccer. I like the adrenaline,"[1] he says.

B HIGHLINING

You can highline in lots of different places, but
15 mountains are popular. You put a line between two high places and walk across. In this photo, American Andy Lewis is walking above a canyon in
20 Utah, USA. It's early evening, so he can't see very well. Also, the wind is strong, so Andy can't walk fast. Highlining is a great adventure.

25 ## C MOUNTAIN BIKING

Perhaps you often go cycling, but can you ride across the top of a 1,000-meter mountain? Professional mountain biker Kenny Belaey rides across South Africa's Table Mountain in this photo.
30 "The landscape is perfect," he says.

D PARAGLIDING

In this photo, Justin Ferrar is flying above Fronalpstock in the mountains of Switzerland. The weather is perfect for paragliding. But paragliding isn't normally relaxing! Extreme
35 paragliders can fly over 3,000 meters high and for very long distances (over 300 kilometers).

¹**adrenaline** (n) /əˈdrenəlɪn/ a chemical in your body. Humans produce it when they are excited (often in sports).

4d Take a year off!

Reading

1 Read the web page and answer the questions.

1 What does the website offer?
2 What are the top three volunteer jobs?

VOLUNTEER WORK

Do you need a break from your everyday work?[1]

Do you want to travel and live in other countries?

Do you want to take a year off between high school and college?

We have hundreds of volunteer jobs for your year off. This week, our **TOP THREE** volunteer jobs are:

1 Help the lions: volunteer in Zambia and help hundreds of orphan[2] lion cubs.[3]

2 Write for a newspaper: an English newspaper in Bolivia needs young, enthusiastic journalists.

3 Teach English: work with young children in schools all over the world.

Call **555-432-7543** now and ask for more information.

[1]**volunteer work** (n) /ˌvɑlənˈtɪrwɜrk/ a job for no money
[2]**orphan** (n) /ˈɔrfən/ a child with no parents
[3]**cub** (n) /kʌb/ a very young lion

2 Work in pairs. Answer these questions.

1 Do people take a year off in your country? What do they do during that time?
2 Do you do any volunteer work near where you live?

Real life talking about abilities and interests

3 ▶ 45 Work in pairs. Listen to someone call the number on the website in Exercise 1. Which volunteer job is she interested in?

4 ▶ 45 Listen again. Look at the expressions for talking about abilities and interests and circle the expressions you hear.

> ▶ **TALKING ABOUT ABILITIES AND INTERESTS**
>
> **Are you good at** teaching?
> **How well can you** speak English?
> **Can you** teach?
> **Do you like** animals?
>
> **I can speak** English well.
> **I can't** go for eighteen months.
> **I'm (not very) good at** writing.
> **I (don't) like** animals.
> **I love** them!

5 Pronunciation sentence stress

▶ 46 Listen to these sentences. Notice the stressed words. Then listen again and repeat.

1 Are you <u>good</u> at <u>writing</u>?
2 I'm <u>good</u> at <u>writing</u>.
3 Can you <u>teach</u>?
4 How <u>well</u> can you <u>teach</u>?
5 I <u>can't</u> speak <u>English</u> very <u>well</u>.
6 Do you <u>like animals</u>?
7 I <u>love animals</u>!

6 Write four questions using the expressions for talking about abilities and interests. Then work in pairs and ask and answer your questions.

7 Work in pairs. Look at the website in Exercise 1 again and practice this telephone conversation.

Student A: You work for the Volunteer Work company. Ask Student B about his or her abilities and interests.

Student B: You want to take a year off. Answer questions about your abilities and interests.

4e You have an email

Writing short emails

1 How do you communicate with people in other places (e.g., by phone, by email, by text message, by online chat)? Do you communicate differently at work and in your free time? Why?

2 Work in pairs. Read these short emails. Which are about work and which are about free-time activities?

> **1** Hi!
> Are you interested in seeing the new Spielberg movie? It starts at 8.

> **2** Dear Sandy,
> The receptionist is very busy today. Do you have any free time? Can you help her?
> Regards,
> Molly

> **3** Ray,
> The party is at 8 p.m. on Friday. Omar thinks it's on Saturday. Can you tell him?

> **4** Hi, I'm at work until six, so do you want to eat out this evening? The new restaurant on Brooke Street has sushi. We can go there.

> **5** Are you good at fixing copy machines? The one in my office doesn't work. Please help!

> **6** Hello Carlos,
> I got an email from some customers in Peru. I wrote a reply to them using an online translator. You can speak Spanish; could you please check it for me?

3 Writing skill reference words

a Work in pairs. Look at email 1 in Exercise 2. The writer uses *it* so he doesn't repeat information. What does *it* refer to?

b Work in pairs. Look at these words from emails 2–6. What do they refer to?

2	her	3	it, him	4 there
5	one	6	them, it	

4 These sentences repeat the same information. Change the **bold** words to the words in the box.

here	him	it	it
one	them	~~there~~	there

1 I like Joe's café. Can we meet **at Joe's café**? _____*there*_____
2 I have your letter. Can you come and get **the letter**? _____
3 Do you like Mexican food? The café downstairs has **Mexican food** at lunchtime. _____
4 I'm in my office, so meet me **in my office**. _____
5 Olav can't finish his work. Can you help **Olav**? _____
6 Matt and Suki are late. Please call **Matt and Suki**. _____
7 I like the new nightclub. Can we go **to the new nightclub**? _____
8 I need a new computer. This **computer** is very old. _____

5 Write two short emails to a friend or someone you work with. Use reference words.

Message 1: Ask for help with something at work.
Message 2: Invite your partner somewhere (e.g., a restaurant, the movies).

6 Work in pairs. Exchange emails with your partner. Does your partner use reference words? Write a reply to each message.

4f Urban biking

Danny MacAskill is a professional bike rider.

Before you watch

1 Work in pairs. Look at the photo and read the caption. What do you think he is doing? Have you seen this activity before?

2 Write three adjectives to describe this activity. Share your adjectives with a partner.

_____ _____ _____

3 Key vocabulary

Read the sentences (1–5). The words in **bold** are used in the video. Match the words with the definitions.

1 There's a problem with my car. I need to get a **mechanic** to look at it.
2 She learned singing for seven years before she became a **professional** singer.
3 The action movie was exciting because the actor did many dangerous **stunts**.
4 His cooking skills are **impressive**. Everything he makes is delicious!
5 Ice-skating is a **challenge** for me because I'm not good at balancing.

a amazing ____
b a difficult task ____
c unusual or risky acts ____
d a person who fixes machines ____
e doing a particular activity as a job ____

While you watch

4 ▶ **4.1** Watch the video. Are these statements true (T) or false (F)?

1	Danny MacAskill is a stunt rider.	T	F
2	Danny had a different job in the past.	T	F
3	The man watching says Danny's performance is dangerous.	T	F
4	Danny is always looking for difficult places to ride his bike.	T	F
5	The easy part of riding across the bridge is going down.	T	F
6	Danny tries many times, but he can't ride down the bridge.	T	F

5 ▶ **4.1** Watch the video again. What can Danny do with his bike? Check (✓) the things that you see.

☐ jump from one spot to another
☐ ride on one wheel
☐ ride hands-free
☐ ride on walls
☐ cycle backward
☐ do a backflip
☐ climb a bridge
☐ jump from one bicycle to another

After you watch

6 Vocabulary in context

a ▶ **4.2** Watch the clips from the video. Choose the correct meaning of the words and phrases.

b Complete a summary of the video using the words in the box.

at last	look
conquer	see / differently

Danny MacAskill is a bike rider from Scotland. He rides on the streets of Edinburgh. He says that it makes him ¹_____ the city streets _____ now. Danny also says that he wants to ²_____ for new challenges. In the video, Danny tries to climb a bridge with his bike. It was difficult at the beginning, but ³_____ , after many tries, he climbed onto the bridge. Danny managed to ⁴_____ his challenge.

7 Work in pairs and answer these questions.

1 Do you know any other extreme sports?
2 What can people do in those sports?

UNIT 4 REVIEW AND MEMORY BOOSTER

Grammar

1 Complete the sentences with the *-ing* form of these verbs.

go	listen	play	swim	watch

1 I love _____ . It's great exercise!
2 He likes _____ video games.
3 She doesn't like _____ to the gym.
4 They love _____ to jazz music.
5 We don't like _____ baseball on TV.

2 Write sentences about these people and their free-time activities.

1 Shelly / watch TV (never)
   Shelly never watches TV.
2 Chris / watch TV (often)
3 Annette / go to the movies (once a month)
4 Shelly / play video games (sometimes)
5 Chris / play video games (every day)
6 Chris / go to the movies (sometimes)
7 Annette / play video games (rarely)

3 Match the questions with the answers. Write a–e in the blanks.

1 Can you speak Italian? ____
2 Can you swim fast? ____
3 I can play the guitar. Can you? ____
4 I can't sing very well. Can you? ____
5 How well can you play soccer? ____

a No, I can't, but my friend can sing very well.
b No, but I can run fast.
c Yes, I can speak a little, but not very well.
d Not very well.
e No, but I can play the piano.

I CAN	
talk about likes and dislikes	
use adverbs and expressions of frequency	
use *can/can't* for talking about ability	

Vocabulary

4 Which words cannot follow the verbs in **bold**? Cross out the incorrect word in each group.

1 **play**	tennis	golf	running
2 **do**	yoga	camping	exercises
3 **go**	fishing	cycling	soccer
4 **watch**	the guitar	videos	a movie
5 **listen to**	the gym	the radio	music
6 **meet**	friends	family	sports

5 ▶▶ MB Work in pairs. Play Collocation Tennis. Take turns saying one of these verbs. Your partner matches it with a noun, and wins one point for a correct collocation. Try to win five points.

do	go	have	make	meet
play	read	speak	use	watch

6 Complete the sentences with these words.

ball	mountain	snow	teams

1 You play baseball and tennis with a _____ .
2 You ski on _____ .
3 In soccer, two _____ play each other.
4 You can go climbing on a _____ .

I CAN	
use verb + noun collocations	
talk about free-time activities and sports	

7 ▶▶ MB What do these people like doing in their free time? Check your answers on page 46.

Real life

8 Circle the correct options to complete the conversation.

A: I'd like a job for the summer.
B: OK. Are you good ¹ *in / at* English? I have a job for an English teacher.
A: I can speak English ² *good / well*, but I don't like teaching. Is there anything else?
B: What about tennis? How well can you ³ *do / play*?
A: Not ⁴ *very well / a little*.
B: ⁵ *Can / Do* you like animals?
A: Yes, I love them!

9 ▶▶ MB Complete these questions. Then work in pairs. Take turns asking and answering them.

Do you like …?   How often do you …?
Are you good at …?   How well can you …?

I CAN	
ask and talk about abilities and interests	

Unit 5 Food

La Casa de la Abuela

Street food in Oaxaca, Mexico

FEATURES

1 Work in pairs. Look at the photo and read the caption. Answer these questions.

1 What kind of food do you think the woman cooks?
2 What kind of street food can you buy in your country?

2 ▶ 47 Work in pairs. Listen to a travel writer talking about the food in the photo. Answer the questions.

1 Why does she say she has a great job?
2 Where does she always go when she arrives in a new city?
3 Why is Oaxaca one of her favorite places?
4 What street food does she think is the best?

3 ▶ 47 Complete the sentences with these food verbs. Then listen again and check.

cook	eat	~~make~~	serve	smell	taste

1 All the street cooks ____make____ the food by hand.
2 Then they _____ it on a real fire.
3 So when you walk up the street, you can _____ the food from the different stalls.
4 The cooks _____ the tortillas with a local hot sauce.
5 They _____ delicious.
6 I can _____ them at any time of day—for breakfast, lunch, or dinner!

4 Work in pairs. Tell your partner about your favorite dish.

5a Famous for food

Vocabulary food

1 Match the words with the pictures (1–16).

cheese _____	chicken _____	fries _____	eggs _____
fish _____	juice _____	lemons _____	nuts _____
onions _____	oranges _____	pasta _____	pepper _____
potatoes _____	shrimp _____	rice _____	salt _____

2 Work in pairs. Complete these sentences so they are true for you. Use the food words from Exercise 1 or other food words you know. Compare your sentences with your partner.

1 I really like _____ , but I don't like _____ .
2 I often eat _____ , but I rarely eat _____ .
3 I sometimes cook _____ , but I never cook _____ .
4 I know what _____ taste(s) like, but I don't know what _____ taste(s) like.

3 Pronunciation /tʃ/ or /dʒ/

▶ **48** Listen to these words. Do you hear /tʃ/ or /dʒ/ ? Listen again and repeat.

1	**ch**icken	/tʃ/	/dʒ/
2	**j**uice	/tʃ/	/dʒ/
3	**ch**eese	/tʃ/	/dʒ/
4	oran**g**e	/tʃ/	/dʒ/

Listening and speaking famous for food

4 Work in pairs. Match the dishes (1–6) with the countries (a–f). Then check your answers on page 155.

1	pizza	○	○	a	Italy
2	ceviche	○	○	b	Indonesia
3	satay	○	○	c	Peru
4	kabsa	○	○	d	Poland
5	pierogi	○	○	e	India
6	curry	○	○	f	Saudi Arabia

5 ▶ **49** Listen to three people describing a dish from their country. Match the speakers (1–3) with the photos (a–c) on page 59.

Speaker 1 _____
Speaker 2 _____
Speaker 3 _____

6 ▶ **49** Listen again. Match the three dishes (a–c) with the sentences (1–7). More than one answer is possible.

1 It's popular in more than one country. _a, b, c_
2 There's meat in it. _____
3 You make it with fish. _____
4 You cook it. _____
5 You serve it with rice. _____
6 You serve it with salad. _____
7 You eat it hot. _____

7 Think of a popular dish in your country and answer these questions. Then tell your partner about the dish.

1 What is the name of the dish?
2 What do you make it with?
3 What can you add to it?
4 Do you eat it hot or cold?
5 Do you serve it with another dish?

Grammar countable and uncountable nouns with *a/an*, *some*, and *any*

> **COUNTABLE and UNCOUNTABLE NOUNS WITH *A/AN*, *SOME*, and *ANY***

*Cook the chicken with **an onion**.*
*You need **some meat** and **some onions** and **tomatoes**.*
*I don't use **any carrots**.*
*Do you have **any bread**?*

For more information and practice, see page 166.

8 Work in pairs. Look at the grammar box. Look at the nouns in **bold.** Which nouns in **bold** can you count? Which nouns can't you count?

9 Look at the grammar box again. Circle the correct option (a–b) to complete these rules.
1 We use *a/an* before:
  a countable nouns   b uncountable nouns
2 We use *some* and *any* with:
  a singular nouns   b plural nouns and uncountable nouns
3 We normally use *any* in:
  a affirmative sentences
  b negative sentences and questions

10 ▶ 50 Choose the correct options to complete the conversation about curry. Then listen and check.

A: I'd like to make chicken curry this evening. What do you think?
B: Sounds good.
A: OK, well, we need ¹*any / some* chicken. Can you buy ²*a / some* kilo when you go to the supermarket?
B: Sure.
A: And we need ³*a / some* tomatoes.
B: Right. And we don't have ⁴*any / some* onions. I'll get some. Is there ⁵*any / some* rice?
A: Yeah, I think there's ⁶*any / some* rice in the cabinet.
B: OK. And I'll buy ⁷*a / some* cooking oil. So, we need ⁸*any / some* chicken, tomatoes, onions, and oil. Anything else?

11 Work in pairs. You and your partner have two recipes you want to make. You both have some ingredients. Find out what your partner has and what you need from the supermarket.

Student A: Turn to page 154.

Student B: Turn to page 156.

Speaking my Life

12 Work in groups. Plan a special meal for six people. Choose three different dishes. Then make a list of the ingredients you need to make them.

*A: We need **some** …*
*B: And we also need **a** …*
*A: Do we need **any** …?*

13 Tell the class about your meal and the ingredients you need.

Our three dishes are … We need …

5b Top five food markets

Reading

1 Where do you like shopping for food? Check (✓) the option(s).

☐ at a supermarket
☐ at a market
☐ from lots of different stores
☐ I don't like shopping!

2 Work in pairs. Read the article about markets around the world. Answer the questions.

1 How old is St. Lawrence market?
2 What food can you buy at St. Lawrence market?
3 What is hot at Castries Market?
4 What is upstairs at Kreta Ayer Wet Market?
5 What can you hear at La Vucciria?
6 What days is Haymarket open?

3 Discuss these questions as a class.

1 Do you have a food market in your town or city? What days is it open?
2 Can you buy fresh food and local dishes there? What kind?
3 What other street markets are in your town or city? What do they sell?

Grammar *a lot of* and *much/many*

▶ *A LOT OF* and *MUCH/MANY*

There**'s a lot of** different food.
There **are a lot of** / **many** shops here.
There **aren't many** markets.
There **isn't much** food.
Do you eat **a lot of** / **many** apples?
No, **not a lot** / **not many**.
Do you eat **a lot of** / **much** cheese?
No, **not a lot** / **not much**.

For more information and practice, see page 166.

4 Look at the grammar box. Complete the rules for *a lot of, much,* and *many*.

1 We use _____ with both countable and uncountable nouns.
2 We use _____ only with countable nouns.
3 We use _____ only with uncountable nouns.

▶ 51

Top ⑤ | Food markets

Food markets are great places to find interesting local food. Here are our top five markets from around the world.

❶ **St. Lawrence, Toronto, Canada**

St. Lawrence food market, in Toronto, is 200 years old. There are a lot of shops with every kind of meat and seafood.

❷ **Castries Market, St. Lucia**

Naturally, the island of St. Lucia in the Caribbean has a market famous for fish and fruit. Try the local sauce—it's very hot and spicy!

❸ **Kreta Ayer Wet Market, Singapore**

There's a lot of different food here and there are many great food stalls upstairs. Go at around 6 a.m. and have some tasty noodles for breakfast.

❹ **La Vucciria, Palermo, Italy**

There aren't many markets in the world with live music. But in Palermo, musicians play and sing as shoppers buy sausages and fresh pasta.

❺ **Haymarket, Boston, US**

This market is almost 200 years old and famous with food lovers. It's open during daylight hours every Friday and Saturday, but it's good to go early. There isn't much food for sale late in the day!

St. Lawrence food market

5 Underline a part of each sentence that can be replaced with *much* or *many*, and write the replacement word.

   1 I don't eat <u>a lot of</u> fast food. *much*

   2 There aren't a lot of local markets in my region.

   3 Do you buy a lot of snacks for the kids?

   4 There isn't a lot of milk in the fridge.

   5 She doesn't put a lot of salt on her food.

   6 Do you eat a lot of strawberries in the summer?

6 Work in pairs. Complete these sentences in your own words and tell your partner.

  I eat a lot of …   I don't eat much …
  I don't eat many …

Listening and vocabulary
quantities and containers

7 ▶ 52 Work in pairs. Listen to a shopper at one of the markets from the article. Which market is it?

8 ▶ 52 Listen again. Answer the questions.

   1 How many bananas does he buy? ____

   2 How many kilos of rice does he buy? ____

   3 How many bottles of sauce does he buy? ____

9 Look at the pictures and complete the descriptions (1–8) with these words.

bag	bottle	glass	kilo
box	piece	slice	can

  1 a _____ of sauce   5 a _____ of pasta

  2 a _____ of chocolate   6 a _____ of tuna

  3 a _____ of pizza   7 a _____ of meat

  4 a _____ of water   8 a _____ of rice

Grammar *how many / how much*

▶ **HOW MANY / HOW MUCH**

A: **How many** bananas do you want?	B: Six, please.
A: **How much** rice do you want?	B: A kilo.

For more information and practice, see page 166.

10 Look at the grammar box. Which question asks about countable nouns? Which asks about uncountable nouns?

11 Complete these questions with *much* or *many*.

   1 A: How _____ apples would you like?
      B: Six, please.

   2 A: How _____ sugar do you want?
      B: Two kilos.

   3 A: How _____ boxes of pasta do you want?
      B: Just one.

   4 A: How _____ cheese would you like?
      B: Half a kilo, please.

Speaking myLife

12 Work in pairs. Practice conversations at a food market. Take turns asking for these things.

  • five apples and some cheese

  • some bread and a bottle of sauce

  • four cans of tuna and six slices of cake

13 Have a new conversation at a food market. Ask for the foods you like to eat.

5c An eater's guide to food labels

Reading

1 Work in groups. What food do you eat every week? List seven things. Then number the things on your list in order from 1 to 7. Tell the rest of the group what you eat.

1 – very good for you
7 = not very good for you

I eat salad about three times a week because it's very good for you. Once a week, I eat a burger and fries, but fries aren't very good for you.

2 Work in pairs. Look at the photos of food labels on page 63. Answer the questions.

1 What information is on the labels on cans and boxes of food?
2 Do you ever read labels? Why or why not?

3 Read the blog post about food labels and circle the correct options (a–b).

1 Food with the words *superfood* or *natural* on the label ____ .
   a is always good for you
   b often costs more money than other food
2 The *best before* date means you should eat the food ____ .
   a before the date
   b after the date
3 In low-fat foods, there is often a lot of ____ .
   a sugar
   b good fat
4 "Traffic lights" on food labels ____ .
   a use two colors
   b help you choose healthy food

Word focus *mean*

4 The writer uses the word *mean* in the blog post. Match the sentences (1–2) with the uses of the word *mean* (a–b).

1 Red **means** the food is unhealthy. ____
2 The word *healthy* **means** the food is good for you. ____

a to explain a word
b to say what something shows or tells you

5 When do you say these phrases with *mean*? Match the sentences (1–4) with the uses (a–d).

1 Do you know what I **mean**? ____
2 I see what you **mean**. ____
3 Your pizza is delicious. I **mean** it! ____
4 We went out for dinner last Friday—I **mean** last Saturday. ____

a to check the other person understands you
b to say you are serious
c to correct something you said
d to say you understand

6 Work in pairs. Answer these questions.

1 What does the word *vegetarian* mean?
2 What do the three colors on traffic lights mean to car drivers?
3 How often do you say things you don't really mean? Why?

Critical thinking ways of giving advice

7 The writer's main aim in the blog is to give the reader advice. Match the sentences with the ways of giving advice (a–c). Underline the key words.

a gives strong advice
b makes a suggestion
c says something isn't necessary

1 <u>You could</u> look at the price first, or <u>you could</u> read the label. *b*
2 <u>Check</u> the rest of the label. *a*
3 Make sure you look carefully at the list of ingredients before you buy. ____
4 You can still eat it afterwards. ____
5 You don't need to throw the food away. ____
6 Remember that some types of fat are important for health. ____
7 When the label has the number of calories in one portion, be careful. ____

Writing and speaking *my* Life

8 Work in pairs. Write three more pieces of advice about healthy eating. Use the words and phrases from Exercise 7. Then read your advice to another pair.

Make sure you eat lots of vegetables.

AN EATER'S GUIDE TO
FOOD LABELS

▶ 53

You're in your local supermarket. There are hundreds of packages, bags, jars, and cans of food in front of you. Which ones do you choose? You could look at the price first, or you could read the label to
5 find out if it's healthy. But do food labels really tell us everything about the food we eat?

Superfood

The word *superfood* is popular nowadays. It's usually food with lots of vitamins,[1] and it's often more expensive than other food. But *superfood* doesn't mean much—anyone can write *superfood* on any type of food, so check the rest of the label.

Natural

Like *superfood*, *natural* is another popular word on labels (and it often adds to the cost). It usually means that everything in the food is healthy and from nature, but this is not always true. Make sure you look carefully at the list of ingredients before you buy.

Best before

The *best before* date means the food is best before this date, but you can still eat it afterwards. You don't need to throw the food away immediately after the best before date.

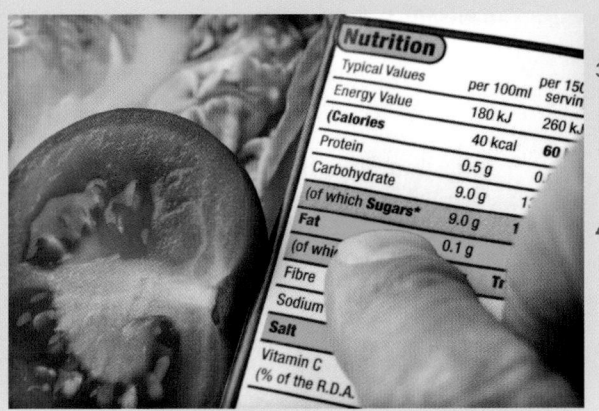

25 Low fat

We often think that fat is bad and that low-fat food is good for you, but this isn't always true. Some low-fat food has a lot of sugar in it, and remember that some types of fat are important for health.

30 Calories and portion size

When the label has the number of calories[2] in one portion,[3] be careful. Your normal portion size is often bigger than the one on the label, so you eat more calories.

DISPLAY UNTIL / USE BY

16 JUN   £3.00

KEEP REFRIGERATED BELOW 5°C

PER PACK		GDA
calories	469	23%
sugars	3.9g	4%
fat	23.4g	33%
saturates	5.6g	28%
salt	2.08g	35%

Traffic lights

35 Some countries use "traffic lights" on labels to help customers with their choices. Red means the food has a lot of fat, salt, or sugar, and is unhealthy. Orange means it's OK, and green means it's very healthy. More and more countries plan to use traffic lights, because they're easy to
40 understand and you don't need to read every word.

[1]**vitamins** (n) /ˈvaɪtəmɪnz/ natural substances in food which the body needs (e.g., vitamin C)
[2]**calorie** (n) /ˈkæləri/ a unit of energy
[3]**portion** (n) /ˈpɔːrʃ(ə)n/ the size of your meal

5d At the restaurant

Vocabulary menus

1 Complete the restaurant menu with these headings.

| Desserts | Drinks | Main course | Appetizers |

Menu

1 _____

Garlic bread	$6.95
Red pepper and tomato soup	$7.50
Shrimp salad	$7.95

2 _____

Spaghetti Bolognese	$13.95
Seafood pizza	$11.95
Steak and fries	$15.50
Mushroom and spinach burger with fries* (*suitable for vegetarians)	$11.95
Chicken satay with Thai noodles	$12.50

3 _____

Apple pie and ice cream	$8.95
Chocolate fudge cake	$7.95
Four cheeses and crackers	$7.50

4 _____

Fresh smoothies (orange, pineapple, strawberry)	$3.95
Bottled water (sparkling or still)	$2.50
Iced tea	$2.50

2 What are some common appetizers, main courses, and desserts in restaurants in your country? Which do you normally order? Tell the class.

3 Look at the menu again and choose a dish or drink from each part. Work in pairs. Tell your partner.

Real life ordering a meal

4 ▶ 54 Listen to two people at the restaurant in Exercise 1. Work in pairs. Answer the questions.

1 What do they order?
2 Look at the menu again. How much does the meal cost?

5 ▶ 54 Look at these expressions for ordering a meal. Who says them: one of the customers (C) or the waiter (W)? Listen again and check.

> **▶ ORDERING A MEAL**
>
> Here is the menu. ____
> Can I get you anything to drink first? ____
> I'd like a bottle of water, please. ____
> I don't want an appetizer. ____
> I'll have a seafood pizza. ____
> I'd also like dessert. ____
> Are you ready to order? ____
> That was delicious. ____
> Can I get you anything else? ____
> Could we have the check, please? ____

6 Pronunciation contractions

a ▶ 55 Listen and repeat these contracted forms.

| I'd | I'd like a coffee. |
| I'll | I'll have a pizza. |

b Practice saying the phrases for ordering a meal with contractions.

7 Work in groups of three. One person is the waiter and two people are customers. Practice a conversation at a restaurant. Use the menu in Exercise 1. Then change roles.

5e What do I do next?

Writing instructions

1 Read the three texts with instructions. Match the texts (1–3) with the places (a–c).

a inside a box ____
b in a cookbook ____
c on a food label ____

1

Y ou can make this cake in about fifteen minutes. First, heat the oven to 200°C. Put the flour in a bowl. Next, add the milk, eggs, butter, and salt.

2

T hank you for buying this *Home Barbecue Grill*. Please follow these instructions:
1 Do not use the barbecue inside a building.
2 Never leave children alone with the barbecue.

3

S tore this bottle of sauce in a cool, dry place. After you open the bottle, use the sauce within three months.

2 Writing skill punctuation

a Match the punctuation marks with their uses (1–6) and find examples in the instructions in Exercise 1.

. (period)
, (comma)
: (colon)

1 between words in a list *comma*
2 at the end of a sentence ____
3 between two or more adjectives ____
4 to introduce a list ____
5 after a sequence word (e.g., *first, next*) ____
6 between two clauses in one sentence ____

b Read the instructions for part of a recipe. Add the missing punctuation.

Fortune cookies are fun at the end of a meal in a Chinese restaurant They're easy to make You need the following pieces of paper three eggs sugar salt and flour First of all write your messages on the pieces of paper Next mix the eggs sugar salt and flour and pour the mixture onto a tray

3 Work in pairs. Write instructions to make your favorite dish. Use some of these verbs in your instructions.

mix   chop   pour

spread   put   slice

4 Exchange your instructions with another pair. Check the punctuation. Would you like to make this dish?

Crates of fruit and vegetables in a market in Cabo San Lucas, Mexico.

Before you watch

1 Work in pairs. Look at the photo and read the caption. Which are fruit and which are vegetables? Do you know any of their names in English?

2 Key vocabulary

Read the sentences (1–6). The words in **bold** are used in the video. Match the words with the definitions (a–f).

1 When you answer a question correctly, you win one **point**.
2 Corn is a type of **cereal**.
3 You hold a flower by its **stem**.
4 Pull up a plant and you can see the **root**.
5 In the fall, the **leaves** on a tree turn red.
6 The **final score** in the game was two-one.

a the part of a plant under the ground _____
b a way of counting the score in a competition _____
c the long, thin part of a plant _____
d the number of points at the end of a game _____
e a type of plant which produces grain such as wheat or rice _____
f the green things on a tree or a plant _____

While you watch

3 You are going to take a video quiz with questions about different pictures on the screen. Before you watch, read the questions and get ready to start.

4 ▶ **5.1** Watch the video quiz and answer the questions below.

5 ▶ **5.2** Watch and check your answers. Count your points and find out your final score.

After you watch

6 Complete the sentences with these words.

cereal	eggplant	leaves
seaweed	stem	wheat

1 Oatmeal is a famous Scottish food. It's made with oats, which are a type of _____ .
2 The British use the French word *aubergine*, but it's called a(n) _____ in the US.
3 Most people eat the root of the turnip, but the _____ are also very good for you.
4 A tomato plant has a tall _____ with lots of flowers and fruit.
5 Flour is made from _____ . You make bread with it.
6 _____ is a traditional food in countries by the sea, like Japan and Korea.

7 Work in pairs. Prepare a short quiz about food by completing these questions with your own words. Decide how many points to give for each question.

1 Do you eat the stems, the leaves, or the roots of …?
2 What type of drink can you make from …?
3 What are three kinds of fruits or vegetables that are …? (a color)
4 Which country or part of the world is famous for …?

8 Write two more quiz questions using any of the question types in Exercise 7.

9 Work with another pair. Take turns asking and answering your quiz questions. Then tell the other pair their score.

		Score
1	What are three types of food you can make from wheat? _____ _____ _____	___ /3
2	Which country has the most types of potatoes? (a) China (b) Peru (c) Italy	___ /1
3	Do you eat the stems, the leaves, or the roots of the asparagus and celery plants? _____	___ /1
4	Do you eat the stems, the leaves, or the roots of the lettuce and cabbage plants?_____	___ /1
5	Do you eat the stems, the leaves, or the roots of the turnip and carrot? _____	___ /1
6	What are the red and purple types of fruit on the screen? _____ _____	___ /2
7	What are the last two kinds of fruit you see on the screen? _____ _____	___ /2
8	What type of plant on the screen makes our food taste hot and spicy? _____	___ /1
9	What type of drink can you make from the bean at the end? _____	___ /1

UNIT 5 REVIEW AND MEMORY BOOSTER

Grammar

1 >> MB Work in pairs. Can you remember the words for these types of food and drink? Are they countable (C) or uncountable (U)?

2 >> MB Are the words in Exercise 1 used with *How much* or *How many?* Write them in the chart below. Then add two more food or drink words.

How much ...?	How many ...?

3 Match the sentence beginnings (1–6) with the endings (a–f).

1 We need   ○   ○   a banana, please.
2 Are there any ○   ○   b kilos of meat.
3 Please buy two ○   ○   c some chicken.
4 Chop an   ○   ○   d onions?
5 I'd like a   ○   ○   e onion.
6 Do we need a ○   ○   f lemon?

4 Choose the correct options to complete the conversation.

A: Do you want an apple?
B: No, thanks. I don't eat [1] *many / much* fruit.
A: Why not? Fruit is good for you.
B: I know, but I prefer other food. I eat [2] *many / a lot of* pasta and pizza. Do you eat [3] *many / much* Italian food?
A: Yes, I do. It's delicious. Are there [4] *a lot of / much* Italian restaurants in your town?
B: No, [5] *not a lot of / not many.*

I CAN	
use countable and uncountable nouns	☐
use *a/an*, *some*, *any*, *a lot of*, and *much/many*	☐

Vocabulary

5 Write these words in the correct group.

bag	chicken	juice	lamb
milk	oranges	carrots	pierogi
potatoes	bananas	satay	can

1 fruit   _____ , _____
2 vegetables   _____ , _____
3 meat   _____ , _____
4 drinks   _____ , _____
5 a dish   _____ , _____
6 a container   _____ , _____

6 >> MB Work in pairs. Think of one more word for each category in Exercise 5.

7 >> MB Use the words in A and B to make phrases using *a ____ of ____* .

A slice	glass	box	can

B tuna	water	pizza	pasta

I CAN	
talk about different types of food	☐
describe quantities of food and drink	☐

Real life

8 Replace the words in **bold** with these phrases.

Are you ready to	I'd like
Can we have	Would you like

1 **Can I get you** anything to drink? _____
2 **I'll have** a bottle of water. _____
3 **Would you like to** order? _____
4 **We'd like** the check, please. _____

9 >> MB Work in pairs. When you go to a café or a restaurant, what do you like to order:

• for breakfast?
• for lunch with a friend from school or work?
• for a special dinner to celebrate something with family and friends?

I CAN	
order a meal	☐

Unit 6 Past lives

Past and present

FEATURES

1 ▶ 56 Work in pairs. There is a connection between the two photos. What do you think it is? Listen and find out.

2 ▶ 56 Listen again and underline the correct options.

1 Chris took black and white photos in the nineteen *fifties and sixties / seventies and eighties*.
2 The first photo is from *1980 / 1981*.
3 The second photo is from *2015 / 2016*.

3 ▶ 57 Match the phrases for talking about periods in time (1–5) with the years. Then listen, check, and repeat.

1 the nineteen seventies	○ ○	1960–1969
2 the end of the twentieth century	○ ○	1989–1999
3 the beginning of the twenty-first century ○	○	1800–1899
4 the sixties	○ ○	1970–1979
5 the nineteenth century	○ ○	2002

4 Work in pairs. Match these people and events with the periods of time (1–5) in Exercise 3.

a the first photographs ____   d The Beatles ____
b the euro currency ____   e the first websites ____
c the first cell phones ____

6a Famous faces

Reading

1 Which people and places are on the notes and coins in your country? Are they:

- kings, queens, or presidents?
- scientists, musicians, writers, or artists?
- places or buildings?

2 Read the article about faces and places on money. Match the paragraphs (1–3) with the pictures (a–c).

3 Read the article again. Are these statements true (T) or false (F)?

1 George Washington was an American president. ____
2 His face is on every ten-dollar bill. ____
3 Euro notes have famous faces on them. ____
4 Some euro notes have pictures of presidents. ____
5 Frida Kahlo and Diego Rivera were artists. ____
6 Their faces are on different Mexican notes. ____

Grammar *was/were*

> ▶ **WAS/WERE**
>
> George Washington **was** the first president of the United States of America.
> His face **wasn't** on the US dollar until the nineteenth century.
> The new notes **were** different from traditional money because there **weren't** any famous people on them.
> When **was** he born?
> **Were** they famous?

For more information and practice, see page 168.

4 Work in pairs. Look at the grammar box. Answer these questions.

1 Are the sentences about the past or the present?
2 What is the base form of the verbs in **bold**?
3 Which form do we use for *you / they / we*?
4 Which form do we use for *I / he / she / it*?

FAMOUS FACES

▶ 58

1 George Washington was the first president of the United States of America. He was born in 1732 and lived during the American Revolution. He died in 1799, but his face wasn't on the US dollar until the nineteenth century. Now, his face is on the famous US one-dollar bill.

2 On January 1, 2002, there was a new currency in Europe—the euro. The new notes were different from traditional money because there weren't any famous people on them. Instead, there were pictures of different types of buildings from different times and places across Europe.

3 Frida Kahlo painted and studied art when she was young. On August 21, 1929, she married the artist Diego Rivera and they lived and worked in Mexico City. During the nineteen thirties, they traveled around the world. Their paintings were famous in many countries. Today, Frida and Diego's faces are on the Mexican 500-peso note.

a

b

c

5 Circle the correct options to complete the text about Queen Elizabeth.

The famous face of Queen Elizabeth II is on many different notes. When she ¹ *was / were* a child, she ² *was / were* on the Canadian dollar. That was in 1936. By 1953, there ³ *was / were* nine countries with her face on their notes, but—surprisingly—the Queen's face ⁴ *wasn't / weren't* on the British pound note until 1960. For a long time, there ⁵ *wasn't / weren't* any happy faces of the Queen on pound notes, but finally, in 2002, there ⁶ *was / were* a happy face on the Scottish five-pound note.

6 Work in pairs. Ask and answer questions to complete texts about other people on currencies.

Student A: Turn to page 153.

Student B: Turn to page 155.

Vocabulary time expressions

7 Number these time expressions in order from past to present.

_____ a yesterday
_1_ b during the nineteenth century
_____ c the sixties
_____ d last Monday evening
_____ e this morning
_____ f last March
_____ g on January 1st, 2000
_____ h a week ago

8 Write *was/were* questions with these words. Then work in pairs. Ask your questions and use time expressions in your answers.

1 When / your grandparents born?
2 When / your last vacation?
3 Where / you on January 1st this year?
4 What month / you born in?
5 Who / some famous people in the twentieth century?

Grammar simple past regular verbs

▶ **SIMPLE PAST REGULAR VERBS**

We use the simple past to talk about finished actions and events.
They **worked** in Mexico City.
He **lived** in the eighteenth century.
She **studied** art.
They **traveled** around Europe.

For more information and practice, see page 168.

9 Work in pairs. Look at the sentences in the grammar box. What do we usually add to regular verbs to make the simple past? What is different about the verbs *live* and *study*?

10 Complete the sentences with the simple past form of the verbs.

1 Barack Obama _____ (live) in the White House from 2009 to 2017.
2 The actress Natalie Portman _____ (study) at Harvard University.
3 The artist Georgia O'Keefe _____ (paint) during the twentieth century.
4 The composer Arthur Honegger _____ (die) in 1955.
5 Angela Merkel _____ (work) as a scientist before she was Chancellor of Germany.
6 My parents _____ (start) their business before I was born.

11 Pronunciation *-ed* endings

a ▶ 59 Sometimes *-ed* adds an extra syllable to verbs in the simple past. Listen to these regular verbs and write the number of syllables.

1 live _1_   lived _1_
2 paint _1_   painted _2_
3 like ___   liked ___
4 want ___   wanted ___
5 work ___   worked ___
6 start ___   started ___
7 play ___   played ___
8 visit ___   visited ___

b ▶ 59 Listen again and repeat.

Speaking and writing *my* Life

12 Write five sentences about someone's life (e.g., someone in your family or a famous person). Then work in pairs. Tell your partner about this person.

6b Visiting the past

Listening

1 Work in pairs. Look at the two photos. Why do you think the caves are important to the woman?

2 ▶ 60 Listen to part of a TV documentary and check your answer to Exercise 1.

3 ▶ 60 Listen again and complete these sentences with a word from the documentary.

1 The caves are in the Mustang region of northern _____ .
2 Humans began living in the caves about a _____ years ago.
3 Many people lived in them until the _____ century.
4 The caves were warm and _____ .
5 Yandu Bista was _____ in a cave.
6 In the end, her family moved to the town, but she says, "I liked living in a cave _____ ."

Grammar simple past irregular verbs and negatives

▶ **SIMPLE PAST IRREGULAR VERBS**

Many common verbs have irregular forms in the simple past. These forms do not end in *-ed*.
go → went, bring → brought, build → built, do → did, have → had, make → made
I/You/She/They **grew up** in a cave.
I/You/She/They **didn't have** enough money.

See page 182 for a list of irregular verbs.

For more information and practice, see page 168.

4 Work in pairs. Look at the grammar box. Answer these questions.

1 Do all verbs in the simple past end in *-ed*?
2 Does the verb change in the third person (*he/she/it*)?
3 What auxiliary verb do you use for negative sentences?

5 ▶ **61** Complete the sentences with the simple past form of the verb. (Some verbs are regular and some are irregular.) Then listen and check.

1 Humans _____ (begin) living in the caves about a thousand years ago.
2 Many people _____ (live) in them until the fifteenth century.
3 They _____ (build) houses and _____ (move) to towns.
4 Yandu Bista _____ (be) born in a cave.
5 She _____ (grow up) there with her family.
6 They _____ (not have) water in the cave.
7 She _____ (go) to the river every day and _____ (bring) water up the mountain.

6 Complete the sentences with the simple past form of these irregular verbs.

be	begin	grow up	have	leave

1 I _____ born in 1939.
2 I _____ in a big city with my family.
3 I _____ school when I was four years old.
4 I _____ a job on weekends.
5 I _____ home when I was 16.

7 Rewrite the sentences in Exercise 6 so they are true for you. You can use the negative form of the simple past and change other words. Then read your sentences to your partner.

Grammar simple past questions

▶ **SIMPLE PAST QUESTIONS**

What **did** *you* **do** *over the weekend? I* **met** *some friends.*
Where **did** *you* **go**? *We* **went** *to a museum.*
Did *you* **go** *to the movies?* **Yes, I did. / No, I didn't.**

For more information and practice, see page 168.

8 Look at the grammar box. What auxiliary form do you use in simple past questions?

9 ▶ **62** Complete this conversation with *did* or *didn't*. Then listen and check.

A: Hi. How was your weekend?
B: It was great, thanks.
A: What ¹_____ you do?
B: I went to Osaka.
A: Oh, ²_____ you go shopping?
B: No, I ³_____ . I went to a museum.
A: Oh, OK. What ⁴_____ you see there?
B: An exhibition about the lives of people from the fifteenth century. It was fantastic!
A: ⁵_____ you go with anyone?
B: I ⁶_____ go with anyone, but I met an old friend afterward for lunch.

Speaking *my* Life

10 Work in pairs. Imagine you both visited an interesting place over the weekend. Ask and answer questions about your visits.

Student A: Turn to page 153.

Student B: Turn to page 156.

11 Write six short sentences about what you did yesterday, using the simple past form of these irregular verbs.

get up	go	meet	have	buy	take

*I **got up** at six o'clock.*

12 Work in pairs. Ask and answer questions about your day. Find out what was the same and what was different.

A: **Did** *you* **get up** *at six yesterday?*
B: *No, I* **didn't**. *I* **got up** *at seven.*
A: *I* **got up** *at six, so that's different.*
B: *Where* **did** *you* **go**?
A: *To the gym.*
B: *Me too! / I also* **went** *to the gym.*

6c Lifelogging

Reading

1 Look at the sentences about what someone did last week. Complete the sentences with these verbs. Then tell your partner which sentences are true for you.

| made | posted | took | wore | wrote |

1   I _____ in my diary.
2   I _____ photos and shared them with friends.
3   I _____ a fitness tracker and went running.
4   I _____ a video with my phone.
5   I _____ comments on social media.

2 Do you keep a diary? Why or why not? Tell the class.

3 Read the article and match the paragraphs (1–4) to the topics (a–d).

a   the first *lifelogger* _____
b   the diary of Samuel Pepys _____
c   people who keep a diary today _____
d   the benefits of lifelogging _____

4 Work in pairs. Read the article again and answer these questions.

1   What did Samuel Pepys write about in his diary?
2   What percentage of people keep a diary nowadays?
3   Who are more likely to keep a diary—men or women?
4   Who was the first *lifelogger*?
5   How do many people record and share their lives nowadays?
6   In the future, why might people look at our photos, videos, and comments?

Word focus *write*

5 Look at these expressions with *write*. What type of word comes after *write* in each expression? Is it a preposition or an article + noun?

1   write about history
2   write in a diary
3   write to your grandparents
4   write down a word

6 Work in pairs. Answer these questions.

1   What things do you write every day or every week? (e.g., a diary, a blog, comments on social media)
2   What do you write about? (e.g., everyday topics, school subjects, work)
3   Who do you often write to? (e.g., friends, family) How do you write to these people? (e.g., by email, text message, social media, letter)
4   Did you write down any new words in your English class today? If so, which ones?

Critical thinking **for or against?**

7 Read these comments about lifelogging and social media. Which comments are for lifelogging (F)? Which are against (A)?

1   You can share photos with family and friends. _____
2   People spend all their free time looking at their phone. _____
3   Fitness trackers make people do more exercise. _____
4   It's interesting and fun to look at your past. _____
5   Sometimes people write bad things about others. _____
6   Historians can learn about people from their photos and videos. _____

8 What's your opinion? Are you for or against lifelogging? Why? Tell your partner.

Speaking *my* Life

9 Prepare a survey about lifelogging.

- Work in groups. Write five or six questions for the survey.
  How many photos of your life do you take every day?
- Interview people in other groups. Take turns to ask and answer your questions.
- Tell your group your results. Are the students in your class all lifeloggers?

LIFELOGGING

a twenty-first century diary

▶ 63

1 In the seventeenth century, Samuel Pepys wrote the most famous diary in the English language. He began the diary in 1660 and finished it in 1669. Pepys wrote about important events in the history of England and about the lives of famous people. His diary also described the everyday lives of his family and other people in London. So his diary is very useful for historians in the twenty-first century.

2 Today, some people still keep diaries. In a recent survey of 500 people, 23% said they wrote in their diary regularly; one in five men and one in four women. This included over 35% of people between the ages of 18 and 34. People between the ages of 35 and 64 don't often keep a diary—probably because they are busy with careers and family life—but 35% of people over 65 keep a diary.

3 In the twenty-first century, a lot of people want to share their lives. They record the things they do with digital technology. This is called *lifelogging*. In 2000, Gordon Bell became famous as the first lifelogger. He wore a camera around his neck that automatically took a picture every 30 seconds. In this way, Bell made a digital diary of his life. Nowadays, everyone is a lifelogger—we take photos of what we had for breakfast, post comments on social media about the news, and make videos of events in our lives. We also wear fitness trackers so we know how much exercise we got and where we went.

4 So, just as modern historians read the diary of Samuel Pepys and learn about life more than three hundred years ago, maybe historians in the future will look at our photos, videos, and comments and learn about our lives in the twenty-first century.

6d How was your evening?

Listening

1 ▶ **64** Listen to three conversations. Write the conversation number (1–3) next to each activity.

a We went to a café and ate a burger. ____
b I stayed up late and watched a movie. ____
c My friend had a party. ____
d I met a friend's family. ____
e We walked along the river. ____
f I couldn't fall asleep. ____
g I went to the gym. ____

Vocabulary opinion adjectives

2 The speakers use opinion adjectives. Write these words and phrases in the correct place in the chart.

~~fantastic~~	not bad	It was fun.
nice	boring	Terrible!
~~OK~~	fine	not very good
It was funny.	Great!	

☺☺	☺	😐	☹
fantastic		OK	

3 Pronunciation intonation

a ▶ **65** Listen and repeat the words and expressions from Exercise 2. Use the same intonation.

b Work in pairs. Ask each other these questions and answer with opinion adjectives.

- How was your evening?
- How was your weekend?
- How was your last vacation?
- How was your …?

Real life asking what people did

> ▶ **ASKING WHAT PEOPLE DID**
>
> **How was …?**
> How was your evening / your weekend / your vacation?
> Did you have a good evening / weekend? Did you have a good time? Did you have fun last night?
> (It was great / fun / OK.)
>
> **Activity**
> Was it a special event / party? (Yes, it was my friend's …)
> What did you do? (I went for a walk. / I watched TV. / Not much.)
>
> **The place**
> Where did you go? (To a café. / To a party. / To the movies.)
> Where was it? (In the city. / At a friend's house.)
>
> **People**
> Who were you with? Who did you meet / go with?
> (A friend. / Friends. / My family.)
> Were there many people there?
> (Yes, lots! / No, not many.)

4 ▶ **64** Read the expressions for asking about past events and complete the conversations with the missing words. Then listen and check.

1 A: Hi! [1]_____ your evening?
  B: It was great, thanks.
  A: [2]_____ you go?
  B: To a new café in town. We ate a burger and then walked along the river.
  A: [3]_____ you with?
  B: My brother and his friend from when he was at school.

2 A: How was your weekend?
  B: Fantastic! My friend had a party at his house. It was great.
  A: [4]_____ his birthday?
  B: No, he passed his college exams, so he was really happy!
  A: That's nice. [5]_____ many people there?
  B: Yes, there were. I met his family for the first time. It was fun.

3 A: I'm so tired.
  B: Why? [6]_____ you do last night?
  A: Not much. I stayed up late and watched a movie. It was kind of boring, so I went to bed, but I couldn't fall asleep for a long time.
  [7]_____ a good evening?
  B: It was fine. I went to the gym, and I was in bed by ten.

5 Work in pairs. Take turns asking your partner what they did at these times. Ask questions about the activity, the place, and the people.

- last night
- last weekend
- last vacation

6e Thanks!

Writing thank you messages

1 Do you ever write a "thank you" note, email, or letter to people? If yes, is it for any of these reasons?

- after a meal at someone's house
- when someone gives you a present
- to a client or customer at work
- after you stay with someone

2 Read the card, email, and letter. Why does the writer say "thank you" each time?

Hi!

Thanks for coming to my party. I really liked the present! It was a fun night!

See you again soon.

Love,
Ginny

b

Dear Nadia,

Thank you for your work in Rio. The conference was very successful. In particular, we enjoyed the meal on the last night!

Everyone on the team sends their thanks.

See you again next year.

Best regards,
Sanjit

c

Dear Mr. Sato,

Thank you very much for attending our Spanish course last year. We hope it was useful.

Please find attached some information about our courses for the next academic year.

I look forward to hearing from you in the future.

Yours sincerely,

AM Ruiz

Course Administration

3 Writing skill formal and informal expressions

a Complete the chart with expressions from the messages in Exercise 2.

	a	b	c
greet the person	*Hi!*		
thank the person			*Thank you very much for …*
talk about future contact		*See you again next year.*	
end the message			

b Which message (a–c) uses very formal expressions? Which message uses very informal expressions?

4 Choose a situation (1–3) and write to thank the person. Decide if you need formal or informal expressions.

1 You were in the US and someone invited you to their home. You met his family and friends and you had lunch with them.
2 You were on a ten-day visit to a college in Vietnam. Someone at the college showed you around Ho Chi Minh City on the weekend and helped you during your visit.
3 You work for a sports equipment company. A customer bought some products from you this year. Email him some information about your company's new products for next year.

5 Work in pairs. Exchange your "thank you" messages. Does your partner:

- greet the person?
- thank the person?
- talk about future contact?
- end the message?
- use the correct formal or informal expressions?

An ancient object in the Museo del Oro
in Bogotá, Colombia

Before you watch

1 Look at the photo and read the caption. Why do you think this object is important? Why do people like looking at this type of object in a museum?

2 Key vocabulary

Read the sentences. The words and phrases in **bold** are used in the video. Match the words with the definitions (a–g).

1 Put your new dress in the **wardrobe**.
2 This old family photograph **reminds** me of my grandparents.
3 When I was a child, I had a **scary** teacher.
4 I was **scared** of my old teacher.
5 This painting **belonged** to my father.
6 New York is an **incredible** city.
7 **Wow!** I love your new dress!

a was the possession of _____
b afraid or worried that something bad is going to happen _____
c making you feel afraid or worried _____
d makes you remember something _____
e really great _____
f an expression you use when you are surprised or excited about something _____
g a cabinet in a bedroom for clothes _____

While you watch

3 You are going to watch a video with three people talking about objects from their past. Before you watch, match these sentences (a–f) with the objects (1–3).

1 The dress   2 The book   3 The bust

a "It was his school book." ____
b "He's very serious and very scary." ____
c "I started to wear it a lot." ____
d "He has this incredible nose and chin." ____
e "It's very important to me because it reminds me of my mom." ____
f "It's called *Tom Brown's School Days*." ____

4 ▶ **6.1** Watch the video and check your answers to Exercise 3.

5 ▶ **6.1** Watch the video again and match the time expressions with the events.

1 She was born in Moscow. _b_
2 She got married. ____
3 She wore the dress. ____
4 Her daughter found the dress in a wardrobe. ____
5 The book was written. ____
6 Her great grandmother's first husband died. ____
7 Mr. Montgomery gave the book to Charles Ellisdon. ____
8 He visited his grandparents every Sunday. ____
9 Dante was a writer in Italy. ____
10 He lives in the living room. ____

a in 1901
b in 1955
c in the nineteenth century
d in the seventies
e in the thirteenth and fourteenth century
f nowadays
g on July 31st, 1890
h the day after her wedding
i when he was a child
j years later

After you watch

6 Vocabulary in context

▶ **6.2** Watch the clips from the video. Choose the correct option to complete the sentences.

7 Think of a special object from the past in your home. Plan and write a short presentation about the object using time expressions, the simple past, and some of these expressions.

> This is …
> It's very important/special to me because …
> It reminds me of …
> It's a piece of my family history.
> It looks …
> I like looking at it because …

8 For the next lesson, bring in the object or a photo of the object. Give a short presentation about it and explain:

- what it is.
- its history.
- why it's important to you.

UNIT 6 REVIEW AND MEMORY BOOSTER

Grammar

1 **>> MB** Work in pairs. Answer the questions about the people in the pictures.

- Who was this person?
- Where was he/she from?
- What did he/she do?

2 Complete the text with the simple past form of the verbs.

Marco Polo ¹_____ (grow up) in Venice in the thirteenth century. When he ²_____ (be) seventeen, he ³_____ (travel) with his father and uncle. They ⁴_____ (go) from Venice to Persia, and finally to China. Polo ⁵_____ (live) in China for seventeen years and ⁶_____ (work) for the Khan (or Emperor). Twenty-four years later, he ⁷_____ (return) to Venice and ⁸_____ (write) a book about his journeys in Asia. The book ⁹_____ (become) famous across Europe because of the stories. Marco Polo ¹⁰_____ (die) in 1324.

3 Write questions about Marco Polo using these words and verbs from Exercise 2. Use the simple past form.

1 Where / Marco Polo / in the thirteenth century?
2 When / he / with his father and uncle?
3 Which parts of the world / they / to?
4 How many years / he / in China?
5 Who / he / for?
6 When / he / to Venice?
7 What / he / a book about?

4 **>> MB** Work in pairs. Ask and answer the questions from Exercise 3.

I CAN	
use the simple past	
ask and answer questions about the past	

Vocabulary

5 **>> MB** Work in groups. How many time expressions can you make with these words? You have two minutes. You can use words more than once.

before	2001	Wednesday	this
twentieth	last	March	on
sixties	week	evening	in
century	ago	month	February 28th

6 **>> MB** Choose five time expressions from Exercise 5 and write five sentences about the past.

7 Cross out one incorrect word in each group.

☺☺	fantastic	great	fine	very good
☺	fun	OK	nice	funny
☺	boring	fine	not bad	OK
☹	terrible	fun	boring	not very good

I CAN	
use time expressions	
use opinion adjectives	

Real life

8 Work in pairs. Make questions with the words.

1 evening / how / your / was /?
2 special / was / party / a / it /?
3 last / where / you / go / did / night / ?
4 you / were / with / who / ?
5 were / lots / of / there / there / people/ ?

9 Match the answers to the questions in Exercise 8.

a To the movies. ____
b Yes, my friend graduated from college, so he had a party. ____
c My brother and his family. ____
d No, not many. ____
e It was fun. I went out for a meal with friends. ____

10 **>> MB** Work in pairs. Write a conversation asking about somebody's weekend. Use all these phrases.

Fantastic!	with an old friend
Lots!	OK
Terrible!	in the middle of the countryside

I CAN	
ask what people did	
talk about last night / the weekend, etc.	

Unit 7 Journeys

The long journey

FEATURES

1 Work in pairs. Look at the photo of a ladybug. Why do you think the photo is called "The long journey"?

2 ▶ 66 Listen to a description of the photo. Circle the seven adjectives you hear.

clean	red	cold	dangerous
difficult	dirty	green	easy
fast	hot	huge	long
safe	short	slow	tiny

3 Work in pairs. Find seven pairs of opposite adjectives in Exercise 2.

clean / dirty

4 Work in pairs. Which adjectives in Exercise 2 can you use to describe:

1   your commute to work or school?
2   transportation where you live (e.g., cars, trains)?
3   your city or town?
4   the weather today?

7a Animal journeys

Reading

1 You are going to read an article about the journeys three animals make. Look at the photos and quickly skim the article. Match the animals (1–3) with the distances (a–c).

1 saiga antelope   ○   ○   a 30 meters every year
2 tree frog   ○   ○   b 35 kilometers a day
3 loggerhead turtle   ○   ○   c 14,000 kilometers in fifteen years

2 Read the article and check your answers to Exercise 1.

3 Read the article again and complete the chart.

	Saiga Antelopes	Tree Frogs	Loggerhead Turtles
When do they travel?	*spring*		
Where do they travel to?			
Which adjectives describe the journey?			

▶ 67 **Animal journeys** | Every year, animals around the world go on long and difficult journeys called migrations.

Saiga antelopes live in Central Asia. In the spring, they walk to higher places for food. A male saiga can
5 walk thirty-five kilometers a day—it's faster than a female. The journey is more dangerous for a female saiga because she
10 has her calf—her baby—in the spring.

Tree frogs have shorter journeys than other animals. But for a small
15 frog, the journey isn't easy. In the spring, it climbs thirty meters down a tree, lays its eggs in water, and then
20 climbs back up the tree. For a tree frog, it's a very difficult journey.

Many turtles have a very long journey—longer than other sea animals. They travel all their life. For
25 example, the **loggerhead turtle** leaves the beach as a baby and swims around fourteen thousand kilometers. Fifteen years later, the female turtle returns to the same beach and lays eggs.

Grammar comparative adjectives

> ▶ **COMPARATIVE ADJECTIVES**
>
> We use a comparative adjective to compare two things or groups of things.
>
> *Turtles have long journeys.* → *Turtles have **longer** journeys **than** tree frogs.*
>
> *Tree frogs have short journeys.* → *Tree frogs have **shorter** journeys **than** saiga antelopes or turtles.*
>
> *The female saiga's journey is dangerous.* → *The female saiga's journey is **more dangerous than** the male's.*
>
> Spelling changes: *big* → *bigger, safe* → *safer, easy* → *easier*
> Irregular adjectives: *good* → *better, bad* → *worse*
>
> For more information and practice, see page 170.

4 Work in pairs. Look at the grammar box. Answer these questions about comparative forms.

  1 What two letters do you add to short adjectives to make the comparative?
  2 What word comes before long adjectives?
  3 Which adjectives have an irregular comparative?
  4 What word often comes after a comparative adjective to compare two things?

5 Write the comparative form of these adjectives.

  1 big   _____
  2 small   _____
  3 cheap   _____
  4 expensive _____
  5 cold   _____
  6 hot   _____
  7 dangerous _____
  8 safe   _____
  9 difficult _____
  10 easy   _____
  11 fast   _____
  12 slow   _____
  13 good   _____
  14 bad   _____

6 Complete the sentences with the comparative form of these adjectives.

big	cheap	fast	good	hot	slow

  1 The summer in Mexico is _____ than in Canada.
  2 My journey was _____ than normal because the train was late.
  3 Their new house has three bedrooms. It's _____ than their old house.
  4 Call a taxi. We're late, and it's _____ than walking.
  5 The bus ticket is $10 and the train ticket is $12, so the bus is _____ .
  6 I go to work by bus. It's _____ than going by car because I can read a book.

7 Work in pairs. Make sentences comparing these things. Use a comparative adjective + *than*.

Australia is hotter than Antarctica.

  1 Australia / Antarctica
  2 a car / a bicycle
  3 rock climbing / surfing
  4 travel by air / travel by sea
  5 an elephant / a lion
  6 visiting a city / camping in the country
  7 Paris / New York
  8 train journeys / plane journeys

8 Pronunciation stressed and weak syllables

▶ **68** Listen to the stressed and weak syllables in these sentences. Then listen again and repeat.

              /ə/   /ə/
  1 <u>A</u>frica is <u>ho</u>tter than <u>Eu</u>rope.

                 /ə/   /ə/
  2 Aus<u>tra</u>lia isn't <u>col</u>der than Ant<u>arc</u>tica.

Speaking *my*Life

9 Compare these sentences from Exercise 7. Which sentence is a fact and which is an opinion?

*Antarctica is **colder than** Australia.*
*Rock climbing is **more fun than** surfing.*

10 Work in pairs. Which of your sentences in Exercise 7 are opinions? Say the sentences with these phrases.

I think ...	In my opinion ...

*I think rock climbing is **more dangerous than** surfing.*

11 Write sentences with your opinion. Compare two of these things.

- places or cities
- sports or free-time activities
- types of travel
- types of vacations
- places in the city
- types of transportation
- famous people

12 Work in pairs. Take turns reading your opinions aloud. Do you agree with your partner?

*A: I think Tokyo is **more expensive than** Dubai.*
B: I agree! / I don't agree!

Filmmaker James Cameron with his submarine Deepsea Challenger.

Vocabulary ways of traveling

> ▶ **WORDBUILDING collocations**
>
> We can talk about different ways of traveling with the verbs *walk, ride, drive, fly,* etc. We can also use collocations with verbs + transportation nouns.
> **go by** + *bicycle/train/car*
> **travel by** + *train/bus/plane/boat*
> **take** + *a taxi / a bus / the train*
>
> For more practice, see Workbook page 59.

1 Look at the wordbuilding box. Circle the correct option to complete these sentences.

1 I always *take / drive* a taxi when I go out with friends in the evening.
2 When my family goes on vacation, we always *drive / go* by car.
3 How did you *fly / travel* to Moscow? By train or by plane?
4 When it's raining I normally travel *to / by* work on the train.
5 Let's *travel by / take* the bus downtown.

2 Work in pairs. Ask and answer these questions using the words in Exercise 1.

1 How do you normally travel to work (or school)?
2 How do you normally travel when you go on vacation?
3 What's your favorite way to travel? Why?

Listening

3 ▶ 69 Look at the photo above. Listen to a documentary about James Cameron's journey to the deepest place on Earth and complete the information.

1 The place: *The Mariana Trench*
2 Distance to the bottom: _____
3 Length of journey: _____
4 Type of transportation: _____
5 Number of new species: _____

> **documentary** (n) /ˌdɒkjʊˈment(ə)ri/ a movie about real life
> **species** (n) /ˈspiːsiːz/ type or group of animal

4 ▶ 69 Work in pairs. Compare your notes from Exercise 3. Then listen again, check your notes, and complete any missing information.

Grammar superlative adjectives

> ### SUPERLATIVE ADJECTIVES
>
> We use a superlative adjective to compare one thing with all the other things in a group.
> *The Mariana Trench is **the deepest** place in the ocean.*
> *This fish has **the biggest** teeth of any fish for its size.*
> *Titanic is **the most popular** movie by James Cameron.*
> *Avatar was **the most expensive** movie.*
>
> Spelling changes: *big* → *big**g**est*, *easy* → *eas**i**est*
> Irregular adjectives: *good* → *best*, *bad* → *worst*
>
> For more information and practice, see page 170.

5 Work in pairs. Look at the grammar box. Answer these questions about superlative forms.

1 What three letters do you add to short adjectives?
2 What word comes before longer adjectives?
3 What word usually comes before a superlative adjective?

6 Complete the chart with superlative adjectives.

Adjective	Comparative adjective	Superlative adjective
long	longer	
fast	faster	
expensive	more expensive	
good	better	

7 Complete the text with the superlative form of the adjectives.

New Year is the ¹_____ (important) holiday in China. Millions of people leave the
²_____ (big) cities in China and travel home to their families, so it's the
³_____ (busy) time of year for travel. Many college students go by train, and it's also the
⁴_____ (bad) time of year for driving on the roads. Some people go by plane because it's the ⁵_____ (fast) way to get home, but it's also the ⁶_____ (expensive) because lots of tourists fly into China during the New Year's holiday. They visit the
⁷_____ (popular) places in China, such as the Great Wall. With so many people traveling in China at this time, it's the
⁸_____ (large) human migration in the world.

8 ▶ 70 Work in pairs. Complete the conversation about Ireland with the superlative or comparative form of these adjectives. Then listen and check.

beautiful	cheap	~~famous~~	good
good	hot	popular	small

A: I want to visit Ireland in July, but I only have ten days. What are the best places to visit?
B: Well, Dublin is ¹ *the most famous* city in Ireland, and of course it's also ²_____ with tourists.
A: But I don't want to see lots of other tourists. What's ³_____ city?
B: In my opinion, Galway is the prettiest. In terms of size, the city is ⁴_____ than Dublin, but it's next to the water, so there are great views.
A: How cold is it?
B: July is ⁵_____ month, so it's OK.
A: What about transportation? What's ⁶_____ way to travel around?
B: Buses are ⁷_____ , but I think a car is ⁸_____ than public transportation when you are a tourist. With a car you can stop and see lots of different places on the way.

Speaking my Life

9 Write notes about your country or a country you know well. Use the ideas below or your own ideas.

- the most famous city
- the oldest city
- the most beautiful place
- the most popular place for tourists
- the best place to visit
- the hottest month
- the coldest month
- the cheapest way to travel

10 Work in pairs. Imagine you are going to the country your partner wrote about in Exercise 9.

Student A: Ask questions using the ideas in Exercise 9.

Student B: Answer Student A's questions using your notes from Exercise 9.

Change roles and have another conversation.

*A: What's **the most famous** city in Peru?*
*B: I think it's probably Lima, but I think Arequipa is **the most beautiful** city.*

7c Visit Colombia!

Reading

1 Work in pairs. Look at the photos on page 87. What topics (e.g., food and restaurants in a city) do you think are in the article?

2 Now read the article. Can you find the topics you thought of in Exercise 1?

3 Work in pairs. Read the article again. Match these sentences to the cities (A–D), according to the information in the text.

1 In this city you can take dance lessons from experts. ____
2 There's a cable car that goes over the city. ____
3 No one lives in this city anymore. ____
4 There are two important events every year. ____
5 People in this city like to stop and talk to anyone. ____
6 This city is famous because of an artist. ____
7 It's difficult to get to this city. ____

4 Find words in the article to match these definitions.

1 a type of city or place with ships and boats _____
2 an informal and friendly conversation _____
3 a type of artist who makes large objects, often from stone or metal _____
4 the objects made by the artist in 3 _____
5 a type of transportation that moves over your head (e.g., in the mountains) _____
6 places with music and dancing _____
7 a special public event or celebration, usually every year _____
8 very old _____

Word focus *time*

5 Find these phrases with *time* in the article. Then use the phrases to complete the sentences.

have a good time	have time for
save time	spend time

1 On the weekend, we always _____ with family and friends.
2 I woke up late, so I didn't _____ breakfast.
3 Don't wait for the bus. _____ by taking a taxi.
4 Did you _____ on your trip?

6 Work in pairs and answer these questions.

1 Do you spend most of your time doing your homework?
2 Do you have time for sports and other hobbies?
3 Did you have a good time over the weekend?
4 We *spend time* and *save time*. What's another noun we often use with *spend* and *save*?

7 Imagine you can visit the cities in the article. Which would you like to visit most? Rank the four cities from 1 to 4 (1 = your first choice, 4 = your last choice). Then compare your answers in groups and give your reasons.

Critical thinking writing for the reader

8 Overall, what type of reader do you think the article on page 87 is for? Who would be interested in this article? Tell the class.

9 Now read a different text about the city of Cali. Compare it with the paragraph about Cali in the article. In each paragraph, what choices does the writer make about:

1 the type of reader? (Is it for a tourist, a business person, a student, or someone who likes art?)
2 the type of topics? (Is it about art, history, business, sports, or music and dance?)

Cali is a city where people work hard. There are a lot of businesses there. It has a good airport for visitors, with comfortable hotels. There is good public transportation, but taxis are the fastest way to get around the city. In the evening, Cali has restaurants with traditional and international food.

Writing myLife

10 Plan a paragraph about your town or city. First make choices about:

• the type of reader.
• the type of topic.

Then write your paragraph in 50 words.

11 Exchange your paragraph with a partner. What type of reader did your partner write for, and what is the topic?

A journey to
Colombia's cities

▶ 71

Many visitors to Colombia spend time
in Bogotá, the country's capital city, but
Colombia also has some other great cities.

A *Cartagena* is a port on Colombia's coast. Because the
5 city is by the Caribbean Sea, the food here is a fantastic
mix of seafood and tropical fruit. Also, Cartagena is one
of the friendliest places in the world—everyone has time
for a chat, including waiters in restaurants, store clerks,
taxi drivers, or people walking in the streets.

20 *Cali* is a city where people work hard, but also know
how to have a good time. The city is famous for its music
and dance, and there are lots of concerts and nightclubs.
It's also the home of Colombian salsa: you can take
classes with some of the best dancers in the world. The
25 annual Festival of Pacific Music and the World Festival of
Salsa are in August and September, so these are good
months to visit.

10 *Medellín* is best known for the sculptor Fernando **B**
Botero. He was born here, and you can see
his huge sculptures of people and animals
everywhere in the city. The Botero Plaza is in the
center and has a lot of sculptures by him. You
15 can also walk to other squares to see more. If you
want to save time between places, take the cable
car over the city. And in the afternoon, when
the sun gets very hot, go inside the Museo de
Antioquia to see Botero's paintings.

For a very different kind of Colombian city, take a **D**
four-day trek[1] to *Ciudad Perdida*, which means
30 the "Lost City." You walk through rivers and jungle,
and after three days, you finally climb up 1,241
steps. At the top, you find the stone walls of an
ancient city over a thousand years old with an
incredible view over the mountains.

[1]**trek** (n) /trek/ a long and difficult journey on foot

7d Travel money

Vocabulary money

1 Complete the sentences with these pairs of words.

borrow / cash	buy / ticket
change / dollars	lend / money
pay / credit card	spend / money

1 I need to _____ some _____ into yen.
2 Did you _____ a lot of _____ on that dress?
3 You can _____ by _____ or by cash.
4 I forgot my wallet. Can you _____ me some _____ to buy a drink?
5 Can I _____ some _____ and pay you back later?
6 They want to _____ a train _____ .

2 ▶ **72** Listen to three conversations about money. Match the conversations with the places.

a Conversation 1 ○   ○ in a store
b Conversation 2 ○   ○ in a parking lot
c Conversation 3 ○   ○ at a bank

Real life making requests

3 ▶ **72** Complete the conversations from Exercise 2. Use the expressions for making requests to help you. Then listen and check.

Conversation 1
A: Hello, can I change one hundred dollars into euros?
B: Yes, of ¹c_____ . One moment. One hundred dollars is eighty-nine euros.
A: OK, ²c_____ you give me the euros in tens?
B: ³S_____ . Ten, twenty, thirty, forty, fifty, sixty, seventy, eighty …

Conversation 2
A: Would you like to buy this?
B: Yes, please. And ⁴c_____ I have it in a bag, please?
A: ⁵C_____ . That's twelve euros.
B: Here's my credit card.
A: Oh, I'm ⁶s_____ , but I can only take cash.
B: Oh, no! I don't have any.
A: Don't worry, there's a bank with an ATM around the corner.
B: Oh, thanks.

Conversation 3
A: Oh, no! It's two dollars for parking. I only have a ten-dollar bill.
B: So what's the problem?
A: The machine takes coins. ⁷C_____ I borrow some money?
B: I'm ⁸a_____ I don't have any change. But look! It takes credit cards.
A: I don't have a credit card with me.
B: It's OK. I do.
A: Great. I can pay you back later.
B: Don't worry! It's on me!

▶ MAKING REQUESTS

Requests	**Responding *no***
Can I change …?	I'm sorry, but …
Can you give me …?	I'm afraid I don't …
Could I have …?	

Responding *yes*
Yes, of course.
Sure!
Certainly.

4 Work in pairs. Take turns asking for different things with these pairs of words. Respond *yes* or *no*.

lend / ten dollars	give / a drink
borrow / your phone	pay / credit card
use / your pen	have / some dinner
buy / a ticket	

7e The end of the road

Writing a travel blog post

1 Work in pairs. Read a travel blog post about a bus journey and answer the questions.

1 Where was the writer?
2 How many days was the journey?
3 What could the passengers see?
4 What happened to the bus?
5 Who tried to fix the engine?
6 How did some passengers feel?
7 Why did the writer feel sorry for the bus driver?
8 Why did the writer walk to the border?

Yesterday was the final day of my bus journey from Lhasa to Kodari, on the Nepal border. It's the highest road in the world and it's also a very long journey. We traveled for three days through the Himalayas and you could see the north side of the highest mountain in the world.

In the afternoon, we were only five kilometers from Kodari when suddenly the bus stopped. The driver got out and looked at the engine. For the next three hours, he tried to fix the engine. Some of the other passengers got angry, but he couldn't start the bus.

Finally, all the passengers got out and started to walk to the border. I felt sorry for the bus driver because he looked sad and lonely. But I also wanted a good hotel and a hot meal, so I left the bus, too, and walked to Kodari. Later that night, the bus arrived in the town.

2 Writing skill *so* and *because*

a Look at these sentences and answer the questions.

a I felt sorry for the bus driver because he looked sad.
b I wanted a good hotel and a hot meal, so I left the bus, too, and walked to Kodari.

1 Which sentence gives the reason, then the action?
2 Which sentence gives the action, then the reason?
3 When do you use *so* and *because*?

b Complete the sentences with *so* or *because*.

1 We called a taxi _____ we were late for the meeting.
2 The train was late, _____ we waited on the platform.
3 We had a drink of water _____ it was a very hot day.
4 It started raining, _____ they ran home.
5 We rented a car _____ there were no trains or buses.
6 My friend lent me ten dollars _____ I didn't have any cash.

3 Circle the correct options to complete this travel blog post.

It was the end of our family vacation [1] *and / because* we were very tired. We had a long car trip from San Francisco to Arizona via Los Angeles, [2] *so / but* we left early in the morning. The drive was easy at first [3] *so / because* there wasn't much traffic at that time of day, [4] *but / and* at noon we needed to stop at a garage near Los Angeles [5] *but / because* there was a problem with the engine. The garage couldn't fix the car for 24 hours, [6] *so / because* we needed a hotel for the night. The nearest hotel was at Disneyland. We went there [7] *and / but* it was the best part of the trip!

4 Write a short travel blog post about a trip or a place you visited on vacation. Think about these questions.

- Where were you?
- When was it?
- Who was there?
- What happened?

5 Work in pairs. Exchange your travel blog posts. Use these questions to check your partner's blog post.

- Did your partner answer the questions in Exercise 4?
- Did the description use different conjunctions (*and*, *because*, *but*, and *so*)?

The final journey

In Alaska, the sockeye salmon swims up the river. It's a dangerous journey.

Before you watch

1 Look at the photo and read the caption. Why do you think it is a difficult journey for the sockeye salmon?

2 Key vocabulary

Read the sentences. The words in **bold** are used in the video. Match the words with the definitions (a–f).

1 When I sit in the sun too long, my **skin** burns.
2 The water in this river is very **shallow**.
3 A baby's skin is very **smooth**.
4 When an animal dies, its body **decays**.
5 The chicken **lays** eggs.
6 In fall, the leaves on many trees **turn** red.

a breaks up and goes back into nature _____
b when a female bird pushes an egg from her body _____
c nice to touch, not rough _____
d not deep _____
e the outside part of a human's or an animal's body _____
f change (color) _____

While you watch

3 You are going to watch a video about the final journey of the sockeye salmon. In what order do you think the events (a–g) happen? Number them from 1 to 7.

a The fish try to jump past the brown bears. ___
b The sockeye salmon start their journey up the river. _1_
c The salmon arrive in the shallow water. ___
d The male salmon changes its shape and color. ___
e The female salmon lays her eggs. ___
f The male salmon fight. ___
g The salmon die and decay. _7_

4 🎬 **7.1** Watch the video and check your answers to Exercise 3.

5 🎬 **7.1** Work in pairs. Watch the video again and answer the questions.

1 Which US state are the rivers in?
_____
2 Are the sockeye salmon born in the river or in the ocean?
_____
3 How many salmon finish the long journey?
_____
4 How does the male salmon's skin change?
_____
5 Do scientists know why this happens?
_____
6 Where were the salmon born?
_____
7 What do the males do in the shallow river?
_____
8 What do the females do?
_____
9 Why is it important for the parents' bodies to die and decay?
_____

After you watch

6 Vocabulary in context

🎬 **7.2** Watch the clips from the video. Choose the correct meaning of the words and phrases.

7 🎬 **7.1** Work in pairs. Watch the video again with the sound OFF.

Student A: As you watch, describe the life of the sockeye salmon. Try to use all these expressions in your description.

full of a type of fish	bodies start to change
it can take weeks	turn green/red
one in every thousand	start to fight
the biggest danger	lay their eggs
get past the bears	die and decay

Student B: Listen to Student A and circle the expressions you hear.

Change roles and do the activity again.

UNIT 7 REVIEW AND MEMORY BOOSTER

Grammar

1 Look at the picture below. Complete the sentences with the name of a planet in the picture.

1 _Mercury_ is the closest planet to the Sun.
2 Saturn is a big planet, but _____ is the biggest.
3 Venus is a hot planet, but _____ is the hottest.
4 The journey from Earth to _____ is longer than Earth to Uranus.
5 _____ is the best planet for humans.
6 Mars is smaller than Earth, but _____ is the smallest planet.

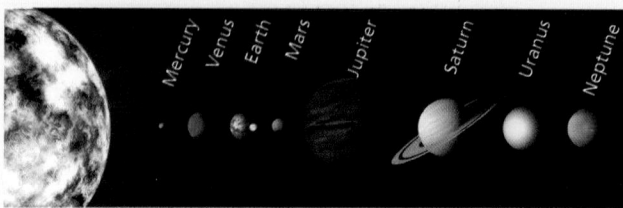

2 ▶▶ MB Work in pairs. Underline nine adjectives in sentences 1–6 in Exercise 1. Which are comparative adjectives? Which are superlative adjectives?

3 Read the information. Then write two comparative sentences using the adjectives.

1 The summer temperature in Qatar is 40°C. It's 20°C in Berlin. (hot / cold)
   Qatar is hotter than Berlin. Berlin is colder than Qatar.
2 A Porsche can travel at 300 km/h. A Mini can travel at 225 km/h. (fast / slow)
3 The Burj Khalifa cost $1.5 billion to build. Taipei 101 cost about $2 billion. (cheap / expensive)
4 The Nile River is 6,650 km long. The Amazon River is 6,712 km long. (long / short)

4 Now read these sentences and compare them with the information in Exercise 3. Then complete them with suitable superlative adjectives.

1 The summer temperature in London is 18°C. London is _the coldest_ city.
2 A Bugatti Veyron can travel at 430 km/h. It's _____ car.
3 This castle costs $10 million. It's _____ _____ home.
4 The Mississippi River is 3,733 km. It's _____ river.

I CAN	
use comparative and superlative adjectives	☐

Vocabulary

5 ▶▶ MB Work in pairs and say the opposite of these adjectives.

cheap	clean	cold	easy
fast	long	safe	tiny

6 ▶▶ MB Write five sentences with adjectives from Exercise 5. Then work in pairs. Take turns reading your sentences, but don't say the adjective. Guess your partner's missing adjective.

A: It's very _____ in the winter.   B: cold

7 Complete these sentences with words related to travel.

1 I often go _____ bus to work.
2 I don't like to _____ by boat because I get seasick.
3 Sometimes I drive to the store and sometimes I _____ the bus.
4 Did you travel _____ Beijing by plane?

8 Circle the correct verbs to complete these sentences.

1 Can I *pay / buy* by credit card?
2 Can you *lend / borrow* me ten dollars?
3 Could I *change / pay* one hundred euros into dollars?
4 *Spend / Take out* some money from that ATM.

I CAN	
use everyday adjectives	☐
talk about ways of traveling	☐
talk about money	☐

Real life

9 Match the two halves of the sentences.
1 Can you lend   ○   ○ a a dollar?
2 Could I borrow   ○   ○ b cash?
3 Could you pay by ○   ○ c me a dollar?
4 Could I have it   ○   ○ d pen?
5 Could I use your ○   ○ e in a bag?

10 ▶▶ MB Write a short conversation between two people. Use two of the requests from Exercise 9 in your conversation.

I CAN	
make requests	☐

Unit 8 Appearance

The Dinagyang Festival in the Philippines

FEATURES

1 Work in pairs. Look at the photo and read the caption. Where is the festival? Which adjectives do you think describe it?

| boring | colorful | crowded | exciting | fun |
| loud | noisy | popular | quiet | relaxing |

2 ▶ 73 Listen to a visitor at the Dinagyang Festival. Are these sentences true (T) or false (F)?

1	The speaker went to a festival in Manila.	T	F
2	The festival is on the fourth Sunday in January.	T	F
3	People wear colorful clothes and make-up.	T	F
4	The music is in one part of the city.	T	F
5	The visitor enjoyed the local food.	T	F

3 Work in pairs. Discuss these questions. Use the adjectives in Exercise 1.

1 What is an important day or festival in your town or city? When is it?
2 What do people do on the day? Do they eat special food?
3 Do people wear special clothes or make-up?

*… is a **popular** festival in my country.*
*There's **loud** music and dancing in the streets.*
*People wear **colorful** clothes.*

8a Global fashion

Vocabulary clothes

1 Work in pairs. Match these words with the photos.

a bag	b belt	c coat	d dress
e jacket	f jeans	g leggings	h shirt
i shoes	j shorts	k skirt	l socks
m suit	n sunglasses	o top	p pants
q sneakers	r T-shirt		

2 Pronunciation /s/ and /ʃ/

▶ **74** Listen to the sounds /s/ and /ʃ/. Then listen to these words and circle the sound you hear.

1 <u>s</u>uit /s/ /ʃ/
2 <u>sh</u>oes /s/ /ʃ/
3 <u>s</u>kirt /s/ /ʃ/
4 <u>sh</u>irt /s/ /ʃ/
5 <u>sh</u>orts /s/ /ʃ/
6 <u>s</u>ocks /s/ /ʃ/
7 <u>s</u>unglasses /s/ /ʃ/

3 Work in groups. Answer the questions.

1 What clothes do you wear every day?
2 What clothes do you only wear in the summer?
3 What clothes do you only wear in the winter?
4 When do people wear suits?
5 When do women wear dresses?

Reading

4 Work in pairs. When you go shopping for clothes or bags, which of these things are most important to you? Discuss your ideas and number them from 1 to 4 (1 = most important, 4 = least important).

- the price ____
- the color ____
- the brand ____
- the country it's from ____

5 Work in pairs. Read the article below about a fashion company. Answer the questions.

1 Which country are the bags from?
2 Where does the company sell the bags?

6 Read the article again and complete the sentences with these people. One is used twice.

fashion designers	local workers	Reese

1 _____ started Rags2Riches.
2 _____ make the products.
3 _____ get a good salary.
4 _____ work with the company.

▶ **75**

GLOBAL FASHION

The two women in the photo are making bags. They work for the company Rags2Riches in the Philippines. Reese Fernandez-Ruiz co-founded[1] the company in 2007 to help workers (mainly women) in the Philippines. The company gives them jobs with a good salary. Rags2Riches is also an environmentally friendly company because it makes new, fashionable bags from old, unused materials.

Rags2Riches is still growing. It has about 1,000 workers and is training more. It has five stores and an online store that sells bags all over the world.

The company works with different well-known designers, such as Rajo Laurel—one of the most famous fashion designers in the Philippines.

[1]**co-found** (v) /ˌkəʊˈfaʊnd/ start a company with other people

Grammar present continuous

7 Work in pairs. Look at the grammar box. Answer the questions.

1 What is the form of the main verb in the present continuous?
2 What auxiliary forms do we use?
3 What time expressions do we use with the present continuous?

8 Complete these sentences with the present continuous form of the verb.

1 I _____ (shop) at the moment.
2 We _____ (not work) in the office today.
3 He _____ (hold) a brown backpack.
4 The company _____ (not make) any money at the moment.
5 _____ you _____ (wear) a suit?

9 Work in pairs. Describe what clothes:
- you are wearing today.
- your partner is wearing.
- your teacher is wearing.

10 Tell your partner what someone in the class is wearing. Don't say the person's name. Can your partner guess who you are describing?

Grammar simple present and present continuous

11 Work in pairs. Look at the grammar box. Answer these questions.

1 Which tense do we use for a fact or a routine?
2 Which tense do we use for an action now or around the time of speaking?

12 Circle the correct options to complete the sentences.

1 At the moment, *I travel / I'm traveling* in Asia.
2 Usually, he *doesn't go / isn't going* to the gym during the week.
3 Today *she visits / she's visiting* an important customer.
4 My sister *likes / is liking* clothes and fashion.
5 These days, the cost of clothes *goes / is going* up.
6 She *doesn't go / isn't going* on vacation very often.

13 Match the questions (1–5) with the answers (a–e).

1 Do you normally wear a uniform? ____
2 I'm doing my homework. Can you help me? ____
3 Is it raining in your town today? ____
4 Who are you working with this week? ____
5 Where do you come from? ____

a Sorry, not now. I'm making dinner. Maybe later.
b Two people from Japan. They're helping us with a new project.
c Spain, but I'm studying in Lima for a year.
d Yes, I do, but today I'm not working, so I can wear a T-shirt and jeans.
e No, it isn't. It's nice and sunny.

Speaking *my*Life

14 Work in pairs. Ask the questions in Exercise 13 and give answers that are true for you. Use the present continuous or the simple present.

8b People at festivals

A

B

Vocabulary face and body

1 Write these words in the correct place on the picture.

arm	beard	eye	foot	hair
hand	head	leg	mouth	shoulder

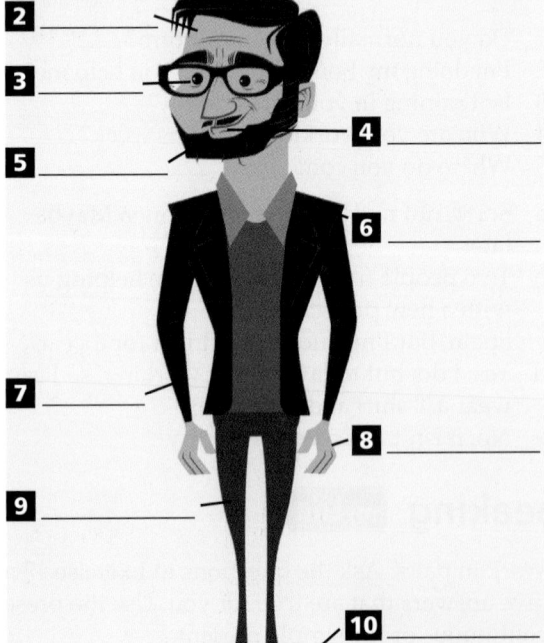

1 _____
2 _____
3 _____
4 _____
5 _____
6 _____
7 _____
8 _____
9 _____
10 _____

2 Complete the sentences with these pairs of words.

arms / legs	hair / eyes
head / ears	hands / neck

1 My sister has long, dark _____ and blue _____ .
2 The music is very loud! My _____ and both my _____ are aching.
3 It's very cold outside. You need gloves and a scarf to keep your _____ and _____ warm.
4 You need strong _____ and _____ for mountain climbing.

3 Pronunciation sound and spelling

▶ 76 Work in pairs. Match the words in A to the words with the same vowel sound in B. Then listen, check, and repeat.

A	head	shoes	beard	eye	feet	nose

B	coat	ears	jeans	leg	tie	suit

head – leg

96

Listening

4 Work in pairs. Look at the two photos on the left from the same festival in Spain. Answer these questions.

1 What are the people doing?
2 What clothes are they wearing?

5 ▶ 77 Listen to a conversation about the two photos. Number the photos (1–2) in the order the people talk about them.

6 ▶ 77 Words for parts of the face and the body are missing from these sentences. Try to recall the words. Then listen again and check.

1 The people at the bottom put their _____ around each other.
2 Other people push them forward with their _____ .
3 Then four people climb up and stand with their _____ on the other people's _____ .
4 People at the bottom have to be strong to hold onto the other people's _____ .
5 These dancers were wearing costumes with big masks over their _____ .
6 The faces are amazing. They have huge eyes and big _____ .
7 He doesn't have any hair, but he has a big black _____ .

Grammar *be vs. have*

> ▶ **BE VS. HAVE**
>
> *She's thin / tall / Vietnamese.*
> *He **has** blue eyes / long hair / a great sense of humor.*
>
> *Do they **have** red hair?*
> *Yes, they **do**. / No, they **don't**.*

For more information and practice, see page 172.

7 Work in pairs. Look at the sentences in the grammar box. Answer these questions.

1 We use *be + adjective / have + adjective + noun* to describe appearance (inherent qualities).
2 We use *be + adjective / have + adjective + noun* to describe specific attributes.
3 With *have* questions, do you answer *Yes, I have*, or *Yes, I do*?
4 In these sentences, does *'s* mean *is* or *has*?
  a She's short.   b He's well-built.

8 Complete this description of dancers at a festival with the correct form of *be* or *have*.

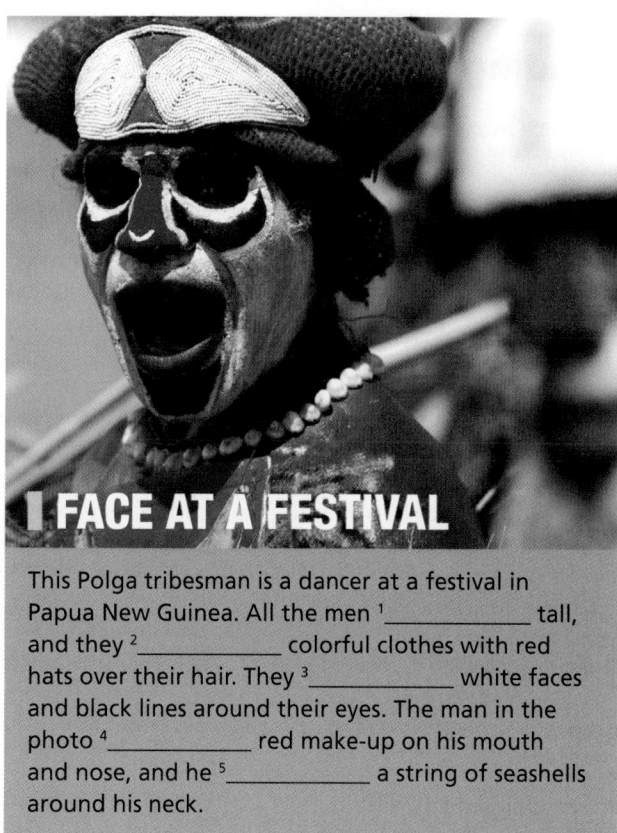

FACE AT A FESTIVAL

This Polga tribesman is a dancer at a festival in Papua New Guinea. All the men ¹_____ tall, and they ²_____ colorful clothes with red hats over their hair. They ³_____ white faces and black lines around their eyes. The man in the photo ⁴_____ red make-up on his mouth and nose, and he ⁵_____ a string of seashells around his neck.

9 Write a short description of the appearance of a famous person you know, using *be* and *have*. Write 50 to 60 words. You can write about these things.

| height | eyes | hair | clothes |

10 Read your description to your partner. Does your partner think your description is accurate?

Speaking *myLife*

11 Work in pairs. Play this game.

Student A: Choose a person in the class, but don't say who it is. Answer Student B's questions.

Student B: Ask Student A questions and guess the person.

Then change roles and play the game again.

A: Is this person female?
B: Yes, she is.
A: Does she have long hair?
B: Yes, she does. / No, she doesn't.
A: Is she tall?
B: Yes, she is. / No, she isn't.

8c Pink and blue

Reading

1 Work in pairs. Compare the two photos in the magazine article.

- Say three things that are the same or similar.
- Say three things that are different.

2 Read the article and match these headings with the paragraphs (1–5).

a Are all girls the same? _____
b Why does this happen? _____
c How it started _____
d Boys' favorite color and toys _____
e Differences between the past and the present _____

3 Look at these words from the article. Match the words (1–7) with the definitions (a–g).

1 toy
2 doll
3 jewelry
4 make-up
5 unusual
6 dinosaur
7 advertisement

a objects you wear on your body, e.g., around your neck, on your ears _____
b an object for children to play with _____
c a picture or a short video to sell a product or service _____
d different from others _____
e a toy that looks like a person or a baby _____
f something you put on your face (to improve or change your appearance) _____
g a large animal that lived millions of years ago _____

Critical thinking is it in the text?

4 Read the article again. Decide if the information in these sentences (1–6) is:

- in the article (✔).
- not in the article (✗).

1 Jeongmee is a photographer from South Korea. ✔
2 She thinks her daughter is similar to other girls of her age. _____
3 The types of toys in the girls' and boys' rooms were different. _____
4 Jeongmee thinks the difference between girls' and boys' toys might be because of television and advertising. _____
5 In the past, children had lots of different colors in their bedrooms. _____
6 Jeongmee thinks pink for girls and blue for boys is bad. _____

Word focus *like*

5 Read the sentences with the word *like*. Replace *like* in each sentence (1–3) with the words that have a similar meaning (a–c).

1 There are blue toys **like** robots, dinosaurs, and superheroes.
2 Girls **like** pink make-up, clothes, or toys for cooking.
3 Many of these girls were **like** Seowoo and had lots of pink things.

a love _____
b similar to _____
c such as _____

6 Complete these sentences in your own words. Then work in pairs. Tell your partner.

1 When I was a child, I liked …
2 In my living room, I have things like …
3 I often wear … , like other people of my age.

Speaking **myLife**

7 Circle the options to complete the sentences with your opinion.

1 The information in the article is *surprising / not surprising*.
2 The article is *interesting / not interesting*.
3 What the article says is *true / not true* in every country.
4 What the article says is *true / not true* for most boys and girls.
5 Boys and girls make different color choices because of *TV and advertising / other things*.

8 Work in groups. Tell one another your opinions from Exercise 7 and give reasons for your answers. Do you agree with your classmates' opinions?

I think the information in the article is surprising because …

In my opinion, it's not true in my country because …

Pink and blue

▶ 78

Jeongmee Yoon is a South Korean photographer. When her daughter Seowoo was five years old, she loved pink, so her mother photographed Seowoo in her bedroom with all her possessions.
5 There were plastic toys, animals, dolls, books, clothes, jewelry, make-up, and things for school. And everything was pink.

The photograph gave Jeongmee an idea. She asked parents if she could photograph their
10 daughters with their possessions. Many of these girls were like Seowoo and had lots of pink things. Jeongmee says, "My daughter is not unusual. Most other little girls in the United States and South Korea love pink clothing
15 and toys."

Next, Jeongmee photographed boys with their possessions, and noticed a difference in the color of objects they showed: the boys' objects were blue. The types of objects were also different.

20 Boys usually had toys like robots, dinosaurs, and superheroes, but girls typically liked pink make-up, clothes, or toys for cooking.

Jeongmee's pink and blue photographs show how important these two colors are in the lives
25 of young children. Jeongmee wonders if parents and children buy products for children in these colors because they see them on television and in advertisements.

The historian Jo Paoletti of the University of
30 Maryland says "pink for girls and blue for boys" wasn't true in the past. In the 19th century, people wore clothes of different colors, so men also wore pink and women wore blue. Jeongmee also noticed that the colors children prefer often
35 changes as they get older.

8d The photos of Reinier Gerritsen

Real life talking about pictures and photos

1 Work in pairs. Do you take a lot of photos on your phone or with a camera? What do you often photograph?

2 Work in pairs. Look at the photo. Discuss the questions.

1 Where are these people? What are they doing? How do they feel?
2 Do you think it is an interesting photograph? Why or why not?

3 ▶ 79 Work in pairs. The photo is by Reinier Gerritsen. Listen to someone talking about him and his photography. Answer the questions.

1 Where are the people in this photo?
2 Why does the person like Reinier's photos?
3 The speaker talks about the people in the photo. Number the people 1–5 in the order the speaker talks about them.

4 ▶ 79 Listen again and match the beginnings of the sentences (1–8) with the endings (a–h).

1 His photos	○	○ a scenes of everyday life.
2 They often show	○	○ b are very interesting.
3 This one	○	○ c the man and woman are talking.
4 On the right,	○	○ d is watching her.
5 The other blonde woman on the left	○	○ e a bit sad.
		○ f I don't normally look at people very closely.
6 She looks	○	
7 Look at the other woman	○	○ g at the back.
		○ h is on the New York subway.
8 I like the photo because	○	

▶ TALKING ABOUT PICTURES AND PHOTOS

General description
This photo shows …
I can see …

Location
on the left/right
in the middle
at the front/back

The people (appearance and actions)
She looks happy/sad/bored/nervous.
He is reading/sleeping/thinking.

Your opinion
I think …
I like it because it's a beautiful picture.

5 Pronunciation silent letters

▶ 80 Listen to these words. Which letter is silent? Listen again and repeat.

interesting	sometimes	everyday
listening	blonde	closely

6 Work in pairs. You are going to describe another photo by Reinier Gerritsen. Look at page 157 and follow the instructions.

8e Short and simple

Writing short messages

1 Work in pairs. Do you use these symbols when you send online messages? What do they mean?

2 Read five short messages from a cell phone. Which symbol can you add at the end of each message? You can use more than one.

1 Good job on passing your exams! ____
2 Thanks for the photos. I love the photo of Sam in the funny costume! ____
3 I'm at the train station but the train isn't here. It's late again! ____
4 Thanks for the invitation to the movie. Yes, I'd love to come. ____
5 It was nice to see you over the weekend. ____

3 Writing skill the KISS rules (keep it short and simple)

a Read the KISS rules for writing short messages.

> 1 Don't add unnecessary information.
>
> 2 Use numbers (not words) where possible.
>
> 3 Don't use long sentences with lots of conjunctions.
>
> 4 Don't use two sentences when you can use one sentence.
>
> 5 Use less formal words and phrases for everyday messages.
>
> 6 Leave out some words such as pronouns and auxiliary verbs.

b Now compare the pairs of sentences (1–4). Circle the sentence (a or b) that follows a KISS rule. Work in pairs and discuss. Which rules does the simpler sentence follow?

1 a I'm sitting in the café at the moment. Would you like to meet me here?
   b Can you meet me now in the cafe?
2 a My English exam is today. Let's speak at 2.
   b I have an English exam today but I'm free at two in the afternoon, so we can speak then.
3 a See you next month.
   b I look forward to seeing you again in a month.
4 a I called earlier but you weren't in. Can you please call me back when you read this?
   b Please call me.

c Read these sentences and rewrite them as short and simple messages.

1 I'm visiting for the day, so would you like to meet me in town?
2 I'm sorry but I'm staying with friends this week, so I'm not at home.
3 I hope you have a good time. I look forward to seeing you in the summer.

4 Work in pairs. You want to arrange to meet this week. Look at these instructions and write the first message. Exchange your messages, read your partner's message, and write a reply.

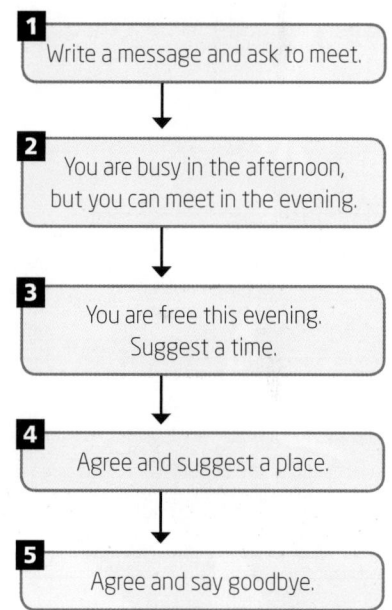

5 Work in pairs. Read and check all your messages again.

- Are all your messages short and simple?
- Did you follow the KISS rules in each message?
- Can you improve any of the messages?

8f Festivals and special events

A parade with musicians in Argentina

Before you watch

1 Work in pairs. Look at the photo and read the caption. Discuss these questions.

1 What are the musicians wearing in the parade?
2 What festivals or special events in your country have music?

2 Key vocabulary

Match these words with the pictures (1–7).

clarinet _____	clown _____	costume _____	glove _____
jewelry _____	mask _____	trumpet _____	

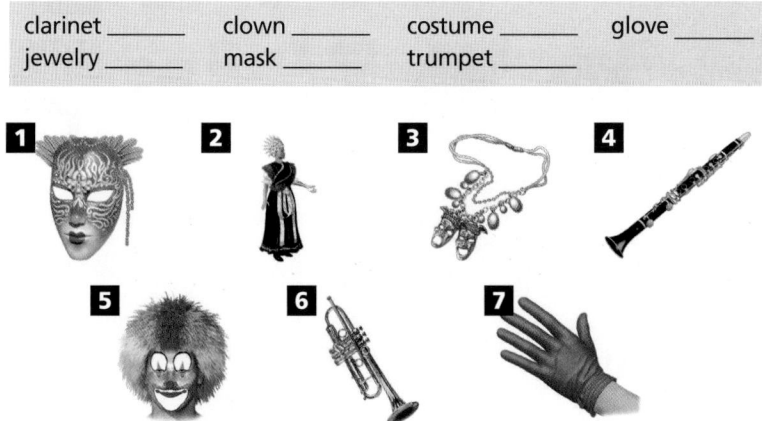

3 Answer these questions about the objects in Exercise 2. Tell the class.

1 Which of these things can you see in your country?
2 When do you see them? (e.g., at festivals, at special events)

While you watch

4 ▶ 8.1 Watch the video. There are five photos in the video and each one shows a festival or a special event. Circle the things you can see in each photo.

1 **Fire Festival:**	make-up	costume	fireworks
2 **Rodeo:**	make-up	jewelry	clown
3 **Parade:**	clarinet	trumpet	drums
4 **Elephant festival:**	make-up	gloves	mask
5 **Carnival:**	mask	gloves	jewelry

5 ▶ 8.1 Work in pairs. Watch the video again. Answer these questions.

Photo 1
1 Which country is the Beltane Fire Festival in?
2 Does the narrator like the woman's costume?

Photo 2
3 Where is the clown from?
4 Is he making the audience laugh or is he listening to his national anthem?

Photo 3
5 Which city is the parade in?
6 How does the speaker describe the music?

Photo 4
7 Where is this photo?
8 What colors can you see on the elephant?

Photo 5
9 Which Italian city are the women in?
10 How often is the carnival?

After you watch

6 Vocabulary in context

▶ 8.2 Watch the clips from the video. Choose the correct options to complete the sentences.

7 Work in pairs. Read these sentences from the video. Are the words in **bold** very positive or very negative? Practice reading the sentences. Stress the **bold** words.

1 She's wearing an **amazing** costume!
2 Those gloves are **wonderful**!
3 The colors are **incredible**.

8 ▶ 8.1 Work in pairs. Play the video again with the sound OFF. Take turns being the narrator. Describe each photo when it is on the screen. Talk about:

- where it is.
- what you can see.
- what you like about it.

9 Read this email. Which event in Exercise 4 is the person writing about?

> Hi!
>
> We're having a great time in Scotland! Last night, we went to a festival. There were lots of people and they were wearing interesting costumes and white make-up. One woman had a white dress and an amazing tall hat. Everyone carried fire torches, so it was an incredible event. I've attached a photo for you to look at.
>
> Bye for now!

10 Choose another festival or event from the video. Imagine you went to it. Write an email to a friend and describe it. Then exchange emails with a partner. Can you guess their festival?

UNIT 8 REVIEW AND MEMORY BOOSTER

Grammar

1 >> MB Work in pairs. Find the photos in Unit 8 to match these sentences.

1 These women live in the Philippines.
2 They are standing on other people's shoulders.
3 He has a blue room.
4 A man is wearing a yellow, orange, and blue costume.
5 She's reading a book.

2 >> MB Work in pairs. Look at Exercise 1 again. Underline the verbs in sentences 1–5 and answer these questions.

- What are the verb forms?
- When do we use them?

3 Complete the sentences with the simple present or present continuous form of the verbs.

1 At the moment, they _____ (work) in Japan.
2 He _____ (always / start) work at nine.
3 What _____ (you / do) now?
4 Currently, she _____ (write) a book about fashion.
5 We _____ (live) in Los Angeles.
6 _____ (you / like) this dress?
7 Why _____ (you / wear) those shoes this evening? They're ugly!
8 A: Where are Eiko and Sam? They're late.
   B: They _____ (drive) here now.

4 Complete the sentences with the correct form of *have*.

1 Penelope _____ blue eyes. (+)
2 I _____ a beard. (–)
3 The two sisters _____ the same dress. (+)
4 He _____ a cap. (–)
5 The dancer _____ white make-up on his face. (+)
6 _____ she _____ brown or blonde hair?

I CAN	
use the present continuous and the simple present	
use *be* and *have* to talk about appearance	

Vocabulary

5 >> MB Work in pairs. Can you remember the words for these pictures?

I CAN	
talk about clothes	
talk about faces and parts of the body	

Real life

6 Circle the correct options to complete these sentences about the photo in Greece.

1 This photograph *shows* / *takes* people in Xanthi, Greece.
2 Everyone is wearing black and white *costumes* / *uniforms*.
3 Some people have *masks* / *make-up* on their faces.
4 Some people are wearing black *hats* / *belts*.
5 The woman *on the right* / *in the middle* doesn't have a hat.
6 She *looks* / *has* happy.

7 >> MB Look at other units in this book and choose a photo with people. Write five sentences to describe the photo and read them to your partner.

I CAN	
describe a picture or photo	

Unit 9 Entertainment

Watching
Photo by Volkan Güney, Istanbul, Turkey

FEATURES

1 Work in pairs. Look at the photo. Where do you think the woman is? Choose from the places below.

at a concert	at a stadium	in a museum
at the movies	at a theater	in an art gallery
at home		

2 ▶ 81 Work in pairs. Listen to somebody talking about the photo. Answer these questions.

1 Where is the woman?
2 What is she watching?
3 What are the people in the video doing?

3 Work in pairs. At which of the places in Exercise 1 can you do these things?

1 look at a painting or a photo *in an art gallery*
2 look at old objects
3 watch a movie
4 watch TV
5 listen to music
6 watch a play
7 watch sports

4 Imagine you are going out this evening. Number the activities in Exercise 3 from 1 to 7 (1 = your first choice, 7 = your last choice). Then compare your answers in groups and give your reasons.

9a The Tallgrass Film Festival

Vocabulary movies

1 Complete these sentences in your own words. Then work in pairs and compare your sentences.

1 I go to the movies … (once a week? once a month?)
2 I usually watch movies … (on TV? on the internet? at a movie theater?)
3 I like watching movies … (with friends? on my own? with a big audience?)
4 The last movie I saw at the movie theater was …

▶ **See** or **watch**?

*I went **to see a movie** last night.* (to talk about the event)
*I like **watching movies** with friends.* (to talk about the activity)

2 Match the types of movies with the photos (a–h).

1 animated	2 comedy	3 documentary	4 fantasy
5 horror	6 action	7 science fiction	8 romantic comedy

3 Work as a class. Think of one movie for each type in Exercise 2. Which types of movies do you like? Which types of movies do you never watch?

Reading

4 Work in pairs. Read the article. What types of films can you watch at the Tallgrass Film Festival?

THE TALLGRASS FILM FESTIVAL
▶ 82

Every year, the Tallgrass Film Festival shows more than 190 movies from 33 different countries. You can see many different movies including science fiction, documentaries, and fantasy. Here are some of the movies this year.

MOTHER
This comedy thriller from Estonia is by the director Kadri Kõusaar. A man is shot in a small Estonian town and his mother tries to find out who did it.

BROTHER
In a drama from Venezuela, two brothers grow up in Caracas with a love for soccer. But life is difficult and sometimes violent for the two boys as they try to become professional players.

APRIL AND THE EXTRAORDINARY WORLD
It's 1941 and April lives with her family in Paris. One day, her family disappears, and April (with her cat) has to find them. Great storytelling and animation for the whole family. (In French with English subtitles.)

5 Read the article again. Are these statements true (T) or false (F)?

1 The festival is once a year.   T   F
2 You can see movies from around the world there.   T   F
3 This year you can see a movie from Estonia.   T   F
4 *Brother* is about two soccer teams in Venezuela.   T   F
5 *April and the Extraordinary World* is a horror movie.   T   F

6 Work in pairs. Which of the movies at the festival would you like to see? Why?

Listening

7 ▶ 83 Work in pairs. Two friends are at the Tallgrass Film Festival. Listen to their conversation and answer the questions.

1 Which movie does Isabella talk about?
2 Where does Charles invite Isabella?
3 Does she answer yes or no?

8 ▶ 83 Listen again and complete the conversation with the verbs you hear.

C = Charles, I = Isabella

C: Hey! Isabella.
I: Hi, Charles. Are you enjoying the festival? I'm going to ¹_____ a ticket for the next movie. It's called *Mother*. Are you going to ²_____ it, too? It starts in ten minutes.
C: No, I'm not, but where are you ³_____ afterward? Didier, Monica, and I are going to ⁴_____ dinner at a Japanese restaurant. Do you want to come?
I: Sorry, but I'm not going to ⁵_____ out late tonight. I'm tired.
C: OK. No problem.
I: Oh, I have to go. Bye.
C: Bye. See you later.

Grammar *be going to* (for plans)

> ▶ **BE GOING TO** (FOR PLANS)
>
> *I'm going to buy* a ticket for the next movie.
> *I'm not going to stay out* late.
> What *are you going to see*?
> *Are you going to see* the movie?
> *Yes, I am. / No, I'm not.*
>
> *going to go* → *going to*
> Instead of *be going to go*, we often say:
> *I'm not going to go* to work tomorrow.
> Where *are you going to go* afterward?

For more information and practice, see page 174.

9 Work in pairs. Look at the grammar box. Answer these questions.

1 Does the form *be going to* + verb (base form) talk about the present or the future?
2 How do we form the negative and question form of *be going to*?
3 How can you say *going to go* in a different way?

10 Work in pairs. Make sentences with *be going to*.

1 we / see a movie at the new theater.
2 I / not buy / a ticket. It's too expensive.
3 you / buy the tickets online or at the theater?
4 where / you / sit?
5 I / not watch / the movie. It starts at midnight.
6 where / you / go / after the movie?

11 Pronunciation /tə/

▶ 84 Listen to the sentences in Exercise 10. Notice the weak vowel sound in *to*. Listen again and repeat.

12 Work in pairs. Complete these sentences in your own words.

1 This evening, I'm going to …
2 This weekend, I'm going …
3 Next weekend, I'm …
4 This summer, …

13 Make questions about your sentences in Exercise 12. Then work in pairs. Ask and answer your questions.

A: *Are you going to see a movie this evening?*
B: *No, I'm not. But I am going to see one this weekend.*

Speaking *my* Life

14 Imagine you are going to a film festival. Choose three movies you want to see and plan your day.

In Cinema 1
2:00–3:30 *Deepsea Challenge*—a documentary by James Cameron about the Mariana Trench
3:55–5:25 *Black Panther*—a Hollywood superhero movie
5:40–7:15 *Mumbai Delhi Mumbai*—a romantic comedy set in two cities in India

In Cinema 2
2:00–4:00 *Wild Tales*—six short, funny movies from Argentina. Includes some violence.
4:15–5:35 *Best Worst Movie*—a fun documentary about one of the worst films in history
5:45–8:15 *Macbeth*—a new movie version of Shakespeare's famous play

In Cinema 3
2:00–4:10 *Howl's Moving Castle*—a classic Japanese animated movie for children and adults
4:15–5:40 *And Your Mother Too*—a movie from Mexico with a mix of comedy and drama
5:45–7:05 *March of the Penguins*—a powerful documentary about the lives of emperor penguins

15 Work in groups. Imagine you are going to the festival with the people in your group. Discuss your plans.

What are you going to see at two o'clock?

9b What's the future for TV?

Vocabulary talking about TV

1 ▶ **85** Listen to seven clips from different TV shows. Match the clips (1–7) with the type of show (a–g).

a a sports program ____
b a comedy show _1_
c a quiz show ____
d a horror movie ____
e a drama series ____
f a wildlife documentary ____
g the news ____

2 Read the comments about different TV shows. Which shows from Exercise 1 (a–g) do they describe?

1 I love the actors in this show. They are all so **funny**! ____
2 It's really **interesting** how they filmed these animals under the ground. ____
3 There's a new episode tonight. I enjoyed the previous episode but it was a little **violent.** ____
4 The movie was so **scary** I couldn't watch it alone. ____
5 This is so **exciting**. They are both playing really well. ____
6 I can never answer the questions, but it's **fun**. ____
7 This is **boring**. I'm not interested in politics. Let's watch a movie instead. ____

3 Work in groups and answer these questions.

1 Which TV shows from Exercise 1 do you often watch?
2 Why do you watch them? (e.g., Are they funny/interesting?)
3 What are you going to watch tonight when you get home?
4 Which do you watch more often? Shows on TV or online videos (e.g., on YouTube)? Why?

Listening

4 ▶ **86** Listen to a report about how young people watch videos and TV. Number a–c in the order the speaker mentions them (1–3).

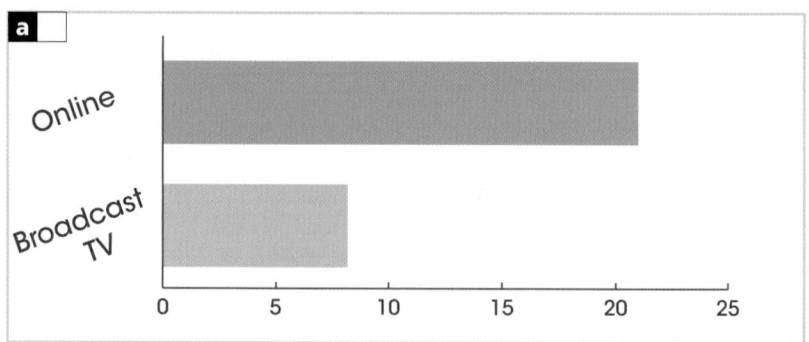

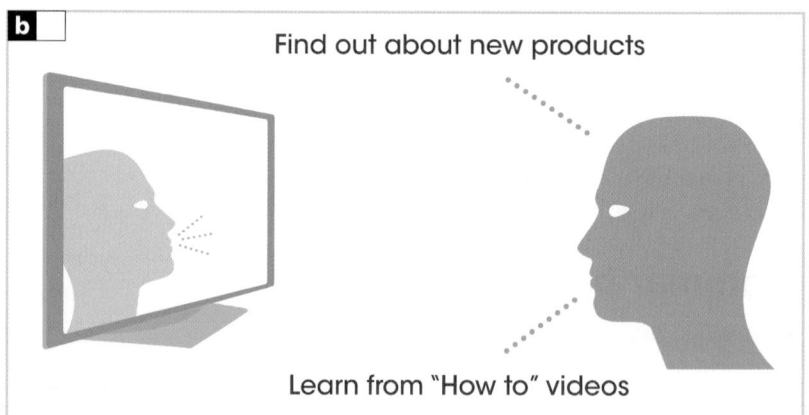

Find out about new products

Learn from "How to" videos

c		Online video	TV
I can watch it when I want to		81%	28%
It has shows I want to watch		69%	56%

5 ▶ **86** Work in pairs. Listen again and answer these questions.

1 Which TV shows does the speaker mention at the beginning?
2 Why do 81% of young people think online TV is better?
3 What topics do people talk about on YouTube?
4 Why do people watch "How to" videos on YouTube?

6 Work in pairs. At the end of the report, the speaker asks, "Are we going to watch TV at all in the future?" What do you think?

We're not going to watch TV in the future because …

Grammar infinitive of purpose

> ▶ **INFINITIVE OF PURPOSE**
>
> We use the infinitive of purpose to give the reason for an action.
> Turn on the TV **to watch the news**.
> Go online **to find a "How to" video**.
> I'm going to record this movie **to watch it later**.
>
> For more information and practice, see page 174.

7 Work in pairs. Look at the grammar box. Answer these questions.

1 Which part of each sentence describes the main action?
2 Which part of each sentence gives the reason? What is the verb form in this part of the sentence?

8 ▶ **87** Read the passage on the right about an interview with the filmmaker Adrian Seymour. Complete the passage with the infinitives of purpose (a–e). Listen and check.

a to make a movie
b to edit the movie
c to find out about his movies
d to take a vacation
e to film wildlife

9 Work in pairs. Match the actions (1–5) with the reasons (a–e). Then make sentences starting with *I'm going to …*

1 read this book about Martin Scorsese ___
2 go to art school ___
3 play this video game again ___
4 buy theater tickets ___
5 watch these videos ___

a to see a play by Shakespeare
b to reach level five
c to find out about his life
d to learn how to play the guitar
e to study painting

I'm going to read this book about Martin Scorsese to find out about his life.

Speaking myLife

10 Think about your plans. Write sentences about where you are going, when, and why. Use some of these ideas.

the movies	tomorrow	on Friday
a concert	on the weekend	next week
a museum	next month	the mall

I'm going to the movies on Friday to see Johnny Depp's new movie.

11 Work in pairs. Take turns telling each other your plans. Ask your partner for the reason or more details.

A: *I'm going to London tomorrow.*
B: *Why are you going?*
A: *To meet some friends.*

Interview with Adrian Seymour

Last week, I spoke to Adrian Seymour
1_____ . Adrian makes movies about nature and animals. This year he's going to Honduras 2_____ about the rain forest. He's going in the summer 3_____ and then he's going back to his office in the fall 4_____ .
So it's going to take about six months in total. Then in the winter, when he's finished the movie, he's going to Indonesia 5_____ !

9c Nature in art

Vocabulary nature

1 Work in pairs. The four pictures (1–4) on the right show nature in art. Answer these questions for each picture.

1 Is the picture modern or traditional?
2 Do you know which country or period in history it is from?
3 What can you see in the picture? Use these words.

birds	flowers	grass	lakes	leaves
mountains	rocks	sea	sky	trees

2 Work in pairs. Do you have paintings or photos in your home? What kind of pictures are they? What do they show? (e.g., people, animals, places)

Reading

3 Read the article and match each artist to the photo of their art (1–4).

4 Read the article again. Check (✓) the sentences that are true for each artist, according to the information in the article.

Critical thinking the writer's preferences

5 Read the sentence below. Does *prefer* mean "like" or "like one thing more than another"?

Many people like Witkiewicz's paintings of people's faces, but I prefer his paintings of nature and landscapes.

6 Work in pairs. Read the article again. Answer these questions.

1 Which of the artists does the writer say she likes?
2 Which of their art does she prefer?

Speaking *my* Life

7 Work in pairs. Discuss the pictures in the article.

- Say which picture you prefer in each of these pairs and why. 1 or 2? 2 or 3? 3 or 4? 1 or 4?
- Which picture do you like the most? Why?

A: Which picture do you prefer? 1 or 2?
B: I prefer 2 because … This is my favorite painting because …

	Stanislaw Witkiewicz	Andō Hiroshige	Beatriz Milhazes	Vincent van Gogh
1 This artist draws the natural environment.	✓	✓	✓	✓
2 This artist is living now.				
3 This artist is European.				
4 This artist also makes sculptures.				
5 This artist is famous for paintings of flowers.				
6 This artist didn't have money when he died.				

Nature in art

▶ 88

Many artists include drawings of nature in their work, but the results can be very different. Here are four of the most famous.

5   _____ *Stanislaw Witkiewicz* (1885–1939) was a Polish artist. You often see his paintings in art galleries in Poland. Many people like Witkiewicz's paintings of people's faces, but I prefer his paintings of nature and landscapes.[1] This one (painted in 1907) shows the Hinczow Lakes in the Tatra mountains. I like this painting because
10 of the green fields and blue water—I'd love to go there.

_____ Japanese art is famous for landscape paintings. You can often see sea and sky, and mountains and trees. *Andō Hiroshige* worked in the nineteenth century and he's one of Japan's most famous artists. He printed and
15 sold thousands of beautiful prints in his lifetime. However, he was poor when he died.

_____ *Beatriz Milhazes* is a Brazilian artist from Rio de Janeiro. She's famous for her colorful paintings of flowers and interesting shapes. She also makes sculptures
20 with different types of natural and man-made materials. Personally, I like all her work, though I prefer her paintings.

_____ *Vincent van Gogh*, the famous Dutch artist, made eleven paintings of sunflowers. They were his
25 favorite paintings because he loved the color yellow. I prefer his other paintings, but many people love these ones. Nowadays, you see them on cards, postcards, and T-shirts. Van Gogh died with no money, but in 1987, someone bought the last sunflower painting for
30 $49 million.

[1]**landscape** (n) /'lændskeɪp/ a painting of an area outside (with trees, rivers, mountains, etc.)

9d Making arrangements

Listening

1 Work in pairs. Look at the photo of some theaters on Broadway, New York. Answer these questions.

1 Is there a theater in your town or city? What kinds of shows are there? (e.g., plays, musicals, dance performances)

2 What was the last show you saw? What was it about?

2 ▶ 89 Work in pairs. Two friends are talking about seeing a show at a Broadway theater. Listen to their phone conversations and answer the questions.

Conversation 1
1 Which show in the photo are they talking about?
2 When is the show?
3 Why isn't Adriana free?

Conversation 2
4 Can Adriana finish work early?
5 What time does the show start?
6 What time are they going to meet?

Real life inviting and making arrangements

3 ▶ 89 Complete the expressions for inviting and making arrangements with these words. Then listen again and check.

| free | great | like | 'd love | meet |
| see | 'm sorry | time | want | |

▶ INVITING AND MAKING ARRANGEMENTS

Inviting
Would you ¹_____ to come?
Are you ²_____ ?
Do you ³_____ to go?

Responding to the invitation
Thanks, I ⁴_____ to.
I ⁵_____ , but I'm working late tonight.
That's ⁶_____ .

Making arrangements
What ⁷_____ does it start?
Let's ⁸_____ at seven.
⁹_____ you at seven.

4 Pronunciation showing enthusiasm

▶ 90 Listen to these phrases for responding to invitations. Underline the word with the most stress. Then listen again and repeat.

1 I'd love to!
2 I'd really like to!
3 That's great!
4 That sounds terrific!

5 Work in pairs. Practice these telephone conversations.

Student A: You have tickets for the musical *Hamilton* tomorrow night. It starts at 8 p.m. Call Student B and invite him or her.

Student B: Answer the phone. You are at work. Listen to Student A's invitation and say yes. Arrange to meet.

Then change roles and have a conversation for the musical *Wicked*. It starts at 8:30 p.m.

9e It looks amazing!

Writing reviews

1 Work in pairs. People often write reviews on websites. Do you ever read them? Why or why not?

2 Match the excerpts from reviews and comments (1–5) with these things.

> an art exhibition _____   a movie _____   music _____
> perfume _____   a restaurant _____

1
I loved her first album, so I was excited about her second. Some of the tracks are good and full of energy, but in others she sounds tired, or even bored! Overall, it's a bit disappointing. _____

2
After the show, we had a meal at this new place downtown. We had seafood for an appetizer and it tasted great. We waited a long time for our main course and when it arrived, it was cold. _____

3
The new exhibition in the gallery has paintings by Picasso when he was very young. They look amazing! You can't believe he was only twenty when he painted them. _____

4
I felt scared at the beginning because it starts in the middle of the night. There are two people in a car and it breaks down. So the people go to a house and a strange man opens the door. But after that it's very funny. I laughed for two hours. _____

5
I bought this because it has the name of my favorite actress on it, but it smells awful! _____

3 Which reviews in Exercise 2 are positive (P)? Which are negative (N)? Write the appropriate letter in each blank.

4 **Writing skills giving your opinion with sense verbs**

a Sense verbs are *look, feel, sound, taste,* and *smell.* We often use sense verbs + adjectives in reviews to give our opinion about something. Underline five sense verbs + adjectives in the reviews in Exercise 2.

b Work in pairs. Which sense verbs could you use to write about these items? You can choose more than one for each item.

> a new building   a new type of sports car
> a new café   a new type of chocolate
> a concert   men's aftershave
> clothes in a store   a video game

c Work in pairs. Which of these adjectives can you use with the verbs *look, feel, sound, taste,* or *smell*? You can use the adjectives more than once.

> angry   beautiful   bored   delicious
> loud   interesting   nice
> soft   terrible   tired

5 Choose two of the items in Exercise 4b. Write a short review or comment for a website about them. Use sense verbs and adjectives.

6 Work in pairs. Exchange reviews. Use these questions to check your partner's reviews.
- Are the reviews positive or negative?
- Did your partner use sense verbs and adjectives?
- Are you now interested in the item in the review?

A musical show for the Carnival in Montevideo, Uruguay

Filming wildlife

The photographer took this photo of an ocelot in Peru using a "camera trap."

Before you watch

1 Work in pairs. Do you watch wildlife documentaries on TV? Why or why not?

2 Work in pairs. Look at the photo. Why do you think ocelots are difficult to photograph?

3 Key vocabulary

Read the sentences. The words in **bold** are used in the video. Match the words with the definitions (a–d).

1 There are **rain forests** across Central and South America.
2 You can use a **camera trap** to photograph animals at night.
3 Leopards are a **species** of big cat like lions and tigers.
4 Adrian works with a **team** who help him.

a something that takes photos when an animal moves in front of it _____
b type or group of animals _____
c places with many trees and different types of wildlife _____
d a group of people working together _____

While you watch

4 ◻️ **9.1** Watch the video with the sound OFF. Number Adrian's actions in the order you see them (1–7).

____ a He's walking through the rainforest.
____ b He's putting a camera trap in a tree.
____ c He's taking a camera trap off a tree.
____ d He's looking for animals in the photos.
____ e He's taking a bath.
____ f He's watching an animal on his computer.
____ g He's climbing up a tree.

5 ◻️ **9.1** Watch the video again with the sound ON. Choose the correct answers for the questions.

1 Where is the rain forest?
  a in Guatemala
  b in Costa Rica
  c in Honduras

2 Where do a lot of the animals live?
  a in rivers
  b in trees
  c under the ground

3 How many camera traps does Adrian put in the trees?
  a six
  b sixteen
  c sixty

4 How long does Adrian wait before he looks at his camera traps?
  a four hours
  b four days
  c four weeks

5 When Adrian looks at the first photos, what does he think?
  a He thinks the cameras don't work.
  b He doesn't think there are any animals.
  c He doesn't know what the problem is.

6 He sees a kinkajou in the pictures. Which three facts are true about kinkajous?
  ☐ They come out at night.
  ☐ They live in rain forests.
  ☐ They also live in the desert.
  ☐ They eat meat and fruit.

After you watch

6 Vocabulary in context

◻️ **9.2** Watch the clips from the video. Choose the correct meaning of the words and phrases.

7 Complete this summary about Adrian Seymour and camera traps using words from the video.

Dr. Adrian Seymour is a ¹filmm_____ and his work is often on nature TV programs. Recently, he went to the Honduran ²r_____ to film animals that humans ³r_____ see. Working with a ⁴t_____ of people, Adrian put camera traps in different places, and waited for four weeks. Then he ⁵c_____ the traps and ⁶s_____ the pictures back at his office.

8 Work in groups. You are a team of filmmakers. A TV channel has a lot of money for a new nature program and it's going to give the money to the team with the best ideas. Plan your new TV program and answer these questions.

1 What are you going to call the TV program?
2 Where are you going to film?
3 What are you going to film? What species of animal(s)? Why?
4 How is your TV program going to be different from other nature programs?

9 Present your ideas to the other teams. Vote on the best idea.

UNIT 9 REVIEW AND MEMORY BOOSTER

Grammar

1 Complete the sentences with *be going to* and the correct form of these verbs.

buy	not drive	take	meet
play	watch	not write	

1 We _____ a movie on TV this evening.
2 Matt and Raul _____ tennis.
3 I _____ friends for dinner.
4 They _____ here because there's a problem with their car.
5 _____ you _____ a vacation this year?
6 Rachel _____ the tickets online before we leave.
7 The author _____ another book ever again.

2 Make five sentences with *be going to* and the infinitive of purpose.

I'm going to	the theater a concert an art gallery a café the mall	to have to see to listen to to look at to buy	a drink. a musical. music. clothes. paintings.

3 >> MB Work in pairs. Tell each other about:

- a plan for this weekend with *be going to*.
- the reason for your plan with the infinitive of purpose.

I CAN	
talk about future plans with *be going to*	
use the infinitive of purpose for giving reasons	

Vocabulary

4 Match these types of movies with the comments (1–6).

animated ____	documentary ____	comedy ____
horror ____	science fiction ____	action ____

1 It's a story in space with aliens.
2 It was very funny, and I laughed for hours afterward.
3 It's all about polar bears and how they live.
4 I couldn't watch the movie. It was very scary!
5 There are fast cars, and the hero always wins.
6 In the past, they drew all the pictures on paper. Nowadays, they make them with computers.

5 Cross out one incorrect word in each group.

1 **types of movies:** animated thriller fantasy news horror
2 **landscapes:** rocks mountains fruit sea sky
3 **plants:** grass birds trees flowers leaves
4 **animals:** kangaroos turtles birds lakes frogs

6 >> MB Work in pairs. Look at the photos and answer these questions.

1 What type of TV shows are they?
2 What words describe these types of shows?
3 When you watch them, how do you feel?

7 >> MB Work in pairs. Discuss these questions.

- What's your favorite TV show at the moment?
- What words describe it?

I CAN	
talk about different types of movies and TV shows	
talk about nature	

Real life

8 Number the lines of the conversation in the correct order (1–8).

<u>1</u> Would you like to see a movie?
____ Sorry, but I'm working late.
____ What time does it start?
____ OK. I'd love to go at nine.
____ There's another showing at nine.
____ Great. Let's meet outside the theater at quarter to nine.
____ At six.
<u>8</u> Right. See you there. Bye.

9 >> MB Work in pairs. Act out a telephone conversation arranging to meet next week. Then change partners and make another arrangement for a different day next week.

I CAN	
invite someone	
make arrangements	

Unit 10 Learning

Walking into a new building
in Yangzhou, China

FEATURES

1 Work in pairs. Look at the photo. What do you think this building is for? What happens here?

2 ▶ 91 Work in pairs. Listen to part of a travel podcast and answer the questions.

   1 Why is Yangzhou famous?
   2 What types of books can you find in the place in the photo?

3 Match the subjects (1–8) with the topics (a–h).

   1 history   ○   ○ a heat, light, and energy
   2 physics   ○   ○ b places in the world
   3 literature   ○   ○ c the past
   4 geography   ○   ○ d living things
   5 biology   ○   ○ e chemicals
   6 mathematics   ○   ○ f computers
   7 chemistry   ○   ○ g numbers
   8 IT (information technology)   ○   ○ h books, poems, plays, etc.

4 Which subjects do/did you study at school? Which subjects are most interesting to you? Why?

10a What have we learned?

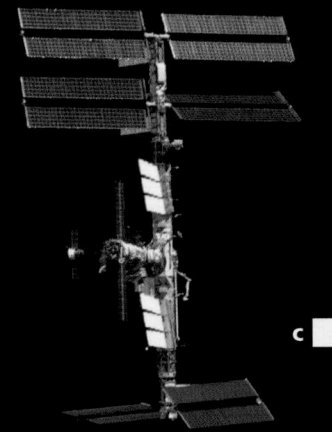

c ☐

a ☐

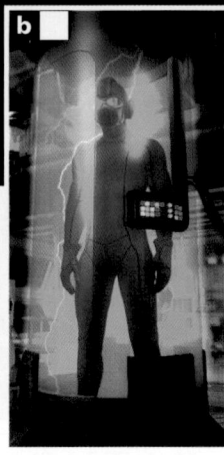

b ☐

Reading

1 Work in pairs. Look at the three pictures. What do you think is happening in each photo?

2 Read the article. Match the paragraphs (1–3) with the photos (a–c).

▶ 92

What have we learned … and what is still to learn?

1 In recent centuries, scientists have learned a lot. They've learned how to send people into space and they've discovered new medicines. More recently, they've designed robots to do routine jobs.

2 However, there are still some things that scientists can't do. For example, some scientists have tried to make objects invisible, but it hasn't worked very well. The car in the photograph has cameras on one side so it shows the images on the other side. But, as you can see, the wheels still aren't invisible.

3 Other scientists are trying to solve the problem of transportation on our busy roads. They've made self-driving cars, but so far they haven't been able to move a human from one place to another without transportation. This is called "teleporting," and scientists don't understand this difficult area of science yet—in fact, it's possible they never will!

3 Read the article again. Is the information in these sentences in the text (✓) or not in the text (✗)?

1 Scientists have learned to do many things. ____
2 Some people have robots in their homes. ____
3 Scientists don't know everything. ____
4 The invisible car isn't completely invisible. ____
5 Self-driving cars work very well. ____
6 Scientists have tried different solutions to transportation problems. ____

4 Work in groups. Discuss the questions and give reasons for your answers.

In the future, do you think we are going to:

1 use robots for housework?
2 make objects invisible?
3 use self-driving cars?
4 teleport humans?

Wordbuilding synonyms and antonyms

> **WORDBUILDING synonyms and antonyms**

Synonyms are words with similar meanings: *learn = study*
Antonyms are words with opposite meanings: *pass ≠ fail*

For more practice, see Workbook page 83.

5 Look at the wordbuilding box. Then circle the best options to complete the sentences.
1 Can you *learn / teach* me how to speak Spanish?
2 Everyone in the class is going to *pass / fail* the test because their English is very good.
3 I can't go out tonight. I need to *study / practice* for a history exam tomorrow.
4 My teacher explained it, but I still don't *know / understand* how it works.

Grammar present perfect

> **PRESENT PERFECT**

I've learned the vocabulary for the test.
He's invented a new robot.
We've discovered a new type of medicine.

I haven't done my homework.
He hasn't passed the exam.
They haven't learned the words.

Note: With regular verbs, add -ed to make the past participle form. See page 182 for a list of irregular past participle forms.

For more information and practice, see page 176.

6 Work in pairs. Look at the grammar box. Answer these questions.

1 Are the sentences talking about an action in the past or present?
2 Do we know exactly when the action happened?
3 In the present perfect, the main verb is the past participle (e.g., *learned*). What is the auxiliary verb?

7 Complete the text with these words.

has	have	haven't	hasn't	has	have

The cell phone [1]_____ changed our lives forever. It [2]_____ become a normal part of our everyday life. In fact, most people [3]_____ forgotten what life was like without it. You probably [4]_____ called from a public telephone box in years. Of course, if you are under 25 years old, life [5]_____ changed at all. Phones [6]_____ always been mobile.

8 Complete these sentences with the present perfect form of the verb.

1 I _____ (pass) all my exams! I'm so happy.
2 There's nobody in school this week. All the teachers _____ (go) on vacation.
3 I _____ (not finish) the assignment. Can I hand it in next lesson?
4 BMW _____ (design) a new type of car. The company's going to sell it next year.
5 He _____ (not do) any homework all year.
6 They _____ (lost) our address. I'll text it to them.
7 I _____ (not see) Tom this week. Is he on vacation?

> **PRESENT PERFECT QUESTIONS and SHORT ANSWERS**

Have you forgotten his phone number?
Yes, I have. / No I haven't.
Has she practiced the piano today?
Yes, she has. / No she hasn't.

Questions with *Have you ever …?*
We often use *Have you ever* to ask about past experiences.
We use *never* in negative answers.
Have you ever studied French?
No, I've never studied French.

For more information and practice, see page 176.

9 ▶ **93** Look at the grammar box. Complete the conversations. Then listen and check.

1 A: [1]_____ you done your homework?
   B: No, I [2]_____ .

2 A: [3]_____ Peter finished his exams?
   B: Yes, he's [4]_____ all of them and now he's waiting for his results.

3 A: Have you [5]_____ studied Arabic?
   B: No, I've [6]_____ studied Arabic.

Speaking myLife

10 Work in pairs. Ask each other *Have you ever …?* questions using these ideas.

be / on TV	invent / something
write / a book	meet / a famous person
fail / test	work / in another country

A: *Have you ever failed a test?*
B: *Yes, I have. I failed my driving test twice!*

10b How good is your memory?

Speaking and reading

1 Work in groups of three. Which things on this list are easy to remember? Which do you often forget?
- people's names and faces
- directions and addresses
- telephone numbers
- dates and facts in history
- food on shopping lists
- the words of a song

2 Work in your group. **Student A:** Turn to page 154. **Student B:** Turn to page 155. **Student C:** Turn to page 157. Memorize the important information in your paragraph, and then write notes on that information in the chart below.

3 Tell the students in your group about the information in your paragraph. Listen to the other students and write notes in the chart.

4 Now read all three paragraphs and compare your notes.

1 How much information have you remembered?
2 How much information have the other students remembered?
3 Which memory techniques have you used before?

	Student A	Student B	Student C
What was the topic of the text?			
What memory techniques did it describe?			

Nelson Dellis has won the USA Memory Championship for the fourth time!

Listening

5 Work in pairs. Look at the photo and read the caption. Answer these questions.

1 Who is the man in the photo?
2 What has he won? Has he ever won it before?

6 ▶ 94 Listen to a news report about Nelson Dellis. Number these topics in the order the reporter mentions them.

___ a the USA Memory Championship
___ b what Nelson can remember
___ c Nelson's memory techniques

7 ▶ 94 Listen again. Answer the questions.

1 How many new names and faces can Nelson memorize?
2 How many different numbers can he hear and repeat?
3 Which years did he win the USA Memory Championship?
4 Which sporting event is the USA Memory Championship similar to?
5 What did he study a few years ago?
6 Who does he teach his techniques to?

Grammar present perfect and simple past

▶ **PRESENT PERFECT and SIMPLE PAST**

*Nelson **has won** the USA Memory Championship four times.*
*He **won** the competition in 2011, 2012, 2014, and again in 2015.*

For more information and practice, see page 176.

8 Look at the grammar box. Circle the correct options to complete these rules.

1 We can use the present perfect and the simple past to talk about the *present / past*.
2 We use the *present perfect / simple past* when we know or say the exact time.
3 We use the *present perfect / simple past* when we don't know or say the exact time.

9 Complete the sentences with two forms of the verb. Use the present perfect and the simple past.

1 My friend _____ his mathematics exam twice! He _____ it last year and this year. (fail)
2 Sally _____ English before. When she was a child, she _____ it at school. (study)
3 Google _____ different driverless cars. In 2016, it _____ a car that traveled 200,000 km with no driver. (make)
4 We _____ a movie over the weekend. I _____ it a few times before, but it was still funny. (see)

Speaking *my*Life

10 In everyday conversations, we often start with a question in the present perfect and then ask another question in the simple past. Write conversations with the ideas in 1–4.

A: *Have you ever studied in another country?*
B: *Yes, I studied in Mexico.*
A: *When did you study there?*

1 Have / take / an English exam?
When / take it?
2 Have / study / science?
Where / study?
3 Have / teach / a subject?
What / teach?
4 Have / learn / to play a musical instrument?
What / learn?

11 Work in pairs. Ask and answer the questions from Exercise 10. Then ask your own questions to find out more about what your partner has learned.

10c Good learning habits

Vocabulary daily habits

1 Work in groups. Discuss these habits (a–j) and decide what you think about each one.

Write (✓) if you think it's a good habit.

Write (–) if you think it isn't good or bad.

Write (✗) if you think it's a bad habit.

a drinking lots of coffee every day ___
b brushing your teeth twice a day ___
c swimming every morning ___
d biting your fingernails ___
e buying the same newspaper every day ___
f eating chocolate ___
g checking your phone during meals ___
h smoking cigarettes ___
i practicing the guitar for thirty minutes a day ___
j learning ten new English words every day ___

2 Work in pairs. Answer these questions.

1 Do you have any of the habits from the list in Exercise 1?
2 Have you ever tried to change a habit? What happened?

Reading

3 Read the article and answer the questions.

1 What was Michael Phelps's habit before a race?
2 What has he won?
3 What examples of useful habits are there in paragraph 2?
4 How does a bad habit form?
5 How long can it take to stop a bad habit?
6 How can you change a habit?

Critical thinking supporting the main idea

4 Each paragraph in the article has a main idea. Match the paragraphs (1–3) with these ideas.

a how we can have good and bad habits ___
b how good habits can help us do something well ___
c how we can change our habits ___

5 The writer supports the main ideas in three different ways. Which paragraph (1–3) uses:

a different examples from everyday life? ___
b information about a real person? ___
c information from research and studies? ___

Word focus *up*

6 Underline two verb phrases with *up* in paragraph 1 and in paragraph 3.

7 Read the sentences. Match the verb phrases with *up* in **bold** (1–5) with their meanings (a–e).

1 He **gets up** at 6:30 a.m. ___
2 They want to **give up** smoking. ___
3 We **wake up** at seven every day. ___
4 The cost of food **goes up** in the winter. ___
5 I always **dress up** for a party. ___

a get out of bed
b wear fun or nice clothes
c stop sleeping
d stop (a bad habit)
e increase

8 Complete these questions with a verb phrase with *up*. Then work in pairs. Ask and answer your questions.

1 When you go out with friends, do you …?
2 In the morning, what time do you …?
3 Which bad habits do you want to …?
4 How often does the cost of transportation …?

Speaking and writing

9 Work in pairs. Choose one of these questions or think of your own question. Write advice about how you can do something well with good habits and routines.

- How can you run a marathon?
- How can you stop drinking too much coffee?
- How can you save more money?
- How can you learn to play a musical instrument like a famous musician?

1 Get up every day at six and eat a healthy breakfast.

Good learning habits

▶ 95

1 People who learn to do something really well almost always have good routines and habits. Take the Olympic swimmer Michael Phelps. Before he retired in 2016, he trained 365 days a year, and he had the same training routine every day. He got up at 6:30 a.m. and had breakfast. He ate exactly 6,000 calories every day. Then he swam for six hours a day. Before a race, he always listened to very loud hip-hop music. Phelps has won 18 Olympic gold medals and 22 Olympic medals in total. That's more than any other person in history.

2 Habits are useful for all of us. We brush our teeth without thinking. Most people travel to school or work the same way every day and don't get lost. And when we want to learn something new—like a musical instrument—it's important to have a daily routine, such as practicing for thirty minutes before breakfast. Of course, habits can also be bad and difficult to change. For example, imagine someone who works in an office. He goes to a café during lunch, and buys coffee and cake. He enjoys it, so he does it again the next day—and the next. Soon it's a habit, and he's spending more money, drinking more caffeine, and eating too many calories.

3 According to researchers at University College London, most people can make something into a habit after 66 days of routine and repetition. Stopping a bad habit (e.g., giving up smoking), however, can take longer—up to 254 days. One conclusion was that the "situation" is important for a habit. So, if you are going to change the habit of having coffee and cake every day, don't go to the café—go for a walk instead. In other words, change the situation and start a new routine.

10d Communication problems

Listening

1 Work in pairs. Look at the photo and discuss the questions.

  1 How does the man feel? What do you think has happened?

  2 Has your cell phone or internet connection ever stopped working? How did you feel?

2 ▶ 96 Work in pairs. Richard works for Omarox Engineering. He answers a telephone call from Omar. Listen and answer the questions.

  1 Where is Omar?

  _____

  2 What time is it?

  _____

  3 What isn't working?

  _____

  4 What is the name of Omar's hotel?

  _____

  5 What is the number?

  _____

  6 Where has Richard put the designs?

  _____

Real life checking and clarifying

3 ▶ 96 Look at these expressions for checking and clarifying. Then match the responses (a–e) with the expressions (1–5). Listen again and check.

> ▶ **CHECKING AND CLARIFYING**
>
> 1 Is that three in the morning? ____
> 2 Was that the Encasa Hotel? ____
> 3 The number is 603-2169-2266. ____
> 4 Is there anything else? ____
> 5 Have you called our colleagues? ____

  a So that's 603-2169-2266?
  b No, in the afternoon.
  c Yes, I have.
  d Yes, one thing.
  e No, the Ancasa Hotel. A for apple.

4 Pronunciation contrastive stress (2)

▶ 97 Listen and underline the stressed word(s) in each response. Then listen again and repeat the responses.

  1 A: Is that three in the morning?
     B: No, in the afternoon.
  2 A: Was that the Encasa Hotel?
     B: No, the Ancasa Hotel.
  3 A: Is that E for England?
     B: No, it's A for apple.

5 Work in pairs. **Student A:** Look at the information below, and prepare for the telephone call. **Student B:** Look at the information on page 155, and prepare for the telephone call. Then practice the telephone conversations.

Student A

Call 1
- You are working abroad, but your cell phone isn't working.
- Call Student B from the Ananda Hotel. Your number is 57-302-570-3022.
- Check that Student B has emailed your presentation for tomorrow's meeting.

Call 2
- Student B is abroad. Answer his/her call.
- Write down information about the hotel (name/number).
- You haven't emailed the video because Student B's email isn't working.

10e Please leave a message after the tone

Vocabulary email addresses and websites

1 ▶ 98 Can you say these email addresses and websites? Listen and check your answers.

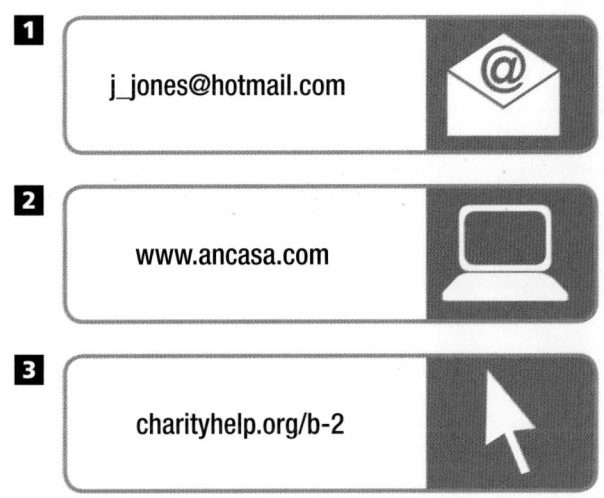

1 j_jones@hotmail.com

2 www.ancasa.com

3 charityhelp.org/b-2

2 Work in pairs. Take turns to say and write down:
- your email address.
- the address of your favorite website.

Writing a telephone message

3 ▶ 99 Listen to a voicemail message and read the written message. There are four mistakes in the written message. Correct them.

> **MESSAGE**
>
> **Name of caller:** Richard Senger
>
> **Message for:** Doctor Omar Al Harbia
>
> **Message:** He can't email the designs. Download them from stk-design.com/a-1 Call him back on his home number (077-234-3785) or email him at rich-sanger@gmail.net.
>
> ★ ★ ★ ★ ★ **Urgent** ☑

4 Writing skill imperatives

When we write messages, we often simplify what the speaker said. In this example, the message is written as an instruction and uses the imperative form.

"He can download them from this address: stk-design.com/e-1" →
Download them from stk-design.com/e-1.

▶ 100 Listen to five voicemail messages. Write down the messages as instructions, using the imperative.

1 *Call Jim back this evening.*
2 _____
3 _____
4 _____
5 _____

5 Prepare to leave a message for a colleague. Include these details.
- your name
- your number
- your email
- ask your colleague to do something

6 Work in pairs. Take turns to read your messages from Exercise 5. Listen to your partner and write down the most important information.

> **MESSAGE**
>
> **Name of caller:** _____
>
> **Message for:** _____
>
> **Message:** _____
>
> _____
>
> _____
>
> _____
>
> _____
>
> ★ ★ ★ ★ ★ **Urgent** ☐

7 Check your partner's written message. Is it clear? Is everything correct (e.g., the spelling, phone numbers, email address)?

10f Baby math

Babies usually start to walk or say their first words by the age of 1, but can they do math at this age?

Before you watch

1 Work in pairs. Look at the photo and read the caption. Do you think babies can do math? Why or why not?

2 Work in pairs. What can babies do? What can't they do? Make a list.

Babies can …	Babies can't …

3 Key vocabulary

Read the passage. Then complete the definitions with the correct form of the **bold** words.

> Dr. Irene Pepperberg is a **psychologist** at Harvard University. She wanted to know how well birds can think and communicate. In 1976, she started an **experiment** with a parrot named Alex. For 30 years, she taught him to recognize objects and colors. The results **revealed** that Alex was a very **smart** bird—he knew colors and shapes, and he could count and say more than a hundred English words. People often think birds aren't very clever, but the **outcome** of Dr. Pepperberg's experiment has changed the way people think about them.

1 A(n) _____ is the result of something.
2 When you _____ something, you show something that was unknown.
3 If you are _____ , you have a clever mind.
4 A(n) _____ studies the mind and behavior of people.
5 A(n) _____ is something scientists do to see if something is true.

While you watch

4 📹 **10.1** Work in pairs. Watch the video. Then answer these questions.

1 What does Karen believe babies can do?

_____

2 What does she do to find out?

_____

3 What result does she get?

_____

4 Does the result support her view?

_____

5 📹 **10.1** Watch the video again. What happens in the second experiment with the baby? Put the events in order (1–6).

____ Karen shows the baby a toy.
____ She shows the baby another toy.
____ The screen goes down.
____ The screen goes up.
____ The baby looks at the result for a long time.
____ She removes the toy behind the screen.

6 📹 **10.1** Complete these sentences about the video using a suitable form of the words in Exercise 3. Then watch the video and check.

1 Yale _____ Karen Wynn believes that human babies are much _____ than we think.
2 To test her theory, Karen did a(n) _____ with babies. She found that babies look longer at things that they find unusual.
3 Karen's research _____ that babies as young as four to six months can add and subtract.
4 Karen says that the _____ of her experiments with babies is similar to findings in a lot of non-human species.

After you watch

7 Vocabulary in context

a 📹 **10.2** Watch the clips from the video. Choose the correct meaning of the words and phrases.

b Work in pairs. Ask and answer these questions.

1 Are you convinced by the results of Dr. Karen Wynn's experiment? Why or why not?
2 Dr. Wynn says that her results are consistent with findings in some non-human species. What other animals do you think are able to count?

8 Work in groups. Design an experiment to test an ability that babies might have. Think about the following questions.

• What ability might babies have?
• What is a way to test this ability? What are the steps?
• What kind of result do you think you will get?

9 In your group, present your experiment to the class. Describe the steps of your group's experiment and predict a result.

UNIT 10 REVIEW AND MEMORY BOOSTER

Grammar

1 Write *Have you ever …?* questions using these ideas.

1 see / the Eiffel Tower?
   Have you ever seen the Eiffel Tower?
2 teach / a subject?
3 learn / to play guitar?
4 ride / a motorcycle?
5 make / a movie?

2 Match these answers with the questions in Exercise 1.

a Yes, I have. I made one about my family for a college project. ____
b Yes, I have. I rode across America on a Harley Davidson last summer. ____
c No, I haven't, but I've helped my younger brother with his homework. ____
d No, I haven't, but I'm going to Paris next year. ____
e No, I haven't, but I'd like to play it one day. ____

3 >> MB Work in pairs. Take turns asking and answering the questions in Exercise 1.

4 Complete the conversation with the present perfect or simple past form of the verbs.

A: ¹_____ (you / ever / visit) Rome?
B: Yes, I have. I was a student at a college there.
A: Really? What ²_____ (you / study)?
B: Art. I also ³_____ (work) in a museum for three months.
A: When ⁴_____ (you / do) that?
B: In 2005.
A: ⁵_____ (you / learn) Italian when you were there?
B: No, I didn't. My parents are Italian, so I ⁶_____ (speak) Italian all my life.

I CAN	
use the present perfect	
ask about past experiences	

Vocabulary

5 These sentences are from different books in a school. Match these subjects to the sentences.

biology	history	geography
chemistry	literature	physics

1 About 60% of the human body is water.
   _____
2 The Mekong River goes through six countries in Southeast Asia. _____
3 Mary Shelley wrote the book *Frankenstein*.
   _____

4 Light travels at 299,792,458 meters per second.
   _____
5 Bolivia became a country in 1825. _____
6 Hydrogen and oxygen makes water.
   _____

6 >> MB Think of an example for these and tell your partner.

• an important fact about the history of your country
• a famous book in the literature of your country
• a scientific discovery in the twentieth century

7 Circle the correct options to complete the sentences.

1 I *study / invent* English every day for an hour.
2 Can you *know / remember* the past tense of the verb "go"?
3 I always *memorize / forget* this word! What does it mean?
4 We can *practice / know* English together by only speaking English.
5 I need to *discover / learn* this list of words before the exam.

8 >> MB Complete this sentence. Then compare with your partner.

This week in my English classes, I've learned …

I CAN	
talk about subjects	
talk about learning	

Real life

9 Put the words in the correct order to make questions for checking and clarifying.

1 Amsterdam? / as / in / A / is / that
2 thirteen / that / thirty? / or / was
3 675-6475? / number / the / is
4 there / anything / is / else?
5 have / sent / the / email? / you

10 >> MB Write down the following.

• the name of a famous person
• the telephone number of your best friend
• the address of someone else in your family

Then work in pairs. Take turns reading your information aloud. Listen and write down your partner's information. Check and clarify the spelling and numbers.

I CAN	
check and clarify information	

The desert in Jordan

FEATURES

1 Work in pairs. Look at the photo. Why do you think the table is in the desert?

2 ▶ 101 Work in pairs. Listen to a man talk about his experience in Jordan. Why was the table in the desert? What happened?

3 Which of these trips did the man in Exercise 2 take?

> a camping trip
> backpacking around the world
> a sightseeing tour
> a package vacation by the beach
> hiking in the mountains

4 Work in groups. Look at the trips in Exercise 3 again and discuss these questions.

- Which vacations do you prefer?
- Which vacations have you done in the past?
- Which vacations are you going to go on in the future?

I prefer package vacations to hiking in the mountains because I like to relax on vacation.
I've never been on a camping trip.
I'm going backpacking around Ireland next summer.

11a Planning a trip

Reading

1 Work in pairs. Discuss these questions.

1 When do you normally plan your vacation? (e.g., a year before, six months before, the week before)
2 What do you do before your vacation? Make a list and compare it with another pair's.

2 Read the information for tourists and other visitors to Australia. Write the headings in the information brochure.

| Road Travel | Weather | Money | Visas | Language |

Information for tourists and visitors to Australia

▶ 102

1 _____

- You have to get a tourist visa before you arrive. You can do this online.
- Tourists can stay for a maximum of three, six, or twelve months.
- You can't work in Australia without a work visa. You have to get a visa from the Australian Embassy in your country or online.

2 _____

- The currency is Australian dollars.
- Most shops, hotels, and banks in large cities accept credit cards.
- In smaller towns, always have cash with you.

3 _____

- Australia is a multicultural country, so there are many different languages.
- Most people speak or understand English.

4 _____

- The climate is different in different areas of the country.
- Summers are very hot and the temperature is often over 40°C. Always use lots of sunscreen and wear a hat.

5 _____

- Tourists don't have to get a new driver's license. But if you stay here for more than one year, you have to take an Australian driving test.

Uluru, Australia

3 Read the comments (1–5) from visitors to Australia. Have the people followed the information in Exercise 2?

1 I've been a tourist here for thirteen months now. I'm going to stay a few weeks longer.   Y   N
2 I got a work visa before I left home.   Y   N
3 I've changed most of my money to US dollars.   Y   N
4 I've been working here for six months. I'm still using my American driver's license.   Y   N
5 I brought sun cream because of the heat.   Y   N

Vocabulary in another country

4 Complete the information about Brazil with these words.

climate	currency	multicultural
right side	temperature	visa
license		

- For employment in Brazil, most people need a work [1]_____ .
- The Brazilian real is the national [2]_____ .
- Portuguese is the official language, but Brazil is a [3]_____ country with over 200 different languages.
- Brazil is a huge country, so the [4]_____ can change between the north and south. However, it's usually warm, and in the summer the [5]_____ is often very high.
- Drive on the [6]_____ of the road.
- You have to carry your driver's [7]_____ when you drive.

5 Work in groups. Discuss these questions about your country or countries. How many answers do you know? Compare your answers with the class.

1 What is the currency?
2 Do tourists need a visa?
3 What's the normal temperature in the summer and winter?
4 Is the climate different in different areas?
5 Which side of the road do you drive on?
6 Do you always have to carry your driver's license?
7 How multicultural is your country?

Grammar *have to / don't have to, can / can't*

▶ **HAVE TO / DON'T HAVE TO, CAN / CAN'T**

You **have to** get a tourist visa before you arrive.
Tourists **don't have to** get a new driver's license.
Tourists **can** stay for a maximum of three, six, or twelve months.
You **can't** work in Australia without a work visa.

For more information and practice, see page 178.

6 Work in pairs. Look at the grammar box. Answer these questions about the verbs in **bold**.

1 Which verb means it is necessary?
2 Which verb means it is possible?
3 Which verb means it is not necessary?
4 Which verb means it is not possible?
5 What form of the verb comes after the verbs in bold?

7 Match the beginnings of the sentences (1–6) with the endings (a–f).

1 I have ____
2 They don't ____
3 He can't ____
4 Tourists can pay ____
5 She can check in ____
6 In my country, you have to ____

a smoke in the airport.
b with dollars in this shop.
c at reception after 3 p.m.
d call 911 for the police.
e to start work at nine every day.
f have to get a visa.

8 Look at these signs and notices for tourists. Circle the correct verbs.

1 You *have to / can* drive on the left.
2 Tourists *can't / don't have to* take photos here.

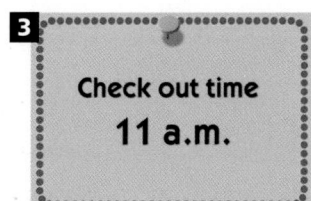

3 Guests *have to / don't have to* leave before 11 a.m.
4 Guests *have to / don't have to* pay.

5 Business class passengers *can't / don't have to* wait.
6 All passengers *have to / can* show their passport.

9 Pronunciation /ˈhæftə/

▶ **103** Listen to the sentences with *have to* and *don't have to*. Notice the pronunciation: /ˈhæftə/. Listen again and repeat.

Writing and speaking *my*Life

10 Work in pairs. Choose one situation (a–c) below and complete the sentences (1–4).

a visiting another country as a tourist
b studying at your language school
c working for your company

1 You have to …   3 You can …
2 You don't have to …   4 You can't …

11 Work with another pair. Tell them your sentences. Can they guess the situation?

11b On vacation

A village near Gunung Mulu
National Park, Malaysia

Vocabulary tourism

What kind of **TOURIST** are you?

Look at the questionnaire below and circle the things that you usually do.

Do you ____

1. a buy a round trip ticket?
   b buy a one-way ticket?
2. a check one or two bags?
   b only take a carry-on bag?
3. a book a hotel in advance?
   b find a hotel after you arrive?
4. a rent a car?
   b use public transportation?
5. a buy souvenirs at tourist shops?
   b shop at local markets?
6. a join a sightseeing tour?
   b travel alone or with a friend?
7. a use a tour guide?
   b plan your own tour?

1 Read the questionnaire from a tourism magazine. Find words in the questionnaire to match these definitions.

1. a ticket for travel to a place and back
   round-trip
2. a ticket for travel to a place (but not back) _____
3. you carry this bag onto the plane _____
4. call for a hotel room (or reserve it online) before you arrive _____
5. special objects you buy on vacation _____
6. give your bag to the airline so they can put it on the plane _____
7. visiting famous and interesting places _____
8. pay to use something (e.g., a car) for a period of time _____

2 Work in pairs. Answer the questions in the questionnaire. Then turn to page 157 and find out what your answers say about you. Tell your partner what kind of tourist you are.

Wordbuilding word families

3 Work in pairs. Look at the wordbuilding box. Make word families with these words.

travel	visit	drive

Listening

4 ▶ 104 Listen to a podcast with travel expert Jan Lanting. What kind of tourist is the podcast for?

5 ▶ 104 Listen to the podcast again. Number these places in the order Jan talks about them (1–3).

_____ a The jungles of Malaysia
_____ b The Arctic
_____ c Rockport, on the coast of Maine

6 ▶ 104 Listen again and make notes about the three places.

	Rockport, Maine, USA	Malaysian jungle	The Arctic
With a tour?	*no*		
Weather and temperature	*cold and it rains*		
Transportation			
Accommodation			

7 Which of the places in Exercise 6 would you like to go to? Why?

Grammar *should/shouldn't*

8 Work in pairs. Look at the grammar box. Answer these questions.

1 What form is the verb after *should* and *shouldn't*?
2 How do you make a question with *should*?
3 Do you use the auxiliary *do/does* in negatives and questions?

9 Work in pairs. Read the sentences. Then use the words in the chart to give advice for each situation.

1 I'm very tired.
2 The sun is shining and the temperature is 40°C.
3 I can't speak the local language.
4 Public transportation is slow to the downtown area.
5 This shop is expensive.
6 Italy has very old and beautiful buildings.
7 I want to visit islands in Vietnam.
8 In Norway, it's very cold in December and January.

You	should	take a vacation. go sightseeing. take a boat. learn some words.
	shouldn't	buy your souvenirs here. take the bus. go in the winter. wear sunscreen.

Word focus *take*

10 We use the verb *take* with different types of nouns. Match these words to the three types.

a a taxi	b an umbrella	c a break

1 *take* + time when you stop work _____
2 *take* + type of transportation _____
3 *take* + an object _____

11 Find five examples of *take* + noun in the Track 104 audioscript at the back of the book.

Speaking and writing *my*Life

12 Work in pairs. Choose a country you know well and write advice for a tourist. Include these topics.

- weather
- famous sites
- local food
- transportation
- language
- shopping

13 Work with another pair. Take turns giving your advice and ask each other questions.

A: You should go to the beach because the weather is hot in this country.
B: Should I take sunscreen?

11c Should I go there?

Reading

1 Work in pairs. Look at the photo of tourists on a ship in Antarctica. Why do you think tourists go there? What do you think they can see?

2 Read the article. Match the paragraphs (1–5) with the topics (a–e).

   a why Antarctica is a good vacation destination ____

   b the writer's problem with most vacation destinations ____

   c negative changes in Antarctica ____

   d which vacations the writer likes and doesn't like ____

   e the positive effect of tourism in Antarctica ____

3 Work in pairs. Read paragraphs 1 and 2 again. Answer these questions.

   1 What does the writer want to do on his next vacation?

   2 What types of vacation does he write about?

4 Do you like the same types of vacation as the writer? Do you agree with him about vacations and other tourists? Why or why not?

Critical thinking reasons for and against

5 Work in pairs. Read paragraphs 3 and 4 again. What reasons does the writer give:

   1 for a vacation in Antarctica?

   2 against a vacation in Antarctica?

6 Work with another pair and compare your lists from Exercise 5. Then read the last line of the article and discuss these questions.

   1 Does the writer have a conclusion? Give reasons for your answer.

   2 What do you think he should do? Why?

Grammar *something, nobody, anywhere*

> **▶ SOMETHING, NOBODY, ANYWHERE**
>
> We normally use *some-* in affirmative sentences and *any-* in negative sentences and questions.
> *I'd like to do **something** exciting.*
> ***Nobody** lives there.*
> *There isn't **anything** in my bag!*
> *Is there **anywhere** in the world without other people?*

7 Look at the grammar box.

a Complete these sentences with *some-*, *any-*, or *no-*.

   1 We use words starting with _____ in a question or with a negative verb.

   2 We use words starting with _____ with a positive verb. The meaning is positive.

   3 We use words starting with _____ with a positive verb, but the meaning is negative.

b Complete these sentences with *-thing*, *-body*, or *-where*.

   1 We use _____ for a person.

   2 We use _____ for a place.

   3 We use _____ for an object or activity.

8 Complete the sentences with *-thing*, *-body*, or *-where*.

   1 There's no_____ interesting to do.

   2 My ticket is some_____ in my bag.

   3 Does any_____ want to go sightseeing?

   4 I'm hungry. I need some_____ to eat.

   5 No_____ in this shop speaks English.

   6 I didn't buy any_____ at the souvenir shop.

9 Circle the correct options to complete the text from a travel magazine.

You should visit
Florence in Italy

Is there [1] *anybody / anywhere* in the world like the city of Florence? Of course, there are other beautiful cities, but—for me—[2] *somewhere / nowhere* else is as beautiful as Florence. There's always [3] *anything / something* to see on every street corner. And the local people are very friendly. If you get lost, you can ask [4] *somebody / something* for directions. And after a long day, you can sit in a café and do [5] *nothing / nowhere*!

Writing and speaking *my*Life

10 Work in pairs. Choose a tourist destination and write a paragraph with the title "You should visit …!"

11 Post your paragraphs around the classroom. Read about the different vacation destinations. Where would you like to go to? Tell the class about your choice.

SHOULD I GO THERE?

▶ 105

Travel writer Carlos Gomm is thinking of taking a vacation in Antarctica. But **should he go there?**

I don't like vacations with hotels, beaches, and swimming pools, and I'm not interested in sightseeing in old cities. So for my next vacation, I plan to do something exciting outdoors. There are so many travel companies on the internet offering that type of vacation. One company offers backpacking trips over the Andes in South America. Another company offers animal safaris[1] in Africa. And you can even go swimming with dolphins with a tour group in Australia.

The problem for me is that when I choose a vacation, I don't want to go somewhere and see lots of other tourists. I want to be the only person there, which is difficult these days. Is there anywhere in the world without other people? What about Antarctica?

3 Antarctica should be perfect for me. It's huge, it's quiet, and it's thousands of kilometers away from other countries. It doesn't have a government and there are no cities, so there's no pollution or noisy traffic. It has lots of wildlife.

4 However, like many places in the world, Antarctica is changing. Fifty years ago nobody lived there, but now between 1,000 and 5,000 scientists live and work there all year, and over 50,000 tourists visit every year. The main way for tourists to visit the continent is by ship. There are no hotels, so cruises are very popular. You can leave the ship during the day and there are guided tours of areas with wildlife. As a result, some people think the numbers of wild animals and birds are decreasing.

5 On the other hand, there is some positive news. Many cruise companies teach their passengers about the wildlife in Antarctica and give money to environmental organizations[2] in the region. These organizations want to help the nature and wildlife of Antarctica so it doesn't change in the future. So what should I do? Should I go to Antarctica, go somewhere else, or stay at home?

[1]**safari** (n) /səˈfɑːri/ a type of trip in Africa to look at animals
[2]**environmental organization** (n) /ɪnˌvaɪrənˈmentlˌɔːgənɪˈzeɪʃn/ a group of people who work to protect nature

11d A vacation in South America

Listening

1 Work in pairs. How do you choose your vacation? Which of these do you use?

- travel books
- travel websites
- videos about places
- advice from family and friends
- a travel brochure

2 ▶ **106** Work in pairs. Listen to two friends talking about a vacation. Answer the questions.

1 Which of the things in Exercise 1 are the friends looking at?
2 Which countries do they mention?
3 What type of vacation does one speaker suggest at the end?

Real life making suggestions

3 ▶ **106** Look at the expressions for making suggestions. Complete these sentences with two words. Then listen again and check.

1 I went on a cruise all the way from Brazil to Argentina. _____ _____ go on that.
2 Yes, but I'm _____ _____ the wildlife.
3 _____ _____ visiting the Andes?
4 But the disadvantage _____ _____ there are lots of other people on a bus tour.
5 But _____ _____ is that you see more with a tour guide.
6 _____ _____ right.
7 Can I _____ _____ suggestion?
8 Actually, that's a really _____ _____ .

▶ MAKING SUGGESTIONS

Suggesting
You should go there for a vacation.
How about visiting the Himalayas?
Can I make a suggestion?
Why don't you go on a tour?
You could travel on your own.

Responding
Yes, but I'm interested in climbing.
But the disadvantage is that it's expensive.
But the advantage is that it's with a tour guide.
Maybe you're right.
That's a really good idea.

4 Pronunciation /ʌ/, /ʊ/, or /uː/

a ▶ **107** Listen and repeat the vowel sounds.

b ▶ **108** Match these words with the sounds from Exercise 4a. Then listen, check, and repeat.

| could ____ | cruise ____ | bus ____ | you ____ | food ____ |
| should ____ | but ____ | love ____ | book ____ | |

5 Work in pairs. Read about these people and discuss the best type of vacation for each of them.

1 Rika has two weeks' vacation to take. She loves traveling, but she doesn't like crowded cities.
2 Ji-woo is a student. She has three months in the summer, but she doesn't have much money.
3 Matheus and Luiza are in their sixties. They don't work anymore and they have lots of free time. They never traveled when they were young.

6 Work in pairs. Imagine you are one of the people in Exercise 5. Take turns telling your partner your situation. Your partner suggests a vacation for you. Respond to your partner's suggestions.

11e A questionnaire

Speaking   *my*Lifo

1 What is most important for you in a hotel? Number the things in this list (1 = most important, 8 = not important).

_____ a good restaurant
_____ good public transportation (to the hotel)
_____ clean and comfortable rooms
_____ internet facilities
_____ friendly staff
_____ gym and swimming pool
_____ parking
_____ a good location (e.g., near the beach or downtown)

2 Work in groups. Compare your answers to Exercise 1.

Writing a questionnaire

3 Work in pairs. Look at an online questionnaire from a hotel to its customers. Answer the questions.

1 Why do hotels give this type of questionnaire to visitors?
2 Which parts of the hotel does it ask about?
3 Would you ask any other questions?

Thank you for visiting our hotel. We hope you enjoyed your stay. Please answer the questions below. Your answers and suggestions are very important to us.

---

1 What was the reason for your visit?
  ○ leisure   ○ business   ○ other

2 How was your room?
  ○ very comfortable   ○ comfortable
  ○ not very comfortable

3 How friendly and helpful were the staff?
  ○ very helpful and friendly   ○ helpful and friendly
  ○ not very helpful and friendly

---

4 Did you use the gym? yes / no

If yes, how would you describe the facilities?

_____

5 Did you eat in the hotel restaurant? yes / no

If yes, can you comment on the food and the service?

_____

6 Would you visit our hotel again? yes / no
7 Would you recommend this hotel to a friend? yes / no
8 What other suggestions do you have to improve our service?

_____

---

4 **Writing skill closed and open questions**

a Good questionnaires use closed questions and open questions. We answer *yes/no* to closed questions, and give longer answers to open questions. Read these questions. Are they open (O) or closed (C)?

1 How was your bus tour?   Ⓞ   C
2 Did the tour guide answer   O   Ⓒ
   all your questions?
3 Were all our staff polite and   O   C
   helpful?
4 Did you book your vacation   O   C
   online?
5 How easy was our website   O   C
   to use?
6 Did you use the hotel   O   C
   swimming pool and gym?
7 Would you recommend   O   C
   this vacation to your
   friends?
8 What other suggestions   O   C
   can you make so we can
   improve our service?

b Does the questionnaire in Exercise 3 use a mixture of open and closed questions? How does it ask for more information after a closed question?

5 Work in pairs. Write a questionnaire for one of these groups.

• passengers at an airport
• customers at a restaurant
• visitors at a sports center

6 Exchange questionnaires with another pair. Imagine you are the passenger, customer, or visitor, and write answers on the questionnaire.

7 Was the questionnaire you answered a good questionnaire? Use these questions to check.

• Was the questionnaire easy to use?
• Did it use both closed and open questions?
• Did it ask for more information after a closed question?

11f Tiger tourism

Tourists at Ranthambore
National Park, India

Before you watch

1 Work in pairs. Look at the photo and read the caption. Where are the people? What do you think they are doing?

2 Work in pairs. Discuss these questions.

1 Where can people see nature and animals in your city or country?
2 What kinds of plants or animals can you see?

3 Key vocabulary

Read the sentences and look at the words and phrases in **bold**. Then match each one to its meaning.

Yellowstone National Park in the US is famous for its **wildlife**—you can see many different types of birds, fish, bears, and so on.

Parks and other green spaces in the city **connect** people **to** nature and give them places to relax.

Like humans, animals **care for** their young by feeding them and keeping them safe.

You can see animals **up close** on a safari tour.

The Eiffel Tower **attracts** more than seven million visitors every year.

1	wildlife	a	to give someone everything they need to be comfortable
2	connect to	b	animals that live in their natural homes
3	care for	c	at a near distance
4	up close	d	to feel close to something or someone
5	attract	e	to bring people to a place

While you watch

4 ▢ **11.1** Watch the video. What is the main message of the video?

a Tigers in India should be free in the wild instead of being kept in zoos for tourists to view.
b Animals in India's national parks are not doing well because there are too many tourists around.
c Tiger tourism in India is a way to help protect tigers and other wildlife in the country.

5 ▢ **11.1** Watch the video again. Complete the chart with activities (a–f) that tourists can and cannot do at the national park.

a walk around freely
b take photos of wildlife
c explore the entire park
d see wild tigers
e feed the animals
f travel with a guide

Tourists can …	Tourists can't …

After you watch

6 Vocabulary in context

a ▢ **11.2** Watch the clips from the video. Choose the correct meaning of the words and phrases.

b Complete these sentences to make them true for you. Then tell your partner your sentences.

1 To me, … is a symbol of …
2 When friends or relatives visit my city, I take them around the …
3 One thing we can do to help in wildlife conservation is …

7 Work in groups. Choose a place in your country where people go to see nature and wildlife (e.g., a national park, a zoo). Imagine you are a tour guide there and you have to introduce the place to visitors. Think about these questions.

- What kind of place is it? (e.g., a park, a nature reserve)
- What is famous there? (Describe two or three things.)
- What can tourists do?
- What are tourists not allowed to do?

8 Present about the place your group chose to another group.

UNIT 11 REVIEW AND MEMORY BOOSTER

Grammar

1 Complete the sentences about a tour guide's job with *have to*, *don't have to*, *can*, or *can't*.

1 I have to wear nice clothes, but I _____ wear a uniform.
2 The tourists _____ smoke on the tour bus, but they can outside.
3 At lunchtime, I _____ eat with the tourists, but I don't have to.
4 I _____ know everything about the city because the tourists ask a lot of questions.

2 Circle the correct options to complete the sentences.

1 This hotel is terrible. We *should / shouldn't* stay here.
2 She doesn't speak the local language. She *should / shouldn't* take a language class before she goes to Italy.
3 You *should / shouldn't* rent a car because it's very expensive.
4 Sometimes the hotels are full, so we *should / shouldn't* book a room in advance.

3 >> MB Write four sentences about your job or studies. Use *should*, *shouldn't*, *have to*, *don't have to*, *can*, or *can't*. Then compare your sentences with a partner.

4 Complete the words in the text with *-body*, *-thing*, or *-where*.

Space **Tourism**

There's always ¹some_____ new to visit on Earth, but maybe you'd like to do ²some_____ really different for your next vacation. Space Adventures is a space tourism company. They sent ³some_____ into space ten years ago. Since then, six more tourists have traveled with the company and hundreds more have reserved flights in the future.

The first female space tourist, Anousheh Ansari

Vocabulary

5 Write these words in the correct category.

camping	hiking	round-trip	one-way
sightseeing	souvenirs	tour guide	tourist

1 Vacation activities _____ , _____ , _____
2 Type of ticket _____ , _____
3 Something you buy on vacation _____
4 Other people on a vacation _____ , _____

6 >> MB Work in pairs. Say three words that:

- are from the same family as the verb *tour*.
- collocate with the verb *take*.
- make a word with *some-*.

Real life

7 Match the suggestions (1–4) with the responses (a–d).

1 How about going on a camping trip? ____
2 You should visit the beach. ____
3 Can I make a suggestion? ____
4 Why don't you go hiking in the mountains? ____

a That's a really good idea. I need some exercise.
b No, thanks. I prefer sleeping in a hotel.
c Yes, but the problem is that it's very crowded in the summer.
d Sure. What is it?

8 >> MB Work in pairs. Ask and answer these questions about your last vacation.

- Where did you go?
- Who did you go with?
- What did you do?
- Would you recommend this vacation?

Unit 12 The Earth

An Inuit man in the Arctic holding a photo of South Carolina
Photo by Ira Block

1 Work in pairs. Compare the two places in the photo. How are they different?

2 ▶ 109 Listen to part of a documentary about the photographer—Ira Block— and the two photos. Complete the sentences with the missing numbers.

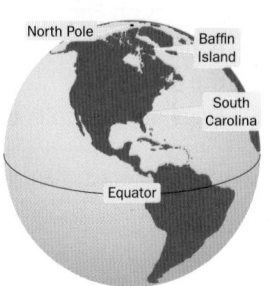

1 The Inuit man lives about _____ kilometers from the North Pole.
2 The US state of South Carolina is about _____ kilometers from the Equator.
3 _____ million years ago, the Arctic probably looked like South Carolina.
4 At that time, the temperature in the Arctic was around _____ °C.
5 Nowadays, the average temperature in the Arctic is around _____ °C.

3 Work in groups. Answer these questions.

1 Is your country nearer to the Arctic, the Antarctic, or the Equator?
2 Where is it spring or summer at the moment? In the Northern or Southern Hemisphere?

12a Climate change

Vocabulary measurements

1 Work in pairs. Match the symbols and their meaning with the type of measurement.

1 % (percentage)   ○   ○ a temperature
2 °C (degrees Celsius) ○   ○ b area
3 km (kilometers)   ○   ○ c distance
4 l (liters)   ○   ○ d weight
5 m² (square meters)   ○   ○ e quantity of water (or liquid)
6 kg (kilograms)   ○   ○ f an amount out of 100

2 Complete these facts about Earth with the symbols from Exercise 1.

Earth Fact File

1 The temperature at the center of the Earth is about 7,500 _____ .
2 The North Pole is over 20,000 _____ from the South Pole.
3 70 _____ of the Earth's surface is water.
4 148,940 million _____ of Earth is land.
5 Objects on Earth weigh less on the moon. A 100 _____ person only weighs 16.5 _____ on the moon.
6 Every day, 914 trillion _____ of rain fall on Earth.

one trillion = one million million (1,000,000,000,000)

▶ **WORDBUILDING word forms**

Words often have more than one form:
  (verb)   (noun)
*It **weighs** 2 kilograms. / The **weight** is 2 kilograms.*
      (adjective) (noun)
*It's 12 meters **high**. / The **height** is 12 meters.*

For more practice, see Workbook page 99.

---

3 Work in pairs. Circle the correct options and answer the questions. Then check your answers on page 157.

1 What's the *long / length* of a marathon?
2 How *deep / depth* is the Mariana Trench?
3 The Burj Khalifa is one of the tallest buildings in the world. What is its *high / height*?
4 How many *kilograms / kilometers* equals one mile?
5 What *percentage / area* of the world's population lives in China?
6 Does a kilogram of metal or a kilogram of plastic *weigh / weight* more?

Reading

4 What is the climate in your country (hot, cold, etc.)? In recent years, has the climate changed? How?

5 Work in pairs. Look at the map on page 143 and read the article below. Answer these questions.

1 What does the map show?
2 How does it show the change?

6 Look at the map again. Are these sentences true (T) or false (F)?

1 The temperature in the Arctic Circle has decreased by 4°C. T F
2 The temperature change in the Northern Hemisphere is greater than in the Southern Hemisphere. T F
3 The temperature in some parts of Antarctica has decreased by 2°C. T F

7 What does the map show about temperature and in your country? Is the information similar to your answers in Exercise 4?

CLIMATE
CHANGE ▶ 110

Climate scientists have measured the temperature and rainfall on every part of the Earth over many years. They look at the changes and predict the future. The map shows the temperature change over 30 years. In most parts of the world, the temperature has increased by a few degrees, and scientists think it will increase in the future.

In conclusion, the changes in climate probably won't stop in the near future.

Grammar *will/won't*

8 Look at the grammar box. Choose the correct options to complete these rules.

1 We use *will/won't* to talk about:
a the past. b the present. c the future.
2 For the third person form (*he/she/it*), we:
a add *-s* to *will*. b don't add *-s* to *will*.
3 The verb after *will* is the base form:
a with *to*. b without *to*.

9 Underline the sentences with *will/won't* + base form of the verb in the article.

10 Work in pairs. Reorder the words to make sentences about the future.

1 it / be / hotter in my country / in the future / will
It will be hotter in my country in the future.
2 increase / the rainfall in this country / in the future / won't
3 I don't think / increase / the number of dry deserts / will
4 be / longer / will / summers / there
5 the percentage of people living in cities / increase / will
6 English / everyone / speak / will
7 gas / won't / people / use / in their cars

11 Work in pairs. Make the sentences in Exercise 10 into questions. Ask your partner for his/her opinion.

A: Will it be hotter in your country in the future?
B: Yes, it will.

12 Pronunciation *'ll*

a ▶ **111** Listen to six sentences. Circle the form of *will* you hear.

1 will / 'll   4 will / 'll
2 will / 'll   5 will / 'll
3 will / 'll   6 will / 'll

b ▶ **111** Look at the Track 111 audioscript at the back of the book. Listen again and repeat.

Writing and speaking
my **Life**

13 Think about your partner's future. Write four sentences about:

• his/her future job.
• his/her future travel.
• his/her future home.
• one other thing about his/her future.

14 Tell your partner your sentences. Does your partner think they will come true?

A: I think you'll become a musician in the future.
B: I don't think I will. I can't play a musical instrument!

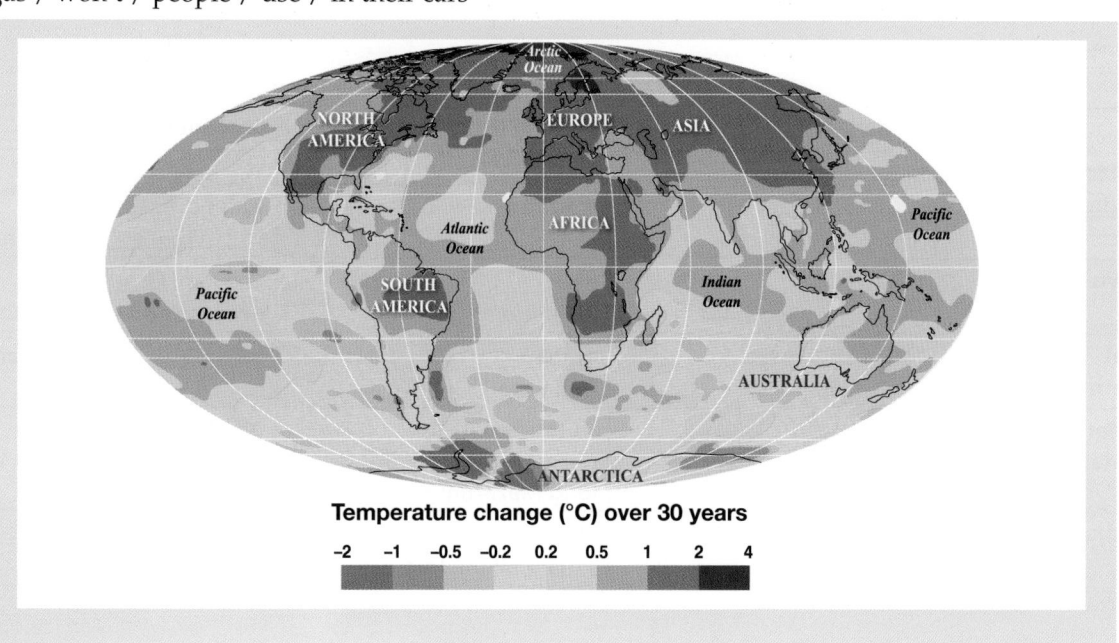

Temperature change (°C) over 30 years

-2   -1   -0.5   -0.2   0.2   0.5   1   2   4

12b The unexplored Earth

Listening

1 Discuss these questions with your class.

   1   Which place on Earth would you like to visit?
   2   Why do you want to go there?

2 ▶ **112** You are going to listen to a radio show about five unexplored places. Work in groups of three: Student A, Student B, and Student C. Listen and complete your sentences in the chart below.

3 In your group, share your information and complete the whole chart.

4 ▶ **112** Listen again. Check and complete the information in the chart.

Vocabulary land and water

5 Work in pairs. Answer these questions about the places in Exercise 2.

   1   Which unexplored places are a body of water?
   2   Which unexplored places are on land?
   3   Which place would you like to explore? Why?

6 Complete the chart with these words.

forest	island	lake
mountain	ocean	river

Areas of water	Areas of land
sea	desert

	Student A	Student B	Student C
The Black Hole of Andros	In the Bahamas in the ¹_____ Ocean	The water is ⁶_____°C.	The hole is very ¹²_____ so it's difficult to ¹³_____ what's in there.
Lake Vostok	In ²_____	It's ⁷_____ square kilometers.	The ice is ¹⁴_____ km deep, so you can't get there.
Mount Dinpernalason	Nobody has ever ³_____ it.	In the ⁸_____ of the Himalayan ⁹_____	It's ¹⁵_____ meters high.
The Merume Mountains	In Guyana in ⁴_____	At the end of the ¹⁰_____ kilometer long Mazaruni River	It's one of the most ¹⁶_____ rivers in the world.
The Foja Mountains	In a ⁵_____ in Papua New Guinea	The forest is ¹¹_____ square kilometers.	There are no ¹⁷_____ of the region.

7 Look at the places in Exercise 6 and think of examples from your country. Which places have you visited? Work in pairs and talk about your places.

There's a forest near my home. We often go there on weekends.

Grammar articles

▶ **ARTICLES**

Definite article
We use *the* with:
- the names of deserts, seas, oceans, and rivers: *the Gobi Desert, the North Sea, the Atlantic Ocean, the Amazon River.*
- plural names or place names with words like *kingdom, states, east/west: the Alps, the Maldives, the United States of America, the United Kingdom, the East Coast.*

No article
We don't use an article with the names of continents, countries, lakes, or a single mountain: *Europe, Brazil, Lake Como, Mount Kilimanjaro.*

For more information and practice, see page 180.

8 Look at the grammar box. Match the places (1–8) with the categories (a–h). Then write *the* or – (no article) for each place.

1 *the* Bahamas
2 _-_ Mount Kilimanjaro
3 _____ Pacific Ocean
4 _____ Africa
5 _____ Nile River
6 _____ Merume Mountains
7 _____ Peru
8 _____ Lake Titicaca

a group of mountains ____
b name of a country ____
c name of a continent ____
d name of a mountain _2_
e name of a river ____
f group of islands _1_
g name of a lake ____
h name of an ocean ____

9 Look at the article and photo of an ancient map. Complete the text with *the* or – (no article).

10 Work in pairs. Turn your book around and look at Al-Idrisi's map. Now north is at the top and south at the bottom. Which continents and countries can you see? Which parts of the world are not on his map?

This map of Earth is from the 12th century. At the time, the king of [1]_____ Sicily wanted a map of the countries around [2]_____ Mediterranean Sea. He paid a man called Al-Idrisi to make one. Al-Idrisi was from [3]_____ Morocco, but he lived in [4]_____ Spain. Al-Idrisi interviewed thousands of travelers for information about the oceans and the continents, including Arabia (now [5]_____ Middle East) and [6]_____ Asia. The map is difficult to understand because old maps used to put south at the top and north at the bottom. So this map shows [7]_____ North Africa at the top and [8]_____ Europe at the bottom.

Speaking *my*Life

11 Work in pairs. Play this guessing game. Think of a place. Your partner guesses the place by asking *yes/no* questions only. The winner is the person who guesses with the fewest questions.

A: Is it a continent?   B: No.
A: Is it in Asia?   B: Yes.

12c Looking for a new Earth

Speaking

1 Work in groups. In the future, do you think humans will live in these places? Choose one answer (a, b, or c) for each place, and give reasons.

> on the moon   on Mars   in the sky   near the sun
> in Antarctica   at the bottom of the ocean

a Yes, definitely!
b Possibly, but I'm not sure.
c No, never!

Reading

2 Read the article. Match the sentences (a–e) to the end of the paragraphs (1–5).

a As a result, they are too hot and gassy, or too cold and icy for human life. ____
b With current space technology, humans will take 766,000 years to travel there. ____
c And how do you find a "new Earth"? ____
d So even if we can't see water on a planet, it's sometimes there. ____
e Humans can live in those temperatures. ____

3 Underline these words (1–6) in the article. Then match them with the definitions (a–f).

1	astronomers	4	orbit
2	planets	5	air
3	star	6	rock

a large round objects in space made of rock and metal, or gas (e.g., the Earth) ____
b a large round object of burning gas in space (e.g., the sun) ____
c people who study the planets and stars in space ____
d going around a planet or star ____
e the gas humans breathe ____
f the solid part of the Earth or a planet ____

4 Work in pairs. Read the article again and answer these questions.

1 When astronomers look for a new Earth, what do they look for in space?
2 When they find a planet, what do they look for?
3 How is Gliese 581g similar to Earth?
4 How is Gliese 581g different from Earth?

Critical thinking the writer's opinion

5 Which statement (a–c) do you think gives the writer's opinion? Underline words and sentences in the text that help you decide.

a The writer thinks we will find habitable planets in the future, but we may not be able to travel to all of them.
b The writer thinks we will find habitable planets in the future, but we definitely won't live on them.
c The writer doesn't think we will find habitable planets in the future.

6 With your partner, ask and answer these questions. Use the phrases for giving opinions.

1 Do you think it's important to find a "new Earth"?
2 Can you imagine life on another planet, or do you think it's impossible?

> In my opinion, …   I think …   I don't think …

Word focus *how*

7 The article asks, "How do you find a 'new Earth'?" Is the question asking about:

a age?
b period of time?
c the distance?
d the way to do something?
e the number?
f price or quantity?

8 Match these question words with a–f in Exercise 7.

> How ____   How far/near ____   How long ____
> How many ____   How much ____   How old ____

Speaking *my* Life

9 Work in pairs. Think of a place you'd like to visit and tell your partner. Take turns asking and answering questions. Use the question words from Exercise 8.

LOOKING FOR A NEW EARTH

▶ 113

1 For thousands of years, humans explored the Earth. Now astronomers are exploring space, looking for new planets or a "new Earth" for humans to live on in the future. But what will a new Earth look like?

2 5 First of all, astronomers look for a star. That's because our own Earth orbits a star (the sun). When astronomers have found a star, they look for planets around it. In recent years, astronomers have found thousands of new planets orbiting suns. Once they 10 find a new planet, it's also important to measure the distance between the planet and the sun. That's because most planets (unlike our Earth) are either too near to the star, or too far away.

3 When they find a planet in a good position, 15 astronomers look for three things: water, air, and rock. Water is important because if humans go there, they will need water to drink and to grow plants. If you can grow plants, then the plants can produce air for humans to breathe.[1] Finally, astronomers also look for rocks, 20 because water is often found under rocks.

4 In recent years, astronomers have found a few planets that are very similar to Earth, and might be habitable.[2] For example, Gliese 581g is a planet at a safe distance from the nearest star. Astronomers also think it has 25 water and rock. The average temperature is between 31 °C and −12 °C: cold, but not colder than Antarctica or the Arctic Circle.

5 However, there are some differences. Gliese 581g is bigger than Earth, and a year on Gliese 581g is only 37 30 Earth days, instead of 365. And the biggest problem is the distance. Gliese 581g is 18 trillion kilometers from Earth.

---

[1]**breathe** (v) /briːð/ to take air in through your nose or mouth
[2]**habitable** (adj) /ˈhæbɪtəbl/ good enough to live in

12d Earth Day

Reading

1 Work in pairs. Read about Earth Day. Answer these questions.

1 What do people do on Earth Day?
2 When and where was the first Earth Day?
3 Why did people go to it?

Real life giving a presentation

2 ▶ 114 Listen to a presentation by a college student. Check (✓) the correct endings to complete the sentences, according to the presentation. Both endings may be correct.

1 Davi is from _____ .
☐ Brazil
☐ the US
2 He talks about Earth Day in the _____ .
☐ past
☐ present
3 People in _____ planted 600,000 trees.
☐ India
☐ China
4 In New Orleans, people put _____ into houses.
☐ energy efficient lights
☐ water-saving systems
5 In Brazil, people picked up trash in the _____ .
☐ cities
☐ countryside

3 ▶ 114 Look at the expressions for giving a presentation. Then listen again. Number the expressions in the order you hear them.

▶ GIVING A PRESENTATION

And finally, in my country, lots of people picked up trash. ____
Today, I'd like to talk about an important day. ____
Thank you very much for listening. ____
Nowadays, more than 175 countries have an Earth Day. ____
In conclusion, I really think Earth Day is important. ____
Good morning, and thank you for coming. ____
My name's Davi, and I'm from Brazil. ____

Friends at Earth Day in Washington, D.C.

April 22nd is Earth Day. For one day every year, people in different countries help the Earth. For example, they clean parks, pick up trash, or plant trees. The first Earth Day was on April 22, 1970 in the US. Over 20 million people went to an Earth Day in their city. There were politicians, teachers, artists, and musicians. As one person said, "We had fun, but we also wanted to help the Earth and the environment."

4 Pronunciation pausing at commas

a ▶ 115 Listen to these sentences from a presentation. Notice how the speaker pauses at the commas. Then listen again and repeat.

1 Today, I'd like to talk about my company.
2 In conclusion, I think it's very important.

b Practice saying the expressions for giving a presentation in Exercise 3. Remember to pause at the commas.

5 Prepare a short presentation. Choose one of these topics and follow the instructions (1–3).

- your local club or organization
- an important day in the year
- your company or place of study
- something you think is important

1 Introduce yourself and your subject.
2 Talk about its history and present.
3 Say why you like it or why you think it's important.

6 Work in groups and give your presentations.

12e Announcing an event

Writing an announcement

1 An announcement gives us information about an event. Which of these announcements do you often read? Have you ever written one?

- an ad for a concert or movie
- a poster for a charity event
- an invitation to a friend's party

2 Work in pairs. Look at the announcement on the poster. Which of these questions does it answer?

- ☐ Who is organizing the event?
- ☐ What is it?
- ☐ Where is it?
- ☐ What date is it on?
- ☐ What time does it start and end?
- ☐ How much does it cost?
- ☐ What activities are there?
- ☐ Is there parking or transportation?
- ☐ What can you buy?
- ☐ Is there food and drink?
- ☐ Where can you read more information?

Newmarket Environmental and Conservation Group

EARTH DAY

Plant 100 trees around Newmarket town center

Theater, music, and art by local performers and artists

Presentations about how to help the environment

Shops selling environmentally friendly products

Hot and cold food

Entrance FREE

Everyone welcome to Earth Day celebration Newmarket Park, April 22

www.NECG.org/earthday for more information

3 Writing skill important words and information

a We don't normally write full sentences on announcements such as posters or notices. Look at the highlighted words in these sentences. They are the words and information on a poster. Which kind of words doesn't the writer use?

1 Everyone is welcome to our Earth Day celebration at Springfield Park on April 22.
2 We are going to plant 100 trees around Springfield Park.

b Underline the key words in these sentences. Then compare your ideas with the poster.

1 There will be presentations about how to help the environment.
2 You can watch local performers, listen to music, and look at art by local artists.
3 Shops are going to be selling environmentally friendly products.
4 You can also buy hot and cold food.
5 Entrance to the event is free.
6 Visit our website at NECG.org/earthday for more information.

4 Work in groups and choose one of these events. Discuss the details (1–9) and plan your event.

- Earth Day in your local park
- a party at work or school
- a charity event to raise money

1 the name of the event
2 the reason for the event
3 the time and date
4 the place
5 the activities
6 the cost
7 food and drink
8 transportation and parking
9 What else?

5 Design and write an announcement for your event as a poster, notice, or ad.

6 Put your announcements on the wall in your classroom. Look at the posters, notices, or ads by other groups. Do they include all the important information? Do they use short sentences?

**Costa Rica exports its
bananas around the world**

Before you watch

1 Work in pairs. Look at the photo and read the caption. What type of food does your country export?

2 Key vocabulary

Read the sentences. The words and phrases in **bold** are used in the video. Match the words with the definitions (a–d).

1 I study **agriculture** at college.
2 This hat **protects** me from the hot sun.
3 Plastic bags are not **environmentally friendly**.
4 My sister didn't have any money for college, but she got a **scholarship**.

a when a school or an organization pays for a student's classes ____
b stops someone or something from being hurt ____
c good for the natural world ____
d the subject of farming ____

While you watch

3 ◻◀ **12.1** You are going to watch a video about Earth University in Costa Rica. Number these actions in the order you see them.

a A teacher and his students are in a classroom. ____
b A cow is eating. ____
c Students are talking and relaxing. ____
d A tractor is in a field. ____
e Students are working on a farm. ____

4 ◻◀ **12.1** Watch the video again and complete the information about the university.

Earth University, Costa Rica

1 Subject: _____
2 Number of students: _____
3 Where students come from: _____ and _____
4 Days a week for study and work: _____
5 Months a year: _____
6 Reason for the banana farm: _____ _____
7 Which country buys their bananas: _____
8 Courses: Farming and _____

After you watch

5 Vocabulary in context

◻◀ **12.2** Watch the clips from the video. Choose the correct meaning of the words and phrases.

6 Work in pairs. Complete these sentences so they are true for you. Then tell your partner.

1 One of my skills is …
2 Once, I sold … and I made a profit.
3 … is the leader of my country.

7 Work in groups. Imagine you are going to make a similar video about a school or college you know well.

Discuss the video and make notes about what you will film (e.g., students working in a classroom) and what you will say (e.g., the number of students, the subjects they study).

As you discuss, write your ideas in this chart.

What will you film?
What will you say in the video?

8 Join another group and explain your ideas for the video.

UNIT 12 REVIEW AND MEMORY BOOSTER

Grammar

1 Complete the conversations with *'ll*, *will*, or *won't*.

1 A: I think we [1]_____ live on the Moon in the future.
  B: No, we [2]_____ . It's impossible.
2 A: [3]_____ the Earth get warmer?
  B: It depends. It [4]_____ in some countries, but it [5]_____ in others.
3 A: [6]_____ deserts get larger?
  B: Yes, I think they [7]_____ .

2 Write *the* or – (no article) for these places.

1 _____ Polynesian Islands
2 _____ Michigan
3 _____ Atlantic Ocean
4 _____ Atlas Mountains
5 _____ Africa
6 _____ Yangtze River
7 _____ Mount Kilimanjaro
8 _____ United Arab Emirates

3 ▶▶ MB In the future, which places on Earth do you think you will visit? Write your top three destinations and compare your list with a partner.

I CAN	
make predictions with *will*	
use the definite article or no article with places	

Vocabulary

4 Work in pairs. Say these symbols in full, e.g., *degrees Celsius*. Then complete the text with them.

°C	m	kg	%	km²

Easter Island is in the southeastern Pacific Ocean and its area is 163 [1]_____ . The climate is warm, with an average temperature of about 20 [2]_____ . The island is famous for 887 statues, called Moai. The largest Moai weighs 74,389 [3]_____ and is 9.8 [4]_____ tall. 3,790 people live on the island. 60 [5]_____ of the population is Rapa Nui. The ancestors of these people built the Moai.

5 Complete the questions about Easter Island with these words. Then find the answers in the text.

tall	big	many	warm

1 How _____ is Easter Island?
2 How _____ is the average temperature?
3 How _____ is the largest Moai?
4 How _____ people live on the island?

6 Circle the correct options to complete these sentences.

1 I'm from Peru and my family always spends the summer by the Pacific *Ocean / Sea*.
2 The Amazon *Lake / River* flows through six countries.
3 Greenland is the largest *forest / island* in the world.
4 We usually think of *mountains / deserts* as hot places, but Antarctica—which is one, too—is very cold.

7 ▶▶ MB Work in pairs. Which of the eight areas of land and water in Exercise 6 do you have in your country? Tell your partner.

I CAN	
talk and ask about measurements	
talk about areas of land and water	

Real life

8 Delete the extra word in each sentence from a presentation.

1 Good morning ~~you~~, and thank you for coming.
2 My name's Eva, and I'm from the Germany.
3 Today, I'm am going to talk about my company.
4 The company has began in 1965.
5 In conclusion, I think the company will to grow in the future.
6 Thank you very much for your listening.

I CAN	
give a presentation	

9 ▶▶ MB You have reached the end of the book! Work in groups and prepare a quiz with 12 questions about the facts in *Life*. Look at each unit and write one question about the information in it.

10 ▶▶ MB Work with another group and ask your twelve questions. Which group answered the most questions correctly?

Unit 6a Exercise 6, page 71
Student A

1 Arthur Honegger is on the Swiss twenty-franc note. Look at the text and complete the questions about him with *was* or *were*.

1 Where _____ he born?
2 _____ he French?
3 Where _____ he from?
4 _____ Arthur and his wife musicians?
5 How long _____ they married?
6 When _____ his music very popular?
7 Where _____ there concerts of his music?

2 Ask your questions and complete the text.

Arthur Honegger was born in ¹_____ in 1892, but he wasn't ²_____ . He was from ³_____ . Arthur and his wife were ⁴_____ . He was a composer, and she was a pianist. They were married for ⁵_____ . At first, Honegger's music wasn't popular, but by ⁶_____ , there were concerts of his music all over ⁷_____ . His face is on the Swiss twenty-franc note.

3 Answer Student B's questions about this person.

Ichiyo Higuchi was Japanese. She was born in 1872. There were five people in her family. Her father was a businessman, but they weren't rich. She was a writer, and her books were very popular. Her face is on the 5,000 yen note.

Unit 6b Exercise 10, page 73
Student A

1 Prepare five questions for your partner with these words.

What / do / over the weekend?
How / get there?
Did / go with anyone?
What / see?
Did / do anything else?

2 Take turns asking and answering the questions. Then complete the chart about Student B.

You	Student B
went to the Natural History Museum	
took the subway	
with a friend from school	
dinosaur bones	
had lunch at the museum	

Unit 2d Exercise 9, page 28
Student B

1 You are the sales clerk.

- Medium T-shirts are $7.50 in different colors.
- Large T-shirts are $8.50 in green, blue, and black.
- Small T-shirts are $7 in red only.

2 Now you are the customer. You'd like a bag.

- Ask about different colors and sizes.
- Ask about the price.

Unit 10b Exercise 2, page 120

Student A

Memorizing names and faces

Do you often forget names and faces? When you meet someone for the first time, listen to them. Repeat their name and use it in the conversation. For example, "It's nice to meet you, Elaine." Look at their face and the clothes they wear. Introduce them to another person and make conversation. With new work colleagues, write down their name, their job, and where you met them.

Unit 1c Exercise 8, page 14

Student A

How many people (live/work/have/speak/use) …?	Spain	The US
population	47 million	
Spanish		13%
a service industry (hotels, banks, etc.)	73%	
cell phones		Everyone
the internet	40 million	

Unit 2a Exercise 11, page 23

Draw six items of furniture in the first room. Then describe your room to your partner. Draw your partner's room in the second room. Afterward, compare your rooms.

1

2

Unit 3b Exercise 12, page 37

Student A

1 Write questions about Joel with these prompts.

1 Who / work for?
2 Where / work?
3 What languages / speak?
4 What time / start work?

2 Ask Student B your questions and complete the fact file.

NAME: Joel Sartore
JOB: Photographer
COMPANY: ¹_____
HOME: Lincoln, Nebraska
PLACE OF WORK: ²_____
CHILDREN: three
LANGUAGE: ³_____
NORMAL WORKING DAY: From ⁴_____ o'clock to six o'clock

3 Answer Student B's questions.

Unit 5a Exercise 11, page 59

mushrooms

flour

Student A

You have a recipe for mushroom pizza.

You have:
- two tomatoes
- some cheese
- some flour
- a pepper
- one potato

You need:
- an onion
- some mushrooms
- some salt
- another tomato
- some olive oil

1 Find out what food your partner has and answer your partner's questions. Take turns asking and answering.

A: Do you have an onion? *B: Yes, I do. I have six.*
B: Do you have any butter? *A: No, I don't.*

2 What do you need to buy?

Unit 10b Exercise 2, page 120

Student B

Memorizing numbers

Do you often forget new numbers such as telephone numbers, house numbers, or PIN numbers? Some people "see" numbers in their brain. Maybe the numbers are in color, or they see the numbers like a picture. You can also repeat the number a few times or learn the numbers in groups. So you might remember the first two numbers because it's your age. And the next three numbers is the house number of a friend. We remember numbers better when we connect them to things we already know.

Unit 6a Exercise 6, page 71

Student B

1 Ichiyo Higuchi is on the 5,000 yen note. Look at the text and complete the questions about her with *was* or *were*.

1 What nationality _____ she?
2 When _____ she born?
3 How many people _____ in her family?
4 What _____ her father's job?
5 _____ they rich?
6 What _____ her job?
7 _____ her books popular?

2 Answer Student A's questions about this person.

Arthur Honegger was born in Paris in 1892, but he wasn't French. He was from Switzerland. Arthur and his wife were musicians. He was a composer, and she was a pianist. They were married for 29 years. At first, Honegger's music wasn't popular, but by the nineteen twenties, there were concerts of his music all over Europe. His face is on the Swiss twenty-franc note.

3 Ask your questions and complete the text.

Ichiyo Higuchi was ¹_____ . She was born in ²_____ . There were ³_____ people in her family. Her father was a ⁴_____ , but they ⁵_____ rich. She was a ⁶_____ , and her books ⁷_____ very popular. Her face is on the 5,000 yen note.

Unit 5a Exercise 4, page 58

pizza – Italy

ceviche – Peru

satay – Indonesia

kabsa – Saudi Arabia

pierogi – Poland

curry – India

Unit 10d Exercise 5, page 124

Student B

Call 1
- Student A is abroad. Answer his/her call.
- Write down information about the hotel (name/number).
- Confirm that you have emailed the presentation for tomorrow's meeting.

Call 2
- You are working abroad, but your cell phone isn't working.
- Call Student A from the Embassy Hotel. Your number is 0043-512-0067241.
- Check that Student A has emailed the video for tomorrow's meeting.

Unit 1c Exercise 8, page 14
Student B

How many people (live/work/have/speak/use) ...?	Spain	The US
population		300 million
Spanish	100%	
a service industry (hotels, banks, etc.)		80%
cell phones	Everyone	
the internet		280 million

Unit 5a Exercise 11, page 59

mushrooms

flour

Student B

You have a recipe for pierogi.

You have:
- six onions
- some salt
- some tomatoes
- some meat
- some olive oil

You need:
- a potato
- some flour
- some mushrooms
- some butter
- some cheese

1 Find out what food your partner has and answer your partner's questions. Take turns asking and answering.

B: *Do you have a potato?*   A: *Yes, I do.*
A: *Do you have any mushrooms?*   B: *No, I don't.*

2 What do you need to buy?

Unit 6b Exercise 10, page 73
Student B

1 Prepare five questions for your partner with these words.

What / do / over the weekend?
How / get there?
Did / go with anyone?
What / see?
Did / do anything else?

2 Take turns asking and answering the questions. Then complete the chart about Student A.

You	Student A
visited the center of Rome	
by bus and by taxi	
with a group of people from work	
the Colosseum	
did some shopping	

Unit 2d Exercise 9, page 28
Student A

1 You are the customer. You'd like a T-shirt.
- Ask about different colors and sizes.
- Ask about the price.

2 Now you are the sales clerk.
- Small bags are $11.30 in pink and blue.
- Large bags are $19.70 in green, yellow, and red.

Unit 11b Exercise 2, page 132

What do your answers mean?

Mostly a answers: You don't have much spare time, so your vacations last a week or two weeks. You plan your vacation months before you go, and your favorite vacations are with other people in tour groups. You like taking lots of clothes and staying in comfortable hotels.

Mostly b answers: You go on long vacations (a month or more) and you don't like planning them. Your favorite vacations are backpacking or hiking. You enjoy meeting local people, eating local food, and staying at small hotels or camping. You usually travel on your own or with one other friend.

Unit 12a Exercise 3, page 142

1. 42.195 km
2. 11 km
3. 829.8 m
4. 1.6 km
5. 20%
6. the same

Unit 8d Exercise 6, page 100

Look at the photo on this page.
Discuss these things.
- The subject of the photo
- The location of people and things
- The people (their appearance and what they are doing or wearing)
- Your opinion of the photo

Unit 3b Exercise 12, page 37

Student B

1 Write questions about Joel with these prompts.

1. What / do?
2. Where / live?
3. Does / have children?
4. What time / finish work?

2 Answer Student A's questions.

> NAME: Joel Sartore
> JOB: [1] _____
> COMPANY: *National Geographic* magazine
> HOME: [2] _____
> PLACE OF WORK: All over the world
> CHILDREN: [3] _____
> LANGUAGE: English
> NORMAL WORKING DAY: From nine o'clock to
> [4] _____ o'clock

3 Ask Student A your questions and complete the fact file.

Unit 10b Exercise 2, page 120

Student C

Memorizing directions and addresses

Some taxi drivers learn hundreds of roads and addresses. How do they do it? Some people see the directions in their head. They see a picture of the roads or the buildings. Other people repeat the names of the roads or the directions. For example, "Turn left at the end, turn right at the movie theater." You can also draw the directions on paper. When you draw, use different colors—the brain remembers more when it sees color.

GRAMMAR SUMMARY UNIT 1

Be (am/is/are)

Affirmative	Negative
I'm a journalist. (I'm = I am)	I'm not a journalist. (I'm not = I am not)
You're a photographer.* (you're = you are)	You aren't a photographer.* (you aren't = you are not)
He's/She's/It's from the US. (he's = he is)	He/She/It isn't from the US. (he isn't = he is not)
We're from Canada. (we're = we are)	We aren't from Canada. (we aren't = we are not)
They're beautiful. (they're = they are)	They aren't beautiful. (they aren't = they are not)

* Remember that we use *you* to refer to a single person or a group of people.

When we speak and in informal writing we normally use contractions of *be* after pronouns. We use an apostrophe (') to show a missing letter. With *is not* and *are not* there are two possible contractions.

> He **isn't** American. = He**'s not** American.
> They**'re not** married. = They **aren't** married.

▶ Exercise 1

Questions	Short answers
Am I a journalist?	Yes, I **am**. No, I'm **not**.
Are you a journalist?	Yes, you **are**. No, you **aren't**.
Is he/she/it from the US?	Yes, he/she/it **is**. No, he/she/it **isn't**.
Are we on Green Street?	Yes, we **are**. No, we **aren't**.
Are they married?	Yes, they **are**. No, they **aren't**.

We often use the *'s* contraction after *who, what, where, when, how,* and *why.*

> **Who's** Richard?
> **Where's** the party?

We never use contractions in positive short answers.

> Are you Michele? ~~Yes, I'm.~~ Yes, I am.

▶ Exercises 2 and 3

Possessive *'s* and possessive adjectives

Possessive *'s*

We use noun + *'s* to show possession.

> The photographer**'s name** is David Doubilet.
> Miguel**'s brother** is a journalist.

After a plural noun, we only add an apostrophe.

> My grandparents**' house** is downtown.

After noun + noun, we only use one *'s*.

> Peter and Magda**'s garden** is beautiful.

Remember that *'s* is also the contracted form of *is*.

▶ Exercise 4

Possessive adjectives

We use possessive adjectives to talk about people in our family and possessions.

> Mehmet is **my** brother.
> **Your** car is nice.
> **His** sister is in China.
> **Her** parents are here.
> It's a restaurant. **Its** name is Happy Food.
> Julie is **our** teacher.
> **Their** family is from the US.

We don't put *the*, *a*, or *an* before possessive adjectives.

> Maria and Valentina are ~~the~~ my cousins.
> Maria and Valentina are **my** cousins.

▶ Exercises 5 and 6

Exercises

1 Complete the sentences with the correct affirmative (+) or negative (–) form of *be*

1 I _____ a doctor. (+)
2 She _____ a student. (–)
3 He _____ from Sweden. (+)
4 I _____ married. (–)
5 They _____ on vacation. (+)
6 We _____ from France. (–)

2 Match the questions (1–6) with the short answers (a–f).

1 Are you a teacher? ____
2 Is he 20 years old? ____
3 Are they from New Zealand? ____
4 Is she single? ____
5 Are you both at the train station? ____
6 Am I late? ____

a Yes, she is.
b No, you aren't.
c Yes, we are.
d Yes, I am.
e No, they aren't.
f No, he isn't.

3 Complete the conversations. Use contractions when possible.

1 A: How old _____ you?
   B: I _____ 28 years old.
2 A: Where _____ she from?
   B: She _____ from the UK.
3 A: _____ they at home now?
   B: Yes, they _____ .
4 A: _____ he at school?
   B: No, he _____ .
5 A: _____ you a nurse?
   B: No, I _____ .
6 A: What _____ your name?
   B: My name _____ Katie.

4 Add an apostrophe or 's in the correct place in the sentences.

1 Lisa ʼs brother is here.

2 This is Hugo house.

3 Abby grandmother is Mary Peters.

4 Anna husband is a journalist.

5 Sara and Pablo father is in Brazil.

6 My parents house is in the center of town.

7 Simon cars are blue and green.

5 Complete the sentences with a possessive adjective.

1 Marco and Samanta are married. _____ hobbies are swimming and running.
2 He's from Germany, but _____ father is from Brazil.
3 We live in the US, but _____ grandparents live in Japan.
4 This is a language school. _____ name is "Study Center."
5 I'm 40 years old and _____ wife is 34 years old.
6 A: What's _____ job?
   B: I'm a filmmaker.

6 Complete the conversation with the words in the box. Use each word once.

her	his	his	my	sister's	your

A: Hello, I'm Maia. What's ¹_____ name?
B: I'm Martina. Where are you from?
A: I'm from Portugal. And you?
B: I'm from Mexico, but ²_____ husband is from England. ³_____ family are all in England.
A: What's ⁴_____ job?
B: He's a photographer.
A: Oh, my sister's a photographer. ⁵_____ name is Silvia. Do you have brothers and sisters?
B: Yes, I do. My ⁶_____ name is Eva.

GRAMMAR SUMMARY UNIT 2

There is/are

We use *there is/are* to talk about things that are in a place.

We use *there's* (= *there is*) before a singular noun and *there are* before a plural noun. We add *any* after *there aren't* and *Are there*.

	Singular	Plural
Affirmative	**There's** an armchair in the living room.	**There are** two armchairs in the living room.
Negative	**There isn't** a chair.	**There aren't any** chairs.
Questions and short answers	**Is there** a television? Yes, **there is**. No, **there isn't**.	**Are there any** pictures? Yes, **there are**. No, **there aren't**.

We use *How many … are there?* to ask about the number of things.

> **How many** people **are there** in your family?
> **How many** rooms **are there** in your house?

Note: we use *there is*, not *there are*, before a list of singular things.
> **There's** a bed, an armchair, and a desk in the bedroom.

▶ **Exercise 1**

Prepositions of place

We use prepositions of place to talk about the position of a thing or a person.
> There are three people **in** the room.
> The computer is **on** the table.*
> The photo is **on** the wall.*
> Your phone is **under** the book.
> The movie theater is **between** the park and the supermarket.
> The chair is **in front of** the television.
> My apartment is **opposite/across from** a school.
> Mexico City is **in the middle of** Mexico.
> The fridge is **on the left/right**.

* Note the two uses of *on*.

*The computer is **on** the table.*

*The photo is **on** the wall.*

▶ **Exercises 2 and 3**

Plural nouns

To make most nouns plural, we add *-s*.
> *car → cars*

After nouns ending in *-ch, -sh, -s, -ss*, and *-x*, we add *-es*.
> *watch → watches*
> *brush → brushes*
> *bus → buses*
> *boss → bosses*
> *box → boxes*

With nouns ending in consonant + *-y*, we change the *-y* to *-ies*.
> *party → parties*

With nouns ending in *-f* and *-fe*, we change the *-f* or *-fe* to *-ves*.
> *life → lives*

Some nouns are irregular.
> *man → men, person → people*

Other nouns have no plural.
> *sheep → sheep*

In adjective + noun and noun + noun combinations, we only make the second word plural.
> *cell phone → cell phones*
> *train station → train stations*

▶ **Exercise 4**

This, that, these, those

We use *this* and *these* to talk about people and things that are near to us. We use *this* + singular noun and *these* + plural noun.
> Is **this** your house?
> **These** are my two brothers.

We use *that* and *those* to talk about people and things that are far from us. We use *that* + singular noun and *those* + plural noun.
> **That's** a big mountain.
> Are **those** your roller skates on the table?

We can also use *this, that, these*, and *those* in front of a noun.
> What's **this book**?
> **Those gloves** are very big.

▶ **Exercise 5**

Exercises

1 Complete the sentences with the affirmative, negative, or question form of *there is/are*. Add *any* when necessary.

1 _____ two bedrooms in my new apartment. (+)
2 _____ a table in the living room. (–)
3 _____ good restaurants in this town?
   Yes, _____ .
4 _____ a garden?
   No, _____ .
5 _____ chairs in the living room. (–)
6 _____ a swimming pool near my house. (+)

2 Choose the correct options to complete the conversation.

A: How is your new house?
B: It's nice. There ¹*are / is* four rooms—a living room, a kitchen, a bathroom, and a bedroom.
A: Is there a yard?
B: No, there ²*isn't / aren't*. But there a park ³*next to / in* the house.
A: And how is your bedroom?
B: It's OK. There's a big bed. There aren't ⁴*any / no* pictures on the wall.
A: ⁵*There is / Is there* a TV in your bedroom?
B: Yes, there is. There is a cabinet ⁶*opposite / under* the bed, and the TV is ⁷*on / between* the cabinet.
A: Are there any windows?
B: Yes, there's a window ⁸*above / in* the cabinet.

3 Look at the picture. Complete the sentences with these words and phrases.

| between | in front of | on |
| on the left | on the right | under |

1 There is a car _____ the house.
2 There is a tree _____ .
3 There is a bird _____ the car.
4 There is a garden _____ .
5 There is a cat _____ the car and the motorcycle.
6 There is a ball _____ the car.

4 Correct the mistakes in the plural forms in these sentences.

1 There aren't any persons in the café.
2 Are there any boxs in his car?
3 There are two babyes in the park.
4 Are there any sandwichs for the picnic?
5 The womans are from Russia.
6 There are nice scarfs in the shop.
7 There are two trains stations in my town.

5 Choose the correct word to complete the sentences. Use the information in parentheses. (N) = the things/people are near. (F) = the things/people are far.

1 A: What's *that / this* on your arm? (F)
   B: It's my new watch.
2 Is *this / that* your key? (N)
3 I like *these / those* boots. (N)
4 Is *this / that* Max's car there in the parking lot? (F)
5 Who are *those / that* people in front of the station? (F)
6 A: Is *this / that* your jacket? (N)
   B: No. It's Eduardo's jacket.
7 Are *these / this* Teresa's glasses? (N)
8 What are *those / these* buildings over there? (F)

GRAMMAR SUMMARY UNIT 3

Simple present (*I/you/we/they*)

Use

We use the simple present to talk about routines and situations in the present.

> *I **go** to work by car.* (routine)
> *Seven million people **live** in St. Petersburg.* (situation)

Form

Affirmative	Negative
*I **live** in Madrid.*	*I **don't live** in Madrid.*
*You **work** in Rome.*	*You **don't work** in Rome.*
*We **eat** lunch at 1 p.m.*	*We **don't eat** lunch at 1 p.m.*
*They **go** to college in Lima.*	*They **don't go** to college in Lima.*

To form the simple present in affirmative sentences, we put the verb after the subject.

> *I* *live* *in Madrid.*
> SUBJECT (MAIN)
>   VERB

In negative sentences, we use two verbs—the negative auxiliary verb *don't* (= *do not*) and a main verb.

> *I* *don't* *live* *in Madrid.*
>   AUXILIARY MAIN
>   VERB VERB

▶ **Exercise 1**

Simple present questions (*I/you/we/they*)

Questions	Short answers
*Do I **have** a car?*	*Yes, I **do**. / No, I **don't**.*
*Do you **live** downtown?*	*Yes, you **do**. / No, you **don't**.*
*Do we **take** this train?*	*Yes, we **do**. / No, we **don't**.*
*Do they **want** lunch?*	*Yes, they **do**. / No, they **don't**.*

To form simple present questions with *I/you/we/they*, we add the auxiliary verb *do* before the subject.

> *Do* *you* *live* *downtown?*
> AUXILIARY SUBJECT MAIN
> VERB VERB

We use the auxiliary verb *do* or *don't* in short answers. We don't repeat the main verb.

> *Do you like this restaurant?* ~~Yes, I like.~~ *Yes, I **do**.*

We can also ask questions with *wh-* words (*who, what, where*, etc.). We put the *wh-* word at the beginning of the sentence.

> ***Where** do you work?*
> ***What** do you want?*
> ***What** time do they arrive?*

▶ **Exercises 2 and 3**

Simple present (*he/she/it*)

Affirmative	Negative
*He **eats** lunch at home*	*He **doesn't eat** lunch at home.*
*Maria **works** in Barcelona.*	*Maria **doesn't work** in Barcelona.*
*The city **has** a lot of traffic.*	*The city **doesn't have** a lot of traffic.*

After *he, she,* and *it*, or other singular names and nouns, we use a form of the verb ending with *-s*.

> *I love Paris.* → *She **loves** Paris.*
> *I live opposite the park.* → *Thomas **lives** opposite the park.*

In negative sentences, we use *doesn't*, not *don't*. The main verb doesn't change.

> *I don't like this park.* → *He **doesn't** like this park.*

Spelling rules

With most verbs, we add *-s* for the third person (*he/she/it*) form.

> *like* → *likes*   *travel* → *travels*   *eat* → *eats*

But with some verbs, we change the spelling.

* With verbs ending in consonant + *y*, we use *-ies*.
  study → *stud**ies***   *try* → *tr**ies***

* With verbs ending in *-ch, -sh, -s, -ss,* and *-x*, we add *-es*.
  watch → *watches*   *finish* → *finishes*

Some verbs are irregular after *he/she/it*.

> *have* → *has*   *do* → *does*   *go* → *goes*

▶ **Exercise 4**

Simple present questions (*he/she/it*)

Questions	Short answers
*Does he **like** classical music?*	*Yes, he **does**.* *No, he **doesn't**.*
*Does she **live** downtown?*	*Yes, she **does**.* *No, she **doesn't**.*
*Does this bus **go** to the airport?*	*Yes, it **does**.* *No, it **doesn't**.*
*Where **does** Leonardo **live**?* *When **does** your train **leave**?*	

We use *does* after *he/she/it* (not *do*). The main verb doesn't change. We use *does* and *doesn't* in short answers.

▶ **Exercises 5 and 6**

Exercises

1 Put the words in order to make affirmative and negative simple present sentences.

1 apartment / live / I / an / in

_____

2 have / don't / a pet / they

_____

3 to work / go / by train / we

_____

4 don't / swimming / like / I

_____

5 eat / in that restaurant / lunch / Julia and Carlo

_____

6 our friends / meet / we / on the weekend / don't

_____

2 Read the sentences and write questions with *you* or *your*.

1 I like going into the city.
   Do you like going into the city _____ ?

2 I'm 32 years old.
   _____ ?

3 I watch TV after work.
   _____ ?

4 My city is polluted.
   _____ ?

5 I like that café.
   _____ ?

6 I live in a small town.
   _____ ?

3 Complete the conversation with the simple present form of the verb.

A: [1]_____ you _____ (go) to work by car?

B: No, I [2]_____ (not have) a car. I go to work by bus. And you?

A: Well, I come by car because I [3]_____ (not live) near my office.

B: What time [4]_____ you _____ (finish) work?

A: At 6 p.m. What [5]_____ you _____ (do) after work?

B: I [6]_____ (like) meeting friends. Sometimes, we [7]_____ (go) to a restaurant for dinner. And you?

A: I drive home because I [8]_____ (be) always tired!

4 Write the third person singular (*he/she/it*) form of the verbs.

1 do   _____
2 watch   _____
3 be   _____
4 go   _____
5 come   _____
6 finish   _____
7 have   _____
8 speak   _____
9 want   _____
10 fly   _____
11 study   _____

5 Complete the sentences with the correct form of *do* to make negative sentences or questions.

1 John and Fay _____ like living in a big city.
2 What time _____ the class start?
3 Jack _____ speak Spanish.
4 What _____ they study in college?
5 She _____ know a lot of people.
6 We _____ watch many movies.
7 _____ he have a sister?

6 Use the words in parentheses to write sentences in the simple present.

1 _____ watching basketball.
   (I / like)

2 _____ pasta for dinner?
   (you / want)

3 _____ on the weekend.
   (we / not work)

4 _____ in the evenings?
   (she / read)

5 _____ work at 7:00 p.m.
   (he / finish)

6 _____ a lot of parks.
   (my town / not have)

7 _____ a lot of different languages. (some people / speak)

GRAMMAR SUMMARY UNIT 4

Like/love + noun or *-ing* form

After the verbs *like* and *love* we use a noun or noun phrase.

> They **love books**. (*books* = a noun)
> They **don't like the same soccer teams**.
> (*the same soccer teams* = a noun phrase)
> Does he **like soccer**? (*soccer* = a noun)

When we use a verb after *like* and *love*, we use the *-ing* form. The *-ing* form is a noun.

> She **likes** swim**ming**.
> They **love** play**ing** computer games.
> I **don't like** danc**ing**.

The *-ing* form can also be part of a phrase.

> Do they like **doing the same things**?

Spelling

With most verbs, we add *-ing* to the main verb.

> watch → watch**ing**   read → read**ing**

But with some verbs, we change the spelling.

- With verbs ending in consonant + *e*, we remove the *e* and add *-ing*.
  > dance → danc**ing**   make → mak**ing**

- With verbs ending in vowel + consonant, we double the consonant and add *-ing*.
  > swim → swim**ming**   run → run**ning**

▶ Exercises 1 and 2

Adverbs of frequency

We use adverbs of frequency to describe how often we do things or how often things happen.

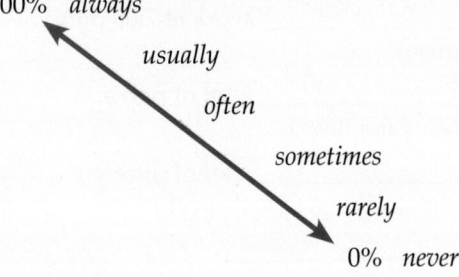

100%   *always*

usually

often

sometimes

rarely

0%   *never*

Position

We put adverbs of frequency after the verb *to be*. We put them before other verbs.

> I**'m usually** at home in the evening.
> They **aren't often** late. (*aren't often* = are not often)
> We **sometimes go** swimming on the weekend.
> Luca **never goes** to the gym.
> We **rarely** go to the movies.

▶ Exercise 3

Expressions of frequency

We sometimes use expressions of frequency instead of adverbs. Some common expressions of frequency are:

> once/twice a day
> three times a week/month/year
> every day/week/month/year, etc.

We usually put expressions of frequency at the end of a sentence.

> I shop online **three or four times a month**.
> Jackie goes running **every day**.

We ask about frequency with *how often*.

> **How often** do you use social media?

▶ Exercises 4, 5, and 6

Can/can't (+adverb)

We use *can* to talk about abilities and things we're able to do. The negative form of *can* is *can't*.

> I **can** swim.
> She **can** dance.
> He **can** speak English.
> We **can't** play the piano.
> They **can't** play tennis.

Sometimes, we use an adverb in a sentence with *can/can't* to describe the main verb.

> I can swim **well**.
> She can dance **very well**.
> He can speak English **a little**.
> We can't play the piano **very well**.
> They can't play tennis **well**.

We don't use the adverb *a little* in negative sentences.

When we ask questions with *can*, we put *can* at the beginning of the question. Sometimes, we also ask questions with *How well*.

> **Can** you play the guitar?
> **How well** can you play the guitar?

▶ Exercise 7

Exercises

1 Write the *-ing* form of the verbs.

1 make   _____
2 watch   _____
3 go   _____
4 come   _____
5 swim   _____
6 shop   _____
7 play   _____
8 write   _____

2 Complete the sentences with the *-ing* form of these verbs.

come	do	listen	play
swim	watch	write	

1 I don't like _____ long emails.
2 She loves _____ TV in the evenings.
3 He likes _____ in the ocean.
4 We love _____ to music in the car.
5 Sandy and Nick always like _____ to our house.
6 Marianne likes _____ taekwondo.
7 I love _____ the piano.

3 Put the adverb of frequency in the correct place in the sentence.

1 I shop online. (sometimes)
_____

2 She has coffee after lunch. (always)
_____

3 Michael is in the gym after work. (usually)
_____

4 I play online games. (never)
_____

5 The students are late for class. (often)
_____

6 He is hungry in the morning. (rarely)
_____

4 Put the words in order to make sentences.

1 go / once / a walk / we / a day / for
_____

2 on vacation / twice / go / a year / they
_____

3 every / use / social media / day / I
_____

4 her friends / she / every / weekend / meets
_____

5 once / visit / or / I / a month / my parents / twice
_____

6 to the gym / I / times / or / go / three / a / week / four
_____

5 Write questions for the sentences in Exercise 4. Use *how often*.

1 _____
2 _____
3 _____
4 _____
5 _____
6 _____

6 Complete the conversation with these words and phrases. Use the *-ing* form of the verbs.

browse	every	go	often	swim
once or twice a month		three or four times a week		

A: What's in your bag?
B: My clothes for the gym. I love
   ¹_____ to the gym after work.
A: How often do you go?
B: I go ²_____ .
A: That's a lot! I like ³_____ .
   But I don't ⁴_____ go to the
   pool—only ⁵_____ .
B: What else do you do in your free time?
A: Well, I love ⁶_____ the
   internet. I do it ⁷_____
   evening!

7 Circle the correct option to complete the sentences.

1 She *can / can't* understand German a little.
2 He's a chef at a restaurant, so he *can / can't* cook very well.
3 We *can / can't* see well because the room is dark.
4 A: *Can / Can't* you speak a foreign language?
   B: No, I *can / can't*.
5 A: What musical instrument can you play?
   B: I *can / can't* play the trumpet.
   A: *Do you / How well* can you play?
   B: I can play it very well.

GRAMMAR SUMMARY UNIT 5

Countable and uncountable nouns with *a/an*, *some*, and *any*

Some nouns are countable. We can count them and they can become plural, for example *car → cars*, *book → books*, and *friend → friends*. Other nouns are uncountable. We can't count them and they cannot normally become plural, for example *bread*, *meat*, and *paper*.

We use *a/an* before singular, countable nouns.
> There's **a banana** on the table.

We use *some* and *any* with uncountable nouns and plural, countable nouns.

- We use *some* in affirmative sentences.
  > We have **some** onions at home.
  > There's **some** bread in my bag.

- We use *any* in negative sentences and questions.
  > We don't have **any** oranges.
  > There isn't **any** juice in the fridge.
  > Are there **any** eggs?
  > Do you have **any** cheese?

When we offer something or ask for something, we use *some*.
> Do you want **some** water?
> Can I have **some** rice?

Sometimes we use *some* and *any* without a noun.
> A: *Do we have any potatoes?*
> B: *Yes, there are* **some** *in the pantry.*
> (some = some potatoes)

> A: *Can we have lamb for dinner?*
> B: *No, we don't have* **any**. *(any = any lamb)*

▶ **Exercises 1, 2, and 3**

A lot of and *much/many*

A lot of, *much*, and *many* are quantifiers. We use quantifiers to talk about quantity or the amount of something.

We use *a lot of* in affirmative sentences with plural, countable nouns and uncountable nouns. We can use *lots of* or *a lot of*—they have the same meaning.
> I always eat **a lot of** fresh vegetables. (a lot of + plural, countable noun)
> There's **a lot of** salt in this food. (a lot of + uncountable noun)

We use *much* and *many* in negative sentences and questions.

- We use *much* with uncountable nouns.
  > There is**n't much** cheese.
  > Do we have **much** food at home?

- We use *many* with plural, countable nouns.
  > There aren't **many** people here today.
  > Are there **many** markets in your city?

We can also use *a lot of* or *lots of* in negative sentences and questions with the same meaning.
> There isn't **a lot of** rice.
> Are there normally **lots of** people at the market?

▶ **Exercise 4**

How many / How much

To ask about quantity, we use *how many* and *how much*.

- We use *how many* to ask about plural, countable nouns.
  > **How many** Italian restaurants are there here?

- We use *how much* to ask about uncountable nouns.
  > **How much** rice do you want?

▶ **Exercises 5 and 6**

Exercises

1 Complete the sentences with *a/an* or *some*.

1 We have _____ pet cat.
2 She wants _____ pasta for dinner.
3 There's _____ car outside my house.
4 He always likes _____ salt on his food.
5 I normally meet _____ friends for lunch.
6 I have _____ apple in my bag.
7 You need _____ rice to make this dish.

2 Choose the best word to complete the sentences.

1 Can I have *some / any* coffee, please?
2 I don't have *some / any* vegetables in the fridge.
3 Are there *any / some* people on the bus?
4 He has *some / any* new boots.
5 Do you want *some / any* tea?
6 She doesn't want *some / any* food because she isn't hungry.

3 Complete the conversation with *a/an*, *some*, or *any*.

A: Are you hungry? Do you want [1]_____ food?
B: Yes, good idea. Can I have [2]_____ sandwiches?
A: No, sorry. I don't have [3]_____ bread. I can make you [4]_____ salad.
B: Thanks, that's perfect. I can help you.
A: OK, we need [5]_____ lettuce, [6]_____ tomatoes, and [7]_____ onion.
B: Oh, no. There aren't [8]_____ tomatoes or onions in the fridge. I have a good idea. Let's go out for lunch! Are there [9]_____ restaurants near here?
A: Yes, there are. Come on, let's go!

4 Choose the correct option to complete the sentences. Sometimes both options are possible.

1 There are *lots of / a lot of* students in the classroom.
2 Do you write *much / many* emails at work?
3 Does the town have *lots of / many* interesting places to visit?
4 We don't have *much / many* milk left.
5 Is there *a lot of / many* sugar in this cake?
6 This dish doesn't have *much / a lot of* cheese.
7 I don't know *many / much* people at this party.
8 They eat *much / a lot of* fresh fruit every day.

5 Complete the questions with *how much* or *how many*.

1 _____ texts do you send in a day?
2 _____ juice do the school children drink?
3 _____ meat do they eat every day?
4 _____ movies does he watch in a week?
5 _____ bags of rice does she have?
6 _____ kilos of flour do we need?
7 _____ water do they drink?
8 _____ sauce do you want with your food?

6 Complete the conversation with these words and phrases.

how many	a	an	any
how much	some	much	some

A: What do we need to buy?
B: Well, we need [1]_____ bottle of olive oil and [2]_____ pasta.
A: [3]_____ pasta do you want?
B: Let's get two packages.
A: OK, here they are. Do we need [4]_____ tomatoes?
B: Yes, get two. Also, we don't have [5]_____ coffee left—there's only half a bag. So let's buy [6]_____ .
A: Here's the coffee.
B: OK, and we also need [7]_____ onion.
A: Only one?
B: Yes, we already have two at home. Right, let's go to check out.
A: OK, [8]_____ bags do we have?
B: One. That's enough.

GRAMMAR SUMMARY UNIT 6

Was/were

We use *was* and *were* to talk about the past. *Was* and *were* are the simple past forms of the verb *be*. We use *were* after *you*, *they*, and *we*. We use *was* after *I*, *he*, *she*, and *it*.

	Affirmative	Negative
I/he/she/it	Pablo Picasso **was** a famous Spanish artist.	Vincent van Gogh **wasn't** rich.
you/they/we	We **were** on vacation last week.	They **weren't** at the gallery.

	Questions	Short answers
I/he/she/it	**Was** Lisa at work yesterday? Where **was** the party?	Yes, she **was**. No, she **wasn't**.
you/they/we	**Were** they at the restaurant? Why **were** you late?	Yes, they **were**. No, they **weren't**.

There are no contractions of *was* and *were*.

▶ **Exercise 1**

Simple past regular verbs

To make the simple past of regular verbs, we add *-ed* to the verb.

walk → walk**ed**   watch → watch**ed**

Simple past verbs never change—we use the same form for all persons (*I, you, he, she, it,* etc.).

I **lived** in Rome.
You **lived** in Rome.
She **lived** in Rome.

Spelling

With some verbs, we change the spelling.

- With verbs ending in *-e*, we add *-d*.
  live → live**d**

- With verbs ending in consonant + *-y*, we change the *-y* to *-ied*.
  study → stud**ied**

- With verbs ending in vowel + consonant, we double the consonant and add *-ed*.
  stop → sto**pped**   plan → pla**nned**

  We never double the consonants *w, x,* or *y*.
  show → show**ed**   play → play**ed**

▶ **Exercise 2**

Simple past irregular verbs

Not all simple past verbs end in *-ed*. Many common verbs are irregular.

go → went   build → built   make → made

We use the same irregular form for all persons (*I, you, he, she, it,* etc.).

I **had** a party.
You **had** a party.
They **had** a party.

▶ **Exercises 3 and 4**

Simple past negatives

In negative sentences in the simple past, we use two verbs—the negative auxiliary verb *didn't* (= did not) and a main verb. The main verb is in the base form.

He	didn't	come	to the exhibition.
SUBJECT	AUXILIARY VERB	MAIN VERB (BASE FORM)	

We don't use the simple past form of the main verb in negative sentences.

We didn't ~~visited~~ **visit** the museum.

▶ **Exercise 5**

Simple past questions

Questions	Short answers
Did you **see** the movie?	Yes, I **did**. No, I **didn't**.
Did she **like** the food?	Yes, she **did**. No, she **didn't**.
Where **did** you **go**?	

To form questions in the simple past, we add the auxiliary verb *did* before the subject. The main verb is in the base form.

Did	you	like	the concert?
AUXILIARY VERB	SUBJECT	MAIN VERB (BASE FORM)	

We use the auxiliary verb *did* or *didn't* in short answers. We don't repeat the main verb.

Did you build this house? ~~Yes, we built.~~ Yes, we **did**.

▶ **Exercises 6 and 7**

Exercises

1 Complete the sentences with the correct form of *was/were*. Use the negative when you see (−) in parentheses.

1 _____ he a famous actor?
2 I _____ a good student at school.
3 A: _____ the bus late yesterday?
 B: No, it _____ . (−)
4 There _____ many people at the concert. (−)
5 _____ the tickets expensive?
6 Clive and Sarah _____ born in the sixties.
7 We _____ at the gym this morning. (−)
8 _____ you at home yesterday evening?

2 Write the simple past form of the verbs.

1	live	_____	6 play	_____
2	work	_____	7 want	_____
3	travel	_____	8 like	_____
4	finish	_____	9 stop	_____
5	start	_____	10 watch	_____

3 Complete the text with the simple past form of the verbs in parentheses.

Gabrielle-Emilie Le Tonnelier de Breteuil
[1]_____ (be) a famous scientist. She
[2]_____ (be) born in Paris, France, in 1706.
She [3]_____ (get) married when she was 19
and [4]_____ (have) three children. But at
the age of 27, she [5]_____ (start) to study
mathematics and physics. She was famous in the
world of science and she sometimes
[6]_____ (work) with the famous French
philosopher Voltaire. She [7]_____ (write)
a translation of a famous book by the British
scientist Isaac Newton, and people still use it
today. She [8]_____ (die) at the age of 42.

4 Write the simple past form of the verbs. Write *R* after the verb if it is regular, and *I* if it is irregular.

1	go	_____	_____
2	grow	_____	_____
3	make	_____	_____
4	do	_____	_____
5	find	_____	_____
6	talk	_____	_____
7	buy	_____	_____
8	see	_____	_____
9	paint	_____	_____
10	write	_____	_____
11	read	_____	_____
12	move	_____	_____
13	have	_____	_____
14	meet	_____	_____
15	listen	_____	_____

5 Write simple past sentences using these ideas.

1 we / not go / on vacation / last year
_____
2 Magda / not like / the movie
_____
3 they / live / in the US / for ten years
_____
4 Mike / make / a big mistake
_____
5 she / not buy / a ticket
_____
6 I / speak / to Bogdan / this morning
_____

6 Write simple past questions using these ideas.

1 you / live / in a house or an apartment?
_____
2 What / they / do last night?
_____
3 Where / Anton / study?
_____
4 you / watch / the soccer game last night?
_____
5 the food / taste good?
_____
6 How / they / build their houses?
_____

7 Complete the conversation with the simple past form of the verbs in parentheses.

A: What [1]_____ (you / do) over the weekend?
B: I [2]_____ (visit) my parents on their farm.
A: I [3]_____ (not know) your parents have a farm!
B: Really? I [4]_____ (grow) up on that farm!
A: Wow! [5]_____ (you / like) living there?
B: Yes, it [6]_____ (be) great! We [7]_____ (play) outside all day with the animals.
A: [8]_____ (you / have) many animals?
B: Yes, we [9]_____ (do). But we [10]_____ (not have) many friends because our farm [11]_____ (not be) near any other houses.

GRAMMAR SUMMARY UNIT 7

Comparative adjectives

We use a comparative adjective + *than* to compare two things or groups of things.

> *A tiger is **faster than** a lion.*
> *Spiders are **more dangerous than** sharks.*

We make comparative adjectives in different ways.

- With most short adjectives (one syllable) we add *-er*.
  cold → colder   high → higher

- With two-syllable adjectives ending in *-y*, we change the *-y* to *-ier*.
  happy → happier   easy → easier

- With long adjectives (two or more syllables) we put *more* before the adjective.
  *difficult → **more** difficult*
  *dangerous → **more** dangerous*

- Some comparative adjectives are irregular.
  good → better   bad → worse

Spelling

With short adjectives ending in *-e*, we add *-r*.
> *safe → safer*

With adjectives ending in one vowel + consonant, we double the final consonant and add *-er*.
> *hot → hotter   big → bigger*

▶ **Exercises 1, 2, and 3**

Superlative adjectives

We use a superlative adjective to compare one thing with all the other things in a group.

> *The elephant is **the heaviest** animal.* (= heavier than all other animals)
> *Sharks are **the biggest** fish in the world.* (= bigger than all other fish)

We often put *the* before a superlative adjective. We make superlative adjectives in different ways.

- With most short adjectives (one syllable) we add *-est*.
  *slow → **the** slowest   short → **the** shortest*

- With two-syllable adjectives ending in *-y*, we change the *-y* to *-iest*.
  *tiny → **the** tiniest   happy → **the** happiest*

- With long adjectives (two or more syllables) we put *most* before the adjective.
  *difficult → **the most** difficult*
  *dangerous → **the most** dangerous*

- Some superlative adjectives are irregular.
  *good → **the** best   bad → **the** worst*

We sometimes use a superlative without a noun when it is clear what we're talking about.

> *I like all his movies, but Titanic is **the best**.*
> (= the best movie)

Spelling

With short adjectives ending in *-e*, we add *-st*.
> *safe → the safest*

With adjectives ending in one vowel + consonant, we double the final consonant and add *-est*.
> *hot → the hottest   big → the biggest*

▶ **Exercises 4 and 5**

Exercises

1 Correct the mistakes in these sentences.

1 My car ride was longer as your bus ride.

2 My sister is more tall than me.

3 She feels happyier in the summer.

4 Today is hoter than yesterday.

5 Cars are dangerouser than planes.

6 He's a gooder cook than me.

2 Write comparative sentences using these ideas.

1 The new restaurant in town / good / the old restaurant.
   _____

2 German / difficult to learn / English.
   _____

3 The book / interesting / the movie.
   _____

4 The weather today / bad / the weather yesterday.
   _____

5 She / busy / than her husband.
   _____

6 Traveling by train / nice / traveling by bus.
   _____

7 Josh's house / big / my house.
   _____

3 Complete the conversations with the comparative form of these adjectives.

| boring   easy   expensive   fast   hot   short |

1 A: Are lions _____ than horses?
   B: No, they aren't. Lions are slower.
2 A: I paid $100 for my shoes.
   B: They are _____ than my shoes. My shoes only cost $60.
3 A: Your hair is _____ than it was yesterday.
   B: Yes, I went to the hairdresser's!
4 A: Was your meeting interesting this week?
   B: No! It was _____ than the meeting last week. I wanted to go to sleep!
5 A: Was the weather nice on your vacation?
   B: Yes, it was _____ than it is here. I went to the beach every day.
6 A: Do you want to walk or go in the car?
   B: It's _____ to walk because there's a lot of traffic on the roads.

4 Complete the sentences with the superlative form of the adjective.

1 The blue whale is the _____ (big) animal on Earth.
2 The giraffe has the _____ (long) neck of all animals.
3 This is the _____ (bad) program on TV.
4 The cheetah is the _____ (fast) animal in the world.
5 Mount Elbrus is the _____ (high) mountain in Russia and Europe.
6 Australian football is one of the _____ (dangerous) sports in Australia.
7 He is the _____ (happy) person I know.

5 Look at the information and complete the sentences using comparative and superlative forms of the adjectives.

Fun animal facts		heavy light
African elephant	5,000 kg	
hippopotamus	2,000 kg	
crocodile	1,100 kg	

1 The African elephant is _____ the hippopotamus.
2 The hippopotamus is _____ the African elephant.
3 The crocodile is _____ .

Airplane tickets to Peru		cheap expensive
AirPeru	$ 550	
Flink Air	$ 690	
Am Travel	$ 725	

4 Am Travel is _____ .
5 Flink Air is _____ Am Travel.
6 AirPeru is _____ .

Lakes		short long
Caspian Sea	1,199 km	
Lake Superior	616 km	
Lake Victoria	322 km	

7 Lake Superior is _____ the Caspian Sea.
8 Lake Superior is _____ Lake Victoria.
9 The Caspian Sea is _____ .

GRAMMAR SUMMARY UNIT 8

Present continuous

Use

We use the present continuous to talk about:

- an action you can see.
  *In the photo, Rajo Laurel **is talking** to a group of designers.*

- an action happening now.
  *A: What **are** you **doing**?*
  *B: I'**m getting** ready for the party.*

- an action happening around the time of speaking.
  *Sara'**s looking** for a new job.*

- a changing situation.
  *Environmentally friendly clothes **are becoming** more popular.*

Form

We form the present continuous with a form of the auxiliary verb *be* + the *-ing* form of the main verb.

Remember the spelling rules for *-ing* verbs. See page 164.

	Affirmative	Negative	Questions and short answers
I	*I'm working.*	*I'm not working.*	*Am I working?* *Yes, I am.* *No, I'm not.*
you/we/ they	*We're working.*	*They aren't working.*	*Are you working?* *Yes, you are.* *No, you aren't.*
he/she/it	*He's working.*	*She isn't working.*	*Is she working?* *Yes, she is.* *No, she isn't.*

Some verbs describe states (for example, *like, love, hate, know, want*). We don't use these verbs with the present continuous.

~~I'm knowing a really nice café near here.~~
*I **know** a really nice café near here.*

With the present continuous we often use time expressions such as *this week/month/year, today, at the moment,* or *this morning.*
*I'm wearing my new dress **today**.*

▶ Exercises 1 and 2

Simple present and present continuous

We use both the simple present and the present continuous to talk about actions and situations in the present.

- We use the simple present to talk about facts and routines.
  *The company **gives** workers a good salary. (fact)*
  *Luca always **wears** a suit to work. (routine)*

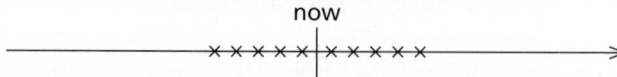

*Luca always **wears** a suit to work.*

- We use the present continuous to describe an action now or around the time of speaking.
  *Luca **is wearing** a blue suit today.*

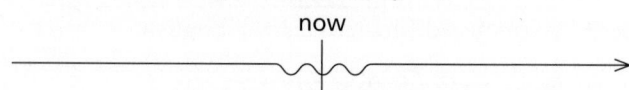

*Luca **is wearing** a blue suit today.*

▶ Exercise 3

Be vs. have

We use *be* with an adjective to describe qualities that are inherent.

*I'**m** tall.*
*He'**s** well-built.*
*The bag **is** red.*
*They'**re** thin.*

We use *have* with an adjective and a noun to describe specific attributes.

*I **have** long arms.*
*He **has** large hands.*
*We **have** short hair.*
*They **have** brown eyes.*

Questions	Short answers
***Are** you tall?*	*Yes, I am.* *No, I'm not.*
***Is** he thin?*	*Yes, he is.* *No, he isn't.*
***Do** you **have** a beard?*	*Yes, I do.* *No, I don't.*
***Does** he **have** short hair?*	*Yes, he does.* *No, he doesn't.*

▶ Exercises 4 and 5

Exercises

1 Write present continuous sentences using these ideas

1 I / wear / my favorite shirt today.
_____

2 you / stay / at a hotel downtown?
_____

3 She / not work / this morning.
_____

4 We / wait / for our train now.
_____

5 Claudia and Martin / watch / TV?
_____

6 I / not go / to class at the moment.
_____

7 They / not stay / here for long.
_____

8 he / learn / a new language?
_____

2 Complete the sentences with the present continuous form of these phrases.

wait for her	rain outside
computer not work	talk to someone else
wear a T-shirt	stay at home today
live with my parents	browse the internet

1 We can't go out because it _____ .
2 It's hot today, so I _____ .
3 He can't speak to you now because he _____ .
4 I'm bored, so I _____ .
5 She needs to leave now because her friend _____ .
6 I don't have a place to live at the moment, so I _____ .
7 Merrick doesn't feel well, so he _____ .
8 Sammir can't work at home today because his _____ .

3 Complete the conversation with the simple present or present continuous form of the verb.

A: Hi! What [1]_____ (do) here?
B: Hi! I [2]_____ (shop).
A: That's nice. I [3]_____ (go) to work!
B: On a Saturday! Why?
A: Oh, I always [4]_____ (work) on Saturday! I usually start at 11 a.m. and I [5]_____ (finish) at 3 p.m.
B: Oh. That's terrible!
A: I know! So, did you buy some new clothes?
B: Not clothes—I bought a new bag! Here, look … [6]_____ (you / like) it?
A: Oh, I love it! [7]_____ (you / go) home now?
B: No, I [8]_____ (want) to buy more things!

4 Complete the sentences with the correct form of *be* or *have*.

1 The boys in my class _____ tall.
2 She _____ long legs.
3 The performers _____ make-up on their faces.
4 His skin _____ tanned.
5 I _____ blue eyes.
6 He _____ well-built.

5 Write questions or answers to complete the conversations.

1 A: Does he have a round face?
   B: No, _____ .
2 A: _____ long hair?
   B: Yes, I do.
3 A: _____ short?
   B: No, they aren't.
4 A: Is she thin?
   B: Yes, _____ .

GRAMMAR SUMMARY UNIT 9

Be going to (for plans)

Use

We use *be going to* to talk about a plan for the future.

I'm going to watch a movie tonight. (= this is my plan)

They are going to travel around the world when they finish their exams.

She's going to look for a better job.

Form

	Affirmative	Negative
I	*I'm going to buy a new TV.*	*I'm not going to buy a new TV.*
you/we/they	*We're going to buy a new TV.*	*They aren't going to buy a new TV.*
he/she/it	*She's going to buy a new TV.*	*She isn't going to buy a new TV.*

	Questions	Short answers
I	*Am I going to buy a new TV?* *What am I going to do tonight?*	*Yes, I am.* *No, I'm not.*
you/we/they	*Are they going to buy a new TV?* *What are we going to do tonight?*	*Yes, they are.* *No, they aren't.*
he/she/it	*Is she going to buy a new TV?* *What is she going to do tonight?*	*Yes, she is.* *No, she isn't.*

We form *be going to* with a form of *be + going to* + main verb (base form). Note that this is like the present continuous form of *go*.

They're going for coffee now. (present continuous)

They're going to leave at 9 p.m. (be going to)

We don't usually say *going to go*. We use the present continuous of *go* instead.

I'm going to go to the store later. → *I'm going to the store later.*

We often use time expressions such as *tonight, this weekend, this summer,* and *next year* with *be going to*.

We're going to visit my sister this weekend.

She's going to move to Edinburgh next year.

▶ **Exercises 1, 2, and 3**

Infinitive of purpose

We use the infinitive of purpose (*to* + base form of verb) to give the reason for an action.

He went home to watch TV.

We're going shopping to buy some new clothes.

They bought tickets to see a musical in New York.

There are two parts of a sentence with the infinitive of purpose:

I called the theater *to buy some tickets for the movie.*

MAIN ACTION REASON FOR ACTION

We also use the infinitive of purpose on its own to answer questions with *why*.

A: Why are you getting up so early?

B: To go for a run.

▶ **Exercises 4 and 5**

Exercises

1 Correct the mistakes in four sentences. Two sentences are correct.

1   I going to meet my friend later.

2   We're going finish work early today.

3   He's going to call you after his appointment.

4   They don't going to watch the soccer game tonight.

5   Tommy's going to take his exams next week.

6   Do you going to travel by car tomorrow?

2 Match the questions (1–8) with the answers (a–h).

1   Is Sara going to come to our house? ____
2   When are we going to watch the movie? ____
3   Who are you going to meet this evening? ____
4   Is he going to get a new car? ____
5   How long are they going to be away? ____
6   Where are you going to have lunch? ____
7   Are you going to work today? ____
8   What are we going to do tonight? ____

a   My friend Poppy.
b   We're going to watch a movie.
c   Yes, he is.
d   For a few hours.
e   No, she isn't. She doesn't have time.
f   Tonight. At about 8:00 p.m.
g   In a café near my house.
h   No, I'm not. I'm going to stay at home.

3 Complete the conversation with *going to* and a verb from the box.

do	not watch	relax	not eat	watch	sit

A: ¹_____ the soccer game tonight?
B: No, ²_____ it because I don't like soccer! What about you?
A: I'm going to a restaurant, but we ³_____ there. The restaurant has a TV outside, so we ⁴_____ at a table and watch the game there. What ⁵_____ after work, then?
B: I ⁶_____ at home and read a book. For me, that's more interesting than soccer!

4 Match the beginnings of the sentences (1–6) with the endings (a–f).

1   I'm going to call the waiter ____
2   He's going to the store ____
3   She's writing her best friend a text message ____
4   Let's go to a café ____
5   I'm calling my doctor ____
6   The student waited until after the lesson ____

a   to make an appointment.
b   to speak to his teacher.
c   to say "happy birthday."
d   to buy a present for his wife.
e   to get coffee.
f   to ask for a menu.

5 Rewrite the two sentences as one sentence. Use the infinitive of purpose.

1   I went to the store. I bought some new shoes.
_____
_____

2   He called the restaurant. He reserved a table.
_____
_____

3   Helen is going to the pool. She's going to take a swim.
_____
_____

4   They went online. They reserved tickets for the movie.
_____
_____

5   She went to the supermarket. She got some food for dinner.
_____
_____

6   I'm going to the library. I'm going to study for my exams.
_____
_____

GRAMMAR SUMMARY UNIT 10

Present perfect

Use

We use the present perfect to talk about an action in the past. We often use it when we don't know exactly when the action happened, or when the timing is not important. The past action is usually important in the present.

Ask Michael for help. He's taken a German class.
(= He took a class in the past. He knows some German now.)

We often use the present perfect to talk about experiences in our lives.

I've visited the US five times.

Form

	Affirmative	Negative
I/you/we/they	*I've failed my exam.* *They've learned a lot.*	*We haven't seen this movie.* *You haven't finished your lunch.*
he/she/it	*He's forgotten the address.* *She's designed a robot.*	*He hasn't done the homework.* *She hasn't come back.*

We form the present perfect with a form of the auxiliary verb *have* + the past participle form of a main verb.

We   've   finished   our work.
AUXILIARY   MAIN VERB
VERB   (PAST PARTICIPLE)

Past participles

Past participles can be regular or irregular.

- With regular verbs, we add *-ed* to the base form. The form is the same as the simple past.
  look (base form)
  looked (simple past)
  looked (past participle)

- Other past participles are irregular. With some irregular verbs, the past participle is the same as the simple past form.
  make (base form)
  made (simple past)
  made (past participle)

- With other irregular verbs, the past participle is different from the simple past.
  write (base form)
  wrote (simple past)
  written (past participle)

See page 182 for a list of irregular past participle forms.

▶ **Exercises 1 and 2**

Present perfect questions and short answers

Form

	Questions	Short answers
I/you/we/they	*Have you seen Sofia?* *Which restaurant have they chosen?*	*Yes, I have.* *No, I haven't.*
he/she/it	*Has the movie finished?* *Why has John left his bag here?*	*Yes, it has.* *No, it hasn't.*

To form questions with the present perfect, we put the auxiliary verb *have* before the subject.

Have   you   finished   dinner?
AUXILIARY   SUBJECT   MAIN VERB
VERB   (PAST PARTICIPLE)

We don't use the main verb in short answers.

Questions with *Have you ever ... ?*

With present perfect questions, we often use *ever* to ask about past experiences.

Have you ever been to Asia? (*ever* = in your life)

We use *never* in negative answers.

No, I've never been there. (*never* = not in my life)

▶ **Exercise 3**

Present perfect and simple past

We use both present perfect and simple past to talk about the past.

I've eaten at this restaurant before. (This happened some time in the past.)
I ate at this restaurant last week. (We know when it happened.)

We always use simple past, not present perfect, when we use a time phrase (e.g., *yesterday, last week, at 2 a.m., in 2005*) to say the exact time the action happened.

I bought a new car last month.

However, we can use present perfect when the time phrase refers to an unfinished period of time (e.g., *today, this week, this month*).

We often start a conversation using the present perfect to talk about general experiences, and then use the simple past to give details.

A: *Have you ever lost something important?*
B: *Yes, I have. Once I left my laptop in a café.*
A: *What happened?*
B: *I went back to the café, but it wasn't there.*

▶ **Exercises 4, 5, and 6**

Exercises

1 Write the past participle form of the verbs. Check (✓) the forms that are the same as the simple past form.

1 do   _____
2 begin   _____
3 be   _____
4 see   _____
5 watch   _____
6 hear   _____
7 speak   _____
8 eat   _____
9 make   _____
10 get   _____
11 buy   _____
12 wake   _____
13 understand _____
14 know   _____
15 learn   _____
16 work   _____

2 Make affirmative and negative present perfect sentences using these ideas.

1 I / not travel / on an airplane.

   _____

2 They / not see / the new movie.

   _____

3 He / forget / his friend's telephone number.

   _____

4 Isabel / start / a language class.

   _____

5 Leo / become / a member of a gym.

   _____

6 She / not eat / her dinner.

   _____

7 We / not play / any games.

   _____

8 Our train / leave / the station.

   _____

3 Complete the questions with the present perfect form of these verbs. Then complete the short answers.

buy	find	finish	meet	write	visit

1 _____ the students _____ their exams? Yes, they _____ .
2 _____ Marcos _____ a new job? No, he _____ .
3 _____ she ever _____ China? Yes, she _____ .
4 _____ they _____ their plane tickets? Yes, they _____ .
5 _____ you ever _____ my friend Carla? Yes, I _____ .
6 _____ you _____ a text message to Sarah? No, I _____ .

4 Choose the correct option to complete the sentences.

1 Have you spoken to Anna *yesterday / today*?
2 Terry *has been / went* to the US in 2003.
3 We *haven't seen / didn't see* our friend Mary at the party last night.
4 My vacation *started / have started* two days ago.
5 I've called her a few times *this week / last week*.
6 Our class *ended / has ended* at 11 o'clock this morning.

5 Number the sentences in order to make two conversations.

Conversation 1
a Yes, I have. I forgot my wife's birthday! She was very angry with me! ____
b Oh, no! Did you buy her something nice afterwards? ____
c Yes, I did. I booked a trip to Paris! ____
d Have you ever forgotten something important? _1_

Conversation 2
e Yes, maybe. I need to go back and look. ____
f Oh, no! When did you last use it? ____
g I've lost my phone! _1_
h OK. Did you leave it in your classroom? ____
i I think I sent a message to a friend during my last class. ____

6 Complete the conversation with the present perfect or simple past form of the verbs.

A: [1]_____ you _____ (see) the news story about this man? It says he [2]_____ (lose) his memory—he can't remember his name or where he's from!

B: That sounds terrible.

A: I know. It says he [3]_____ (go) into a police station yesterday and [4]_____ (ask) for help.

B: And [5]_____ the police _____ (help) him?

A: No, they couldn't. He [6]_____ (not have) any ID, so they couldn't do anything.

B: I'm sure someone is looking for him. A friend or relative.

A: Yes. The police [7]_____ (speak) about him on all the local radio stations today. And they [8]_____ also _____ (put) his photo on Facebook and Twitter. Here's the photo on Facebook.

B: Ah, yes. That's good. I'm sure someone is going to recognize him soon.

GRAMMAR SUMMARY UNIT 11

Have to / don't have to, can/can't

Use

We use *have to*, *don't have to*, *can*, and *can't* to talk about rules and things we need or don't need to do.

- We use *have to* to say that something is necessary.
  I **have to** get up early tomorrow to go to the airport.

- We use *can* to say that something is possible.
  You **can** leave your bag at the train station.

- We use *don't have to* to say that something is not necessary.
  We **don't have to** leave the hotel until noon.

- We use *can't* to say that something is not possible.
  You **can't** visit most beaches on the island without a car.

We never use *don't have to* to say that something is impossible or not allowed. We use *can't*.
  ~~With this visa, you **don't have to** stay more than six months.~~
  With this visa, you **can't** stay more than six months.

Form

	Affirmative	Negative
have to		
I/you/we/they	I **have to** leave early.	I **don't have to** leave early.
he/she/it	She **has to** leave early.	She **doesn't have to** leave early.
can		
I/you/he/she/it/we/they	We **can** change our currency here.	We **can't** change our currency here.

	Questions	Short answers
have to		
I/you/we/they	**Do** you **have to** leave early?	Yes, I **do**. No, I **don't**.
he/she/it	**Does** she **have to** leave early?	Yes, she **does**. No, she **doesn't**.
can		
I/you/he/she/it/we/they	**Can** we change our currency here?	Yes, you **can**. No, you **can't**.

The verb *can* is a modal verb.

- The verb doesn't change after *he/she/it*.
- We don't use the auxiliary *do/does* to make negatives and ask questions.

After *have to*, *don't have to*, *can*, and *can't*, we use the base form of a verb. To make questions with *can*, we put *can* before the subject. To make questions with *have to*, we add *do* or *does* before the subject.

We also use *can* and *can't* to talk about our abilities.
  I **can** speak Spanish. I **can't** speak German.

The full form of *can't* is *cannot*.

▶ Exercises 1, 2, and 3

Should/shouldn't

Use

We use *should* and *shouldn't* to give or ask for advice.
  You **should** visit the MALBA museum when you go to Buenos Aires. (= I think this is a good idea.)
  You **shouldn't** drink the tap water. (= I think this is a bad idea.)

Form

	Affirmative	Negative
I/you/he/she/it/we/they	You **should** stay downtown.	You **shouldn't** stay downtown.

	Questions	Short answers
I/you/he/she/it/we/they	**Should** I stay in the downtown area? Where **should** we go now?	Yes, you **should**. No, you **shouldn't**.

The verb *should* is a modal verb.

- The verb doesn't change after *he/she/it*.
- We don't use the auxiliary *do/does* to make negatives and ask questions.
- The verb after *should* is in the base form.

▶ Exercises 4 and 5

Exercises

1 Complete the sentences with a form of *have to*, and complete the short answers.

1 A: _____ (you / go) to work by car?
   B: No, _____ .

2 _____ (my son / not go) to school today because the school's closed.

3 A: What time _____ (Irene / be) at the train station?
   B: At 4 p.m.

4 A: _____ (people / get) a visa to work in this country?
   B: Yes, _____ .

5 _____ (I / not cook) tonight because we're going to eat in a restaurant.

6 A: _____ (he / turn off) his cell phone during the exam?
   B: Yes, _____ .

7 _____ (Julie / not wake up) early tomorrow because it's the weekend.

2 Complete the sentences with *can/can't* and a correct verb from the box.

eat or drink	leave	park	speak	take	use

1
You _____ your bike here.

2
You _____ loudly here.

3
You _____ your car here.

4
You _____ in this store.

5
You _____ photos here.

6
You _____ your cell phone here.

3 Complete the conversation with *can*, *can't*, or the correct form of *have to*.

A: What time [1]_____ you _____ be at the airport?
B: Two hours before my flight. But we still have lots of time, so we [2]_____ leave immediately.
A: OK. How many bags do you have?
B: Two—a big suitcase and a small bag. But I [3]_____ only take one small bag with me on the plane.
A: [4]_____ you take food and drink on the plane?
B: No, you [5]_____ . You [6]_____ buy food on the plane. It's a new rule!
A: That's terrible! Where can I park the car?
B: You [7]_____ park. Just leave me near the entrance. I can go in by myself.
A: OK, fine.

4 Match the sentences with the advice. Then complete the advice with *should* or *shouldn't*.

1 He feels very tired all the time. ____
2 She has a bad cold. ____
3 There's a lot of traffic on the roads. ____
4 Hanna's face is very red. ____
5 They want to get fit. ____

a They _____ play sports together.
b You _____ take the train.
c He _____ go to bed so late.
d She _____ sit out in the sun all day.
e She _____ go to the doctor's.

5 Complete the conversation with these words.

can	can't	should
don't have to	shouldn't	should

A: We'd like to go on a walking tour of Peru. [1]_____ we book the hotels now?
B: Yes. A lot of tourists go there, so you [2]_____ always find a room if you don't book one in advance. Do you speak Spanish?
A: No, we don't.
B: Well, not everyone speaks English, so you [3]_____ learn a few phrases before you go. But you [4]_____ speak perfectly. People are very helpful.
A: We'd like to go in February. Is that a good time?
B: No, the best time is from May to September. It's not too hot, so you [5]_____ do lots of walking.
A: OK.
B: But you [6]_____ go walking alone. It's easy to get lost! Your hotels will help you find good local guides.

GRAMMAR SUMMARY UNIT 12

Will/won't

Use

We use *will* and *won't* to talk about what we think or know about the future.

> It **will** be 30 degrees this afternoon.
> It **won't** (= will not) rain tomorrow.

We often use I (*don't*) *think + will.*

> **I think** they**'ll** be late.
> **I don't think** you**'ll** like Greece in August—it's so hot.

Note that we don't normally use I *think + won't* as a negative form. We use I *don't think + will* instead.

> ~~I think the weather won't get better this week.~~
> **I don't think** the weather **will** get better this week.

Form

	Affirmative	Negative
I/you/he/she/it/we/they	It **will** be sunny tomorrow.	It **won't** be sunny tomorrow.

	Questions	Short answers
I/you/he/she/it/we/they	**Will** it be sunny tomorrow? Where **will** it be sunny tomorrow?	Yes, it **will**. No, it **won't**.

We normally use the contraction *'ll* after a pronoun.

> There's a lot of traffic today, so he**'ll** probably be late.

Note that the contraction of *will not* is *won't*.

> I **won't** do very well on the exam. I don't understand this topic.

The verb *will* is a modal verb.

* The verb doesn't change after *he/she/it*.
* We don't use the auxiliary *do/does* to make negatives and ask questions.
* The verb after *will* is in the base form.

▶ **Exercises 1, 2, and 3**

Articles

Definite article (*the*)

We use *the* with:

* the names of deserts, e.g., the Sahara Desert
* seas and oceans e.g., the Red Sea, the Pacific Ocean
* rivers, e.g., the Mississippi River
* place names that contain a plural noun, e.g., the Philippines, the Netherlands
* country names that contain the words *kingdom, republic,* and *states*, e.g., The Kingdom of Saudi Arabia, The People's Republic of China, The United States of America
* some geographical areas with the words *east* and *west*, e.g., the West, the Middle East
* *north/east/south/west* to talk about part of a country or place, e.g., the north of Italy, the east of the city

No article

We don't use an article with the names of:

* continents, e.g., Asia
* countries, e.g., France
* states in a country, e.g., Florida
* cities and towns, e.g., Boston
* the names of roads and streets, e.g., First Avenue, Oxford Street
* lakes, e.g., Lake Michigan
* a single mountain, e.g., Mount Everest

▶ **Exercises 4, 5, and 6**

Exercises

1 Choose the correct option to complete the sentences.

1 We think we *will / won't* visit Mount Etna next year. It is easy to go there.
2 I *will / won't* be busy tomorrow, so you should come and see me now.
3 There *will / won't* be many children in the park today because it's raining.
4 She doesn't think she *will / won't* have time to study over the weekend.
5 I think the number of college students *will / won't* decrease because college is so expensive.
6 He *will / won't* come to our dinner party. He has too much work to do.
7 They *will / won't* go camping with us because they prefer to stay in hotels.

2 Find the mistakes in six sentences. Two sentences are correct.

1 My parents will to arrive soon.
2 There will be more things to see in Lisbon.
3 He wills be tired tomorrow morning because he went to bed late.
4 There will be a lot more floods and droughts in the future.
5 We think our customers won't buy the new product.
6 Do factories will produce less pollution in the future?
7 I don't will have time to see you after class.
8 He doesn't think it won't snow this winter.

3 Complete the sentences with *will* and a word from the box.

not remember	pass	have
not use	become	find

1 I'm sure I _____ my driving test. I practiced a lot!
2 _____ Earth _____ hotter in the future?
3 I'm sure he _____ my name. We've only met once.
4 Maria has left her job. But I think she _____ another job soon.
5 _____ you _____ time to see me next week?
6 In the future, we _____ our cars so often because buses and trains will be better.

4 Write the places in the correct column in the table.

Beijing	Czech Republic	Green Road
Himalayas	Indian Ocean	Kalahari Desert
Lake Garda	Lake Victoria	Ganges River
San Francisco	South Korea	

the	no article

5 Complete the sentences with *the* or no article (–).

1 I'd love to go up _____ Mount Olympus one day.
2 She's never been to _____ United Kingdom.
3 They went on a cruise on _____ Nile River.
4 There are many wild animals that live in _____ Arabian desert.
5 We've moved to _____ Budapest.
6 _____ Mediterranean Sea is the best place to go swimming.
7 I live on _____ Portland Street.

6 Find four places where *the* is incorrect and three places where *the* needs to be added.

Millions of tourists visit the Argentina every year because there is a lot to see and do there. Most tourists go to the Buenos Aires to enjoy the great beaches and swim in Pacific Ocean. Tourists who want to go somewhere quieter can visit the Lake Buenos Aires, or Patagonian Desert in Patagonia. It is found in south of Argentina, but a small part is also in the Chile. There, you won't find many tourists, so it's a good place to go if you want to think and be with nature!

Irregular verb chart

VERB	SIMPLE PAST	PAST PARTICIPLE
be	was / were	been
become	became	become
begin	began	begun
bring	brought	brought
build	built	built
buy	bought	bought
choose	chose	chosen
come	came	come
cost	cost	cost
do	did	done
drink	drank	drunk
eat	ate	eaten
fall	fell	fallen
feel	felt	felt
find	found	found
fly	flew	flown
forget	forgot	forgotten
get	got	gotten
give	gave	given
go	went	gone
grow	grew	grown
have	had	had
hear	heard	heard
hurt	hurt	hurt
keep	kept	kept
know	knew	known

VERB	SIMPLE PAST	PAST PARTICIPLE
leave	left	left
let	let	let
lose	lost	lost
make	made	made
meet	met	met
pay	paid	paid
put	put	put
read	read	read
run	ran	run
say	said	said
see	saw	seen
sell	sold	sold
send	sent	sent
sit	sat	sat
sleep	slept	slept
speak	spoke	spoken
spend	spent	spent
swim	swam	swum
take	took	taken
teach	taught	taught
tell	told	told
think	thought	thought
understand	understood	understood
wake	woke	woken
wear	wore	worn
write	wrote	written

Unit 1

▶ 1

I = Interviewer, D = David Doubilet
I: What's your name?
D: David Doubilet.
I: Where are you from?
D: The US. I'm a photographer for *National Geographic*.
I: I really like this photo.
D: Yes, it's in Milne Bay.
I: And who's the diver in the photo? What's her name?
D: Her name's Dinah Halstead.
I: Where's she from?
D: She's from Papua New Guinea. She's a diver and she's also a photographer.

▶ 2

I = Interviewer (man), B = Beverley Joubert
(The words of Beverley Joubert are spoken by an actor.)
I: Hello. What's your name?
B: My name's Beverley Joubert.
I: What's your job?
B: I'm a photographer for *National Geographic*. And I'm also an explorer and filmmaker. I'm married to the man in the photo.
I: What's his name?
B: My husband's name is Dereck. He's also an explorer and filmmaker.
I: In the photo, you are in Australia. Are you from Australia?
B: No, we aren't. We're from Africa—we were both born in South Africa—and we live in Africa. Actually, this picture isn't in Australia, it's in Botswana.

▶ 3

A: Hello. What's your name?
B: My name's Mike Burney.
A: Are you married?
B: Yes, I am. My wife's name is Sally. She isn't here today.
A: What's her job?
B: She's a teacher. I'm also a teacher.
A: Are you both from the United States?
B: No, we aren't. I'm from the US, but Sally is from Canada.
A: And how old are you?
B: I'm thirty-six.
A: Is Sally also thirty-six?
B: No, she isn't. She's thirty-five.

▶ 4

1 I'm thirty-one.
2 Are you from England?
3 No, I'm not.
4 Her name's Helena.
5 We aren't from the US.
6 We're from Canada.
7 No, he isn't.
8 Is he married?

▶ 5

A: Good afternoon. Are you in New Zealand for work or for a vacation?
B: For work. I'm a photographer.
A: I see. What's your address in Auckland?
B: We're at 106a Eglinton Road.
A: We?

B: Yes, I'm with my wife and two children. They're also here.
A: Is your wife also a photographer?
B: Yes, she is, but she isn't in Auckland for work. She's here for a vacation.

▶ 7

1 My parents are Spanish.
2 I am the only boy in my family.
3 What's your name?
4 Where are you from?
5 She is a photographer.
6 His uncle is in the US.
7 Our family is from Asia.
8 Their cousins are both girls.

▶ 9

My family lives in Australia. My mother is from Ireland and her three sisters (my aunts) live there. My father is from Australia and he's a businessman. My sister's name is Orla, and she's a teacher. She's married, and her husband is Tim. He's also a teacher. Their children are Rory and Jack. My best friend is Peter. His father and my father have a company together.

▶ 13

1

R = Rita, M = Miguel
R: Hello, can I help you?
M: Hi. Yes, I'm a new student.
R: What's your name?
M: Miguel.
R: Hi, Miguel. My name's Rita. Nice to meet you.
M: Nice to meet you, too.
R: What's your last name, Miguel?
M: Ferreira.
R: Ferreira? Are you on my list? Um, can you spell that?
M: Sure. It's F-E-R-R-E-I-R-A.
R: OK. Here's some information about the college and your courses. The presentation about the college starts in one hour.
M: OK. See you later.
R: Bye.

2

R = Rita, V = Valérie, M = Miguel
R: Hello. Can I help you? My name's Rita. I work for the college.
V: Hi, I'm Valérie. Nice to meet you.
R: Nice to meet you, too. What's your last name, Valérie?
V: Moreau. That's M-O-R-E-A-U.
R: M, M, M, Mason, Moore, Moreau! OK. Here's some information about the college and your courses. The presentation starts in an hour. Well, you're the second person here, Valérie. There's another student here. He's from Brazil. Miguel?
M: Yes?
R: Miguel. This is Valérie. She's a new student.
M: Nice to meet you, Valérie.
V: Nice to meet you, too.
R: See you both later.
V: Goodbye, Rita. It was nice meeting you.
M: So, Valérie, are you from France?
V: Actually no, I'm from an island in the Pacific Ocean.
M: New Caledonia?
V: That's right!

Unit 2

▶ 14

This photo is by Sarah Leen. It's about people and their possessions. The photo shows all the plastic objects in this family's house. There are seven people in the Stow family and they have hundreds of possessions! I think there are twenty-two balls, fifty shoes and boots, a couch, three TVs …

▶ 16

1 There's a couch.
2 There isn't a rug in this apartment.
3 There are five people in this apartment.
4 There aren't any curtains.
5 Is there a television? Yes, there is.
6 Are there any chairs? Yes, there's one chair.
7 How many pictures are there? There are two.
8 Are there any books? No, there aren't.

▶ 17

There are two pictures on the right wall, and the couch is under them. There's a TV opposite the couch, and there's a plant next to the TV. There's a large rug under the couch. The family is in front of the window. The parents are behind the children.

▶ 18

I = Interviewer, A = Andy Torbet
(The words of Andy Torbet are spoken by an actor.)
I: Hello. Today, I'm in the north of Scotland. We're next to a mountain. It's very beautiful, but it's very cold. I'm here with Andy Torbet. Andy, are you from Scotland?
A: Yes, I am. I'm from Aberdeen.
I: Now Andy, you're a professional climber and you've got a backpack with you today. What's usually in your backpack?
A: Well, this is my hat. It's good because it's cold today, but it's also important when it's hot because of the sun.
I: I see. And what's this here?
A: It's a first-aid kit. It's always in my backpack.
I: Mm. Good idea. And what's that in your hand?
A: It's my camera. I take it everywhere. And these are my climbing shoes.
I: Right. And over there. What are those?
A: My gloves.
I: Right, they *are* important today! OK. So we've got everything. Let's start climbing.
A: Sure. Let's go.

▶ 19

1 maps
2 bottles
3 hats
4 lives
5 cities
6 lunches
7 chairs
8 women

▶ 26

1 It costs three dollars and twenty-five cents.
2 The couch is four hundred and ninety-nine euros.
3 Your ticket is two hundred and eighty yen.

▶ 27

1
A: Hello. Can I help you?
B: Yes. These bags are nice, but they're very small. Are there different sizes?
A: Yes, there are. … These ones are large.
B: Right. Is there a medium size?
A: No. Only two sizes.
B: OK. And are there other colors?
A: Yes, these ones are red.
B: Oh, yes, those are nice! How much are they?
A: They're nineteen dollars and thirty-five cents.
2
A: Hello, can I help you?
B: Yes, I'd like a coffee, please.
A: Large or small?
B: A large one, please.
A: That's three dollars and fifty cents.
3
A: Hello, can I help you?
B: Yes, I'd like a ball, please.
A: A soccer ball? A tennis ball?
B: Sorry, a soccer ball.
A: Well, the soccer balls are over here.
B: Are they all black and white?
A: Um, no. There are a few different colors.
B: Is there a red one?
A: No, there isn't … sorry.
B: Oh. OK, that green one, please.
A: This one?
B: Yes, please. How much is it?
A: It's twenty-one dollars.

Unit 3

▶ 29

Flinders Street train station is in the center of Melbourne, Australia. These clocks show the times of the trains. Every day of the week, over 100,000 people walk under them. It's the most famous place in the city. When people in Melbourne say, "Meet me under the clocks," everyone knows what they mean.

▶ 30

1 It's six o'clock.
2 It's half past three.
3 It's twenty-five past nine.
4 It's quarter to four.
5 It's three minutes past two.
6 It's two minutes to twelve.

▶ 32

J = Journalist, S = Student
J: Do you have a car in New York City?
S: No, I don't. I ride my bike everywhere.
J: Really? Where do you live?
S: In downtown Manhattan.
J: Is it expensive?
S: Yes, it is. Well, the stores are expensive, but there are lots of free places like art galleries and museums.
J: Sounds great. Do you like art?
S: Yes, I do. And I like the theater. This city has great theaters!
J: I'm sure. And what do you do?

S: I'm a college student, and I work in a restaurant at lunchtime. It's popular with tourists, so it's crowded every day.

J: So you're very busy! What time do you finish work?

S: At about three o'clock. After work I go home or in the summer, I go to a park. I really like Central Park. It's beautiful and quiet. I often meet friends there

▶ **33**

1

Beverly Goodman is a marine archaeologist, and she works for *National Geographic*. She has an office, but she doesn't work there very often. She usually works on her boat in the Mediterranean, and looks under the sea for objects from the past.

2

Samuel Diaz is seventeen. It's his last year at school and he has exams soon. Next year he wants to travel around the world, so on weekends he works in a store for extra money.

3

James Harding is a tour guide in London. He doesn't live in London, but he takes tourists around the downtown area. James speaks English, French, and Japanese, so he works with tourists from France and Japan.

▶ **37**

T = Tourist, G = Guide

T: Hello. We'd like to go to the aquarium. Is it near here?

G: It's about fifteen minutes away, but you go past some interesting places on the way. So look at this map. Go straight up Decatur Street and then up Marietta Street. Go across Spring Street and take the first street on the right. Centennial Olympic Park is on the corner. It's very nice. Go past the park and turn left. On the right you can see the World of Coca-Cola.

T: Oh, that sounds interesting.

G: Yes, it is. Go past it and the aquarium is on your right.

T: Great. Thanks a lot.

Unit 4

▶ **38**

1

Well, in my free time I go shopping. I go every Saturday with friends, and we go to the city center. It's fun!

2

After work, I go to the gym. I go about three times a week. After a long day with lots of other people, it's nice to go on your own, and it's good for you, of course.

3

In my free time, I go fishing with my brother. We get up early in the morning and drive to some quiet and beautiful places. It's very relaxing.

▶ **41**

Norbert Rosing's photos of animals are famous. His photos are often in *National Geographic* magazine or on the website. A lot of his photos are of polar bears in the Arctic. Norbert goes to the Arctic once a year. He always goes in the summer. He's sometimes there for a few weeks and sometimes for a few months. He likes the Arctic because there aren't many people and it's one of the last places in the world with no roads. He usually goes by snowmobile and by boat. Between August and November, you can see polar bears every day. Also, in the summer the sun shines twenty-four hours a day

in the Arctic, so Norbert can work at night. In fact, he takes the best photos at night. He rarely works during the day, so he has a lot of free time. He never sleeps at night, so he sleeps for part of the day. Then he reads books, plays video games, or goes for a walk. He's rarely bored!

▶ **45**

T = Travel adviser, S = Student

T: Hello, Volunteer Work. Can I help you?

S: Yes, hello. I'd like some information about your volunteer jobs. I'm a student and I want to travel next year. Do you have any interesting jobs?

T: Sure. We have a job for English teachers. Are you good at teaching?

S: Um, I don't know. I can speak English well, but what other jobs are there?

T: Can you write? There's an English newspaper in Bolivia. They need journalists. But it's for eighteen months.

S: No, I can't go for eighteen months. And I'm not very good at writing. Is there anything else?

T: Do you like animals?

S: Yes, I love them!

T: Well, we have a job in Zambia. It's with lion cubs.

S: Wow! That sounds interesting. What's the job exactly?

Unit 5

▶ **47**

I have a great job because I travel to different countries—I meet new people and visit new places. I really love traveling because I taste lots of different types of food. So when I arrive in a new city, I always go to the local restaurants and cafés. At the moment I'm in Oaxaca. It's one of my favorite places for food. I especially like the street food there. All the street cooks make the food by hand, and then they cook it on a real fire, so when you walk up the street, you can smell the food from the different stalls. Local Mexican tortillas are the best. The cooks serve the tortillas with a local hot sauce. They taste delicious. I can eat them at any time of day—for breakfast, lunch, or dinner!

▶ **49**

1

This is kabsa. It's a popular dish in my country and also in other countries such as Yemen. You need some chicken, although some people make it with fish. Cook the chicken with an onion, some salt and pepper, and other spices. You can add some tomatoes as well. We eat it with rice. I put some nuts and raisins on the top, and sometimes some eggs. It tastes delicious.

2

Ceviche is popular in Peru, but also in countries like Chile. It's easy to make. It's fish, but you don't cook it. You put some juice from a lemon on the fish and this "cooks" it. Sometimes we eat it with onions and maybe some salad as well. You eat it cold.

3

Spaghetti Bolognese is a famous dish all over the world, but the real Bolognese comes from my city of Bologna in Italy. Our city's dish is pasta with Bolognese sauce. People put different things in the sauce, and every Italian has their favorite recipe. For example, some people use carrots. I don't use carrots, but you always need some meat, some onions, and some tomatoes. You usually eat it hot, but when we have some left, I eat it cold for lunch the next day.

▶ 50

A: I'd like to make chicken curry this evening. What do you think?

B: Sounds good.

A: OK, well, we need some chicken. Can you buy a kilo when you go to the supermarket?

B: Sure.

A: And we need some tomatoes.

B: Right. And we don't have any onions. I'll get some. Is there any rice?

A: Yeah, I think there's some rice in the cabinet.

B: OK. And I'll buy some cooking oil. So, we need some chicken, tomatoes, onions, and oil. Anything else?

▶ 52

V = Vendor, C = Customer

V: Hello, can I help you?

C: Yes. I'd like some bananas, please.

V: These are nice and fresh.

C: OK.

V: How many bananas do you want?

C: Six, please.

V: OK. Anything else?

C: Yes. I need some rice.

V: How much rice do you want? A kilo?

C: Yes, a kilo, please.

V: Here you go. And what about some of this sauce? It's local.

C: Is it hot?

V: Yeah, it's hot, but it goes with anything.

C: Yes. OK.

V: How many do you want?

C: Just one bottle … oh actually, two. I can take one back to Korea. And I also need some bread. Do you sell any?

V: No, but there's a place on the other side of the market. So, that's six bananas, a kilo of rice, two bottles of sauce.

▶ 54

A = Man, B = Woman, C = Waiter

A: This is a nice place.

B: Yes, it's one of my favorite restaurants. They have great food here.

C: Good afternoon. How are you today?

B: We're great, thanks.

C: Great. My name's Arthur and I'm your waiter today. So here is the menu. Can I get you anything to drink first?

A: Um, I'd like a bottle of water, please. Sparkling.

B: Yes, good idea.

C: One bottle or two?

B: One between us, thanks.

C: OK.

B: The garlic bread is really good here.

A: Yes, it looks good. But I don't want an appetizer. I'll have a seafood pizza.

B: Really? Are you sure?

A: Well, I'd also like dessert …

B: Right.

C: Hi. Here's your water. Are you ready to order?

A: Yes, I'd like the seafood pizza.

C: OK. Good choice.

B: And I'd like a mushroom and spinach burger.

C: OK. Any appetizers?

B: No, thanks. That's all.

C: OK. So one seafood pizza and a mushroom and spinach burger.

[…]

A: That was delicious.

B: Good. Are you ready for dessert?

A: Actually, I'm full.

C: Hi. How was your meal?

B: Very good, thanks.

C: Can I get you anything else? Some dessert?

A: No, thanks. Could we have the check, please?

C: Oh, sure.

Unit 6

▶ 56

During the nineteen seventies and eighties, Chris Porsz took lots of black and white photographs of local people in his city. Thirty years later, Chris looked for the same people by putting the old photos on his website and in the newspaper. Donna and Steven saw their photo from 1981 and contacted Chris. It shows them as children in front of their old family house. They don't live in the house now, but they live in the same city. They returned to the street and Chris took the second photo in 2015.

▶ 57

1	the nineteen seventies	1970 to 1979
2	the end of the twentieth century	1989 to 1999
3	the beginning of the twenty-first century	2002
4	the sixties	1960 to 1969
5	the nineteenth century	1800 to 1899

▶ 60

The Mustang region is in the Himalayan mountains of northern Nepal. It's famous for its ancient caves. Humans began living in the caves about a thousand years ago. Many people lived in them until the fifteenth century, before they built houses and moved to towns. The caves were warm and dry, and they were safe because of their location.

Even today you can find people who lived in the caves. This woman, Yandu Bista, was born in a cave and grew up there with her family. Life was difficult. They didn't have water in the cave, so she went to the river every day and brought water up the mountain. In the end, her family moved to the town, but she says, "I liked living in a cave better."

▶ 61

1 Humans began living in the caves about a thousand years ago.

2 Many people lived in them until the fifteenth century.

3 They built houses and moved to towns.

4 Yandu Bista was born in a cave.

5 She grew up there with her family.

6 They didn't have water in the cave.

7 She went to the river every day and brought water up the mountain.

▶ 62

A: Hi. How was your weekend?

B: It was great, thanks.

A: What did you do?

B: I went to Osaka.

A: Oh, did you go shopping?

B: No, I didn't. I went to a museum.

A: Oh, OK. What did you see there?

B: An exhibition about the lives of people from the fifteenth century. It was fantastic!

A: Did you go with anyone?

B: I didn't go with anyone, but I met an old friend afterward for lunch.

▶ 64

1

A: Hi! How was your evening?

B: It was great, thanks.

A: Where did you go?

B: To a new café in town. We ate a burger and then walked along the river.

A: Who were you with?

B: My brother and his friend from when he was at school.

2

A: How was your weekend?

B: Fantastic! My friend had a party at his house. It was great.

A: Was it his birthday?

B: No, he passed his college exams, so he was really happy!

A: That's nice. Were there many people there?

B: Yes, there were. I met his family for the first time. It was fun.

3

A: I'm so tired.

B: Why? What did you do last night?

A: Not much. I stayed up late and watched a movie. It was kind of boring, so I went to bed, but I couldn't fall asleep for a long time. Did you have a good evening?

B: It was fine. I went to the gym, and I was in bed by ten.

Unit 7

▶ 66

This photo is by Manoj Chaudhary. He took the photo of this tiny ladybug on a hot day in spring. The grass was very green and he liked the differences in the colors and the sizes. The red ladybug has a slow, long journey as it travels along the grass to a flower at the end. The journey looks very difficult for the ladybug.

▶ 69

James Cameron is a Hollywood movie director. He is famous for lots of different movies. *Titanic* is the most popular movie by James Cameron, and *Avatar* was the most expensive, but he also makes documentaries. *Deepsea Challenge* is a documentary about his journey into the Mariana Trench. The Mariana Trench is the deepest place in the ocean. It's eleven kilometers under the sea and the journey to the bottom took over two hours. Cameron traveled in a one-man submarine with special lights, because the Mariana Trench is also the darkest place on Earth. Cameron filmed many new and strange kinds of sea life on his journey, including fish like the fangtooth. The fangtooth has the biggest teeth of any fish for its size. When Cameron landed on the bottom of the Mariana Trench, he also found 68 new species of animals.

▶ 70

A: I want to visit Ireland in July, but I only have ten days. What are the best places to visit?

B: Well, Dublin is the most famous city in Ireland, and of course it's also the most popular with tourists.

A: But I don't want to see lots of other tourists. What's the most beautiful city?

B: In my opinion, Galway is the prettiest. In terms of size, the city is smaller than Dublin, but it's next to the water, so there are great views.

A: How cold is it?

B: July is the hottest month, so it's OK.

A: What about transportation? What's the best way to travel around?

B: Buses are cheaper, but I think a car is better than public transportation when you are a tourist. With a car you can stop and see lots of different places on the way.

▶ 72

1

A: Hello, can I change one hundred dollars into euros?

B: Yes, of course. One moment. One hundred dollars is eighty-nine euros.

A: OK, can you give me the euros in tens?

B: Sure. Ten, twenty, thirty, forty, fifty, sixty, seventy, eighty …

2

A: Would you like to buy this?

B: Yes, please. And could I have it in a bag, please?

A: Certainly. That's twelve euros.

B: Here's my credit card.

A: Oh, I'm sorry, but I can only take cash.

B: Oh, no! I don't have any.

A: Don't worry, there's a bank with an ATM around the corner.

B: Oh, thanks.

3

A: Oh, no! It's two dollars for parking. I only have a ten-dollar bill.

B: So what's the problem?

A: The machine takes coins. Could I borrow some money?

B: I'm afraid I don't have any change. But look! It takes credit cards.

A: I don't have a credit card with me.

B: It's OK. I do.

A: Great. I can pay you back later.

B: Don't worry! It's on me!

Unit 8

▶ 73

I was in the city of Iloilo in the Philippines last month. I wanted to see the city's annual Dinagyang Festival. The festival is always on the fourth Sunday in January. It's the most famous festival in the Philippines and thousands of local people and tourists come to the city. Groups of local people wear colorful clothes and make-up. You can hear music everywhere, and people dance through the streets. I also ate lots of local food—it was delicious!

▶ 77

A: I have some photographs here from my vacation.

B: Oh, let me see.

A: These two are from Girona in Catalonia. The city has a big festival every year.

B: What are they doing in this one?

A: Oh, this is in the afternoon. They're building a human tower.

B: I see. Why are they wearing different colored shirts?

A: They are in different teams. The people at the bottom put their arms around each other and other people push them forward with their hands. Then four people climb up and stand with their feet on the other people's shoulders. And then the next four go up until they have a tower.

B: Wow! Do they ever fall down?

A: I didn't see them fall down, but people at the bottom have to be strong to hold onto the other people's legs.

B: And what's happening here?

A: This is in the evening. These dancers were wearing costumes with big masks over their heads. I don't know how they were able to dance!

B: The faces are amazing. They have huge eyes and big mouths.

A: That's right. My favorite is this one. He doesn't have any hair, but he has a big black beard. He was very funny.

▶ 79

Reinier Gerritsen is one of my favorite photographers. He's from the Netherlands, but you can often see his photos around the world—in magazines and sometimes in galleries. I have some books by him as well. His photos are very interesting. They often show scenes of everyday life. This one is on the New York subway. It's early morning, so I think most of the people are commuting to work. They're all standing close together, but they aren't talking to one another. Well, on the right, the man and woman are talking, but the others aren't. The woman in the middle is reading her book. And in front of her the woman with blonde hair is listening to music. Then the other blonde woman on the left is watching her. I'm not sure what she's thinking, but she looks a bit sad. Oh, and look at the other woman at the back. She's looking straight at the photographer. I take the train to work every day, but I never think about the other people. I like the photo because I don't normally look at people very closely, but Gerritsen does.

Unit 9

▶ 81

This photo is in Istanbul in Turkey. The woman is in an art gallery, but she isn't looking at a painting. She's watching a short video. The video lasts fifteen minutes and then it plays again. The people in the video are at a theater and they're watching a movie. There's a man standing in the audience, but I don't know why.

▶ 83

C = Charles, I = Isabella

C: Hey! Isabella.

I: Hi, Charles. Are you enjoying the festival? I'm going to buy a ticket for the next movie. It's called *Mother*. Are you going to see it, too? It starts in ten minutes.

C: No, I'm not, but where are you going afterward? Didier, Monica, and I are going to have dinner at a Japanese restaurant. Do you want to come?

I: Sorry, but I'm not going to stay out late tonight. I'm tired.

C: OK. No problem.

I: Oh, I have to go. Bye.

C: Bye. See you later.

▶ 84

1 We're going to see a movie at the new theater.
2 I'm not going to buy a ticket. It's too expensive.
3 Are you going to buy the tickets online or at the theater?
4 Where are you going to sit?
5 I'm not going to watch the movie. It starts at midnight.
6 Where are you going after the movie?

▶ 86

What do you do when you get home in the evening? Perhaps you turn on the TV to watch a new drama series or your favorite comedy show. Or, if you are a teenager or young adult, you probably watch your favorite shows online. That's what the results showed in a survey of teenagers and young adults.

The survey found that people aged 13 to 24 watch 21 hours of video on YouTube or online TV, and only 8.2 hours a week on normal broadcast TV. 81% prefer watching videos online because you can watch them when you want to, and 69% think online shows are better.

So, what is better about the shows? With teenagers, YouTube videos of other people talking about video games, fashion, movies, and music are very popular. In some popular videos, people open boxes to talk about the products inside. And many people watch "How to" videos to learn how to do something new, like playing a new musical instrument or making things.

So, with so many people watching videos online, are we going to watch TV at all in the future?

▶ 87

Last week, I spoke to Adrian Seymour to find out about his movies. Adrian makes movies about nature and animals. This year he's going to Honduras to make a movie about the rain forest. He's going in the summer to film wildlife and then he's going back to his office in the fall to edit the movie. So it's going to take about six months in total. Then in the winter, when he's finished the movie, he's going to Indonesia to take a vacation!

▶ 89

R = Rachel, A = Adriana

1

R: Hi, Adriana. It's Rachel.

A: Hi. Sorry, but I'm at work. I can't really talk now.

R: I know, but I have two tickets for *Phantom of the Opera*. My friend works at the theater and sometimes he gets free tickets. Would you like to come?

A: Thanks, I'd love to. When is it?

R: Tonight!

A: Tonight?

R: Yes, are you free?

A: I'm sorry, but I'm working late tonight.

R: Oh. Can't you ask your manager?

A: I can try.

R: OK. Bye.

2

R: Hello?

A: Hi, Rachel. It's me again. Do you still have the extra ticket?

R: Yes. Do you want to go?

A: Yes, my manager said I can finish early. What time does it start?

R: At seven-thirty, so let's meet at seven outside the theater.

A: That's great. See you at seven.

Unit 10

▶ 91

The city of Yangzhou is famous as a city of learning and culture. Some of China's most famous artists and writers came from here. Now, the city also has the most modern bookshop in the world. When you enter, you feel like you are in a river of books. The books are on the walls, above you, and below you. As you walk toward the center, there are separate rooms with books on every subject: from geography to history, math to chemistry, and biology to children's literature.

▶ 93

1
A: Have you done your homework?
B: No, I haven't.
2
A: Has Peter finished his exams?
B: Yes, he's finished all of them and now he's waiting for his results.
3
A: Have you ever studied Arabic?
B: No, I've never studied Arabic.

▶ 94

Do you always forget names and faces? And how many numbers can you remember? Not many? Well, meet Nelson Dellis. Nelson can listen to the names of 99 people, look at their faces, and memorize every one of them. He can also hear 300 different numbers and then repeat them. Because of his memory, Nelson has won the USA Memory Championship four times. He won the competition in 2011, 2012, 2014, and again in 2015. The USA Memory Championships are like the Olympic Games, but the athletes train their brains and take different memory tests. So how does Nelson do it? He says he doesn't have a special memory. In the past, he often forgot names, dates, and numbers, but a few years ago, he studied memory techniques and practiced for hours and hours every day. Since then, he's won many competitions and has taught his techniques to people all over the US.

▶ 96

R = Richard, O = Omar
R: Hello, Omarox Engineering.
O: Hello, Richard. This is Omar.
R: Hello, Omar. Where are you?
O: I'm in Kuala Lumpur.
R: Great. What time is it there?
O: Er, it's three o'clock.
R: Is that three in the morning?
O: No, in the afternoon. I've just arrived but my cell phone isn't working. I'm calling from a telephone at the hotel.
R: I see.
O: So I want to give you the number of my hotel for the next two days. It's the Ancasa Hotel.
R: One moment. I need a pen. OK. Sorry, was that the Encasa Hotel?
O: No, the Ancasa Hotel. A for apple.
R: Oh, sorry. A-N-C-A-S-A.
O: And the number is six oh three, two one six nine, double two double six.
R: So that's six zero three, two one six nine, two two, six six.
O: That's right.
R: Is there anything else?
O: Yes, one thing. Have you called our colleagues about tomorrow?
R: Yes, I have. They can meet you at three.
O: Good, thanks. I also need the designs, but I can't check email on my phone.
R: I've put them on the company website so you can download them.
O: Oh, that's great. Thanks. Bye for now.

▶ 99

V = Voicemail, R = Richard
V: Hello. This is the Ancasa Hotel. Please leave a message after the tone.
R: Hello. This is Richard Sanger calling. That's S-A-N-G-E-R. This is a message for Doctor Omar Al Harbia. Please tell him I can't email the designs, so they are on the designer's website. He can download them from this address. It's STK-design—that's S-T-K dash design—dot com slash e dash one, once again that's S-T-K dash design dot com slash e dash one. And can he call me back on my home number? That's 0770-234-3785. Or email me at rich-sanger@gmail.com. Please give him this message before he leaves this morning. It's urgent.

▶ 100

1 Can you call Jim back this evening?
2 I'd like you to email the date of the meeting.
3 Can you meet Mrs. Rivers at the airport?
4 Would you book a room for two nights at the hotel?
5 Can you buy two new cell phones?

Unit 11

▶ 101

When I was nineteen, I took a year off between high school and college. I saved some money and then went backpacking around the world. My favorite memory is when I was traveling in the desert in Jordan and I met some local people. They were called Bedouin and they lived in tents in the desert. They were very friendly and invited me for tea. It was a hot afternoon, but they put a table outside and made hot tea. We all sat in the middle of the desert, drank tea, and watched the sun go down. It was wonderful!

▶ 103

1 You have to drive on the left.
2 Guests have to leave before 11 a.m.
3 Guests don't have to pay.
4 Business class passengers don't have to wait.
5 All passengers have to show their passport.

▶ 104

I = Interviewer, J = Jan
I: Hello, and welcome to your weekly podcast from indietravelinfo.com. With me today is travel writer Jan Lanting with more suggestions for the independent traveler. Jan, today I want to start with your advice for travelers this year. Can you give us some suggestions for good places to visit?
J: Yes. First of all, you don't have to leave the US. Last week, I took a short break on my own to Rockport on the coast of Maine. It's a beautiful place.
I: What's the best way to travel there?
J: You can take a bus, but I think you should rent a car. Then you can drive along the coast.
I: What's the weather like at this time of year?
J: Kind of cold, and sometimes it rains, so you should take a coat.
I: I think I'd prefer to go somewhere warmer!
J: OK, well you should fly to Malaysia. It's always quite hot there.
I: Sounds great. With a place like Malaysia, should I book a hotel before I go?

J: In the big cities, hotels are often busy, so you should book in advance. But in the countryside, it's no problem. You can always find a room. I also recommend taking a tour into the jungle.

I: The jungle?!

J: That's right. You can see lots of amazing animals and plants.

I: Should I go with a tour guide?

J: Yes, you should! It's dangerous on your own.

I: Sure. Now for our final destination. The Arctic?

J: That's right. The Arctic.

I: Isn't it cold?

J: Yes, it is. Also, you shouldn't go in the winter because it's dark, but in the summer the days are longer and it's a little warmer, so you should go then.

I: But how do you get there?! Should I go on my own or with a tour?

J: You have to go with a travel company. When I went, I took a cruise ship from Norway and slept in a nice cabin on the ship.

▶ 106

A: That looks interesting.

B: Yes, it's a travel brochure.

A: Oh, really?

B: Yes, I have a month in South America so I'm looking at places to go.

A: I went there last year. It's an amazing part of the world. I went on a cruise all the way from Brazil to Argentina. You should go on that.

B: Yes, but I'm interested in the wildlife.

A: How about visiting the Andes? That was part of my bus tour in Chile.

B: But the disadvantage is that there are lots of other people on a bus tour. I like traveling on my own.

A: But the advantage is that you see more with a tour guide. And you visit places other tourists don't normally go to.

B: Hmm. Maybe you're right.

A: Can I make a suggestion? If you have a month, why don't you go on a tour for two weeks and then you could travel on your own afterward?

B: Actually, that's a really good idea.

Unit 12

▶ 109

This Inuit man lives on Baffin Island in Canada. It's in the Arctic, about two and a half thousand kilometers from the North Pole. Ira Block took the photo, and the Inuit man is also holding another photo by Ira Block. Ira took this second photo in the US state of South Carolina, which is about two and a half thousand kilometers from the Equator. Ira took the two photos because about fifty-six million years ago, the Arctic probably looked like South Carolina today. At that time, the temperature in the Arctic was around twenty-five degrees Celsius. Nowadays, the average temperature in the Arctic is around minus ten degrees.

▶ 111

1   I will visit space in my lifetime.
2   I think I'll learn Spanish.

3   Will you visit me one day?
4   The percentage of people in the countryside will decrease.
5   I don't think there'll be more snow this winter.
6   It'll rain here tonight.

▶ 112

Humans seem to have been everywhere on Earth. So are there any places left? Well, if you're looking for an adventure, here are my top five unexplored places.
First of all, there are two lakes. The Black Hole of Andros is in the Bahamas in the Atlantic Ocean. The water temperature is 36 degrees Celsius, and it's very dark, so it's difficult to see what's in there.
My second lake is Lake Vostok in Antarctica. Lake Vostok is 14,000 square kilometers and freezing cold. Unfortunately, it's been under a sheet of ice for 15 million years. The ice is 3.7 kilometers deep, so it's impossible to get to, though scientists have taken water from it.
If you're a climber, there are lots of mountains in the world that nobody has climbed yet. For example, there's Mount Dinpernalason in the east of the Himalayan mountains. It's 6,135 meters high.
Or you could explore the Merume Mountains in Guyana in South America. But they are at the end of the 500-kilometer-long Mazaruni river, so that's for someone who likes boats and maybe swimming—it's one of the most dangerous rivers in the world.
Then there are also the Foja Mountains in a forest of Papua New Guinea. The forest is 8,100 square kilometers in size, and the bad news is that there are no maps of the region so you'll have to make one while you're there!

▶ 114

Good morning, and thank you for coming. My name's Davi, and I'm from Brazil. Today, I'd like to talk about an important day in my year called Earth Day.
Earth Day began on April 22nd in 1970. Over 20 million people went to Earth Day in different cities across the US. There were politicians, teachers, artists, and musicians. Since that day in 1970, Earth Day has become famous all over the world.
Nowadays, more than 175 countries have an Earth Day. Lots of people do different things. Last year, people in China planted 600,000 new trees. In New Orleans in the US, they put 300,000 energy efficient bulbs into houses. And finally, in my country, lots of people picked up trash in the cities and in the countryside.
In conclusion, I really think Earth Day is important. Next year, I hope you will do something on Earth Day. Thank you very much for listening.

NATIONAL GEOGRAPHIC
L E A R N I N G

Life Student's Book 2, **2nd Edition**
John Hughes, Helen Stephenson, Paul Dummett

Vice President, Editorial Director: John McHugh

Publisher: Andrew Robinson

Senior Development Editor: Derek Mackrell

Development Editor: Melissa Pang

Director of Global Marketing: Ian Martin

Senior Product Marketing Manager: Caitlin Thomas

Media Researcher: Rebecca Ray, Leila Hishmeh

Senior IP Analyst: Alexandra Ricciardi

IP Project Manager: Carissa Poweleit

Senior Director, Production: Michael Burggren

Production Manager: Daisy Sosa

Content Project Manager: Beth McNally

Manufacturing Planner: Mary Beth Hennebury

Art Director: Brenda Carmichael

Cover Design: Lisa Trager

Text design: emc design ltd.

Compositor: Doubleodesign Ireland, Ltd

American Adaptation: Kasia McNabb

For product information and technology assistance, contact us at
Cengage Learning Customer & Sales Support, cengage.com/contact

For permission to use material from this text or product, submit all requests online at **cengage.com/permissions**
Further permissions questions can be emailed to
permissionrequest@cengage.com

Student Book + App: 978-1-337-90563-3
Student Book + App + My Life Online: 978-1-337-90569-5

National Geographic Learning
20 Channel Center Street
Boston, MA 02210
USA

National Geographic Learning, a Cengage Learning Company, has a mission to bring the world to the classroom and the classroom to life. With our English language programs, students learn about their world by experiencing it. Through our partnerships with National Geographic and TED Talks, they develop the language and skills they need to be successful global citizens and leaders.

Locate your local office at **international.cengage.com/region**

Visit National Geographic Learning online at **NGL.Cengage.com/ELT**
Visit our corporate website at **www.cengage.com**

CREDITS
Although every effort has been made to contact copyright holders before publication, this has not always been possible. If notified, the publisher will undertake to rectify any errors or omissions at the earliest opportunity.
Text: p9 Source: 'Interview with David Doubilet', reprinted with permission; p10 Source: 'Interview with Beverley Joubert', reprinted with permission; p15 Source: 'The Face of Seven Billion', National Geographic, March 2011; p22 Source: 'Interview with Andrew Torbet', reprinted with permission; p27 Source: 'A Word of Parts', by Peter Gwin, National Geographic, February 2005; p34 Source: 'Pictures: Twelve Car-Free City Zones', National Geographic, November 16, 2011; p46 Source: 'A Thing or Two About Twins', by Peter Miller, National Geographic, January 2012; p48 Source: 'Interview with Norbert Rosing', reprinted with permission; p51 Source: 'Extreme Photo of the Week: Highlining', National Geographic; Source: 'Extreme Photo of the Week: Mountain Biking', National Geographic; Source: 'Extreme Photo of the Week: Cliff Diving', National Geographic; p60 Source: 'Top 10 Food Markets' National Geographic, September 13, 2001, from the National Geographic Book 'Food Journeys of a Lifetime'; p62 Source: 'An Eater's Guide to Food Labels', by Georgina Gustin, National Geographic: The Plate, May 11, 2016; p70–71 Source: 'She's Right on the Money', by Whitney Dangerfield, National Geographic, October 2005; p72 Source: 'Sky Caves of Nepal', National Geographic, October 2012; p74 Sources: 'Has the UK Lost Its Inner Bridget Jones', Penheaven.co.uk and 'Learning British Timeline', Bl.uk; p84 Source: 'Great Migrations', National Geographic, November 2012; p86 Source: 'Destinations: Columbia', National Geographic Traveler, articles by Michael Parker Stainback, October 10, 2016; Emma Thomson, August 24, 2015; p94 Source: 'Rags to Riches: A Fashionable Way to Empower Poor Filipinos', by Gary Strauss, National Geographic, November 9, 2016; p99 Source: 'Artworks', Jeongmeeyoon.com; p106 Sources: '14th Annual Tallgrass Film Festival Oct 12-16, 2016', Prod5.agileticketing.net and 'Tallgrass Film Association', Tallgrassfilm.org; p108 Source: 'Acumen Report Constant Content', Sanbox.break.com; p108–109, 173 Source: 'Interview with Adrian Seymour', reprinted with permission; p120, 154-156 Source: 'Memory', by Deborah Neffa, National Geographic, November 2007; p121 Source: 'Mental Athletes Increase Brain Size in 15th US Memory Championship', by Nicole Glass, National Geographic, March 28, 2012; p135 Source: 'Continental Divide', by Costas Christ, National Geographic Traveler, March/April 2012; p153, p154 Source: 'Photographer: Joel Sartore', National Geographic.
Cover: VCG/Getty Images.
Photos: 6 (t) © Michael Melford/National Geographic Creative; 6 (ml) © Frans Lanting/National Geographic Creative; 6 (mr) John Michaels/Alamy Stock Photo; 6 (b) © Winfield Parks/National Geographic Creative; 7 (l) © Ira Block/National Geographic Creative; 7 (r) Mike Goldwater/Alamy Stock Photo; 8 (tl) © David Doubilet/National Geographic Creative; 8 (tm) © Sarah Leen/National Geographic Creative; 8 (tr) © Michael William/Shutterstock.com; 8 (mtl) © Bill Hinton Photography/Getty Images; 8 (mtm) © Tino Soriano/National Geographic Creative; 8 (mtr) © Chris Porsz; 8 (mbl) © Manoj Chaudhary; 8 (mbm) Mario Babiera/Alamy Stock Photo; 8 (mbr) © Volkan Güney; 8 (bl) © Shao Feng/Li Xiang/X+Living (www.xl-muse.com); 8 (bm) © Gary Arndt; 8 (br) © Ira Block/National Geographic Creative; 9 © David Doubilet/National Geographic Creative; 10 © Beverly Joubert/National Geographic Creative; 12 © Kenneth Garrett/National Geographic Creative; 14 © Fritz Hoffmann/National Geographic Creative; 15 © Bryan Christie Design LLC; 16 © Photofusion/Getty Images; 17 (t) © sturti/Getty Images; 17 (b) © Junial Enterprises/Shutterstock.com; 18 Gavin Hellier/Alamy Stock Photo; 21 © Sarah Leen/National Geographic Creative; 22 (all) © Courtesy of the artist Yeondoo Jung; 24 (backpack) © bogdan ionescu/Shutterstock.com; 24 (first aid kit) © Elnur/Shutterstock.com; 24 (water bottle) © Edi Eco/Shutterstock.com; 24 (camera) © Bill Fehr/Shutterstock.com; 24 (pens) © Olga Kovalenko/Shutterstock.com; 24 (boots) © George Dolgik/Shutterstock.com; 24 (phone) © Maxx-Studio/Shutterstock.com; 24 (hat) © Kletr/Shutterstock.com; 24 (knife) © Galcka/Shutterstock.com; 24 (gloves) © Nadezhda Bolotina/Shutterstock.com; 24 (torch) © Nataliya Hora/Shutterstock.com; 24 (map) © HomeStudio/Shutterstock.com; 24 (right col: t, bl) © Andy Torbet; 24 (right col: br) © Chris Packham; 27 (t, b) © Ignacio Ayestaran/National Geographic Creative; 28 Matthew Kyte/Alamy Stock Photo; 30 Daniel Slavov/Alamy Stock Photo; 31 © Vimeo/Ted Chung; 32 © The Athenaeum; 33 © Michael William/Shutterstock.com; 34 (t) © Jon Hicks/Getty Images; 34 (ml) © Nadiia Gerbish/Shutterstock.com;

Printed in China by CTPS
Print Number: 02   Print Year: 2019

34 (mr) travelbild-asia/Alamy Stock Photo; 34 (b) © Tyrone Turner/National Geographic Creative; 36 Courtesy of Beverly Goodman; 39 © Sean Gallagher/National Geographic Creative; 40 © Joseph Sohm/Shutterstock.com; 41 (l) © Julia Shepeleva/Shutterstock.com; 41 (r) © Andrew Watson/Getty Images; 42 Blackout Concepts/Alamy Stock Photo; 44 RM Asia/Alamy Stock Photo; 45 © Bill Hinton Photography/ Getty Images; 46 (t) © Helen and Morna Mulgray; 46 (m) © Barry Brecheisen/Getty Images; 46 (b) © Mike Marsland/WireImage/Getty Images; 47 © Kzenon/Alamy Stock Photo; 48 (t, b) © Norbert Rosing/National Geographic Creative; 51 (t) © Pascal Pochard-Casabianca/AFP/GettyImages; 51 (m) Aurora Photos/Alamy Stock Photo; 51 (bl) © Caters News Agency Ltd; 51 (br) © Sylwia Duda/Getty Images; 52 © wizdata/Shutterstock.com; 53 (l) © StockLite/Shutterstock.com; 53 (r) © logoboom/Shutterstock.com; 54 Martin Godwin/Hulton Archive/Getty Images; 56 (l) © Helen and Morna Mulgray; 56 (m) © Barry Brecheisen/Getty Images; 56 (r) © Mike Marsland/WireImage/Getty Images; 57 © Tino Soriano/National Geographic Creative; 58 (1) © Oran Tantapakul/Fotolia.com; 58 (2) © Bianca/Fotolia.com; 58 (3) © Peter Polak/Fotolia.com; 58 (4) © Lorenzo Buttitta/Fotolia.com; 58 (5) © James Insogna/Fotolia.com; 58 (6) Westmacott/Alamy Stock Photo; 58 (7) © thongsee/Fotolia.com; 58 (8) © kritchanut/Fotolia.com; 58 (9) © leftleg/Fotolia.com; 58 (10) © studio_ms/Fotolia.com; 58 (11) © Aaron Amat/Fotolia.com; 58 (12) © Whitebox Media/Fotolia.com; 58 (13) © yakovlev/Fotolia. com; 58 (14) © Larisa Siverina/Fotolia.com; 58 (15) © Natika/Fotolia.com; 58 (16) © danheighton/Fotolia.com; 59 (l) © marco mayer/Shutterstock.com; 59 (m) Simon Reddy/Alamy Stock Photo; 59 (b) © Bon Appetit/Alamy Stock Photo; 60–61 Ian Dagnall/Alamy Stock Photo; 61 (5) Steve Cukrov/Shutterstock.com; 61 (7) mavo/Shutterstock.com; 63 (t) Diana Angstadt/Contributor/Getty Images; 63 (bl) Brian A. Jackson/Shutterstock.com; 63 (br) UrbanImages/Alamy Stock Photo; 64 © gilaxia/Getty Images; 65 (t) © J. Helgason/Shutterstock.com; 65 (ml) © AVAVA/Shutterstock.com; 65 (mm) © Marcell Mizik/ Shutterstock.com; 65 (mr) © stockyimages/Shutterstock.com; 65 (m) © stefanolunardi/Shutterstock.com; 65 (bm) © Yuri Arcurs/Shutterstock.com; 65 (br) © Tony Northrup/Shutterstock.com; 66 © Ira Block/National Geographic Creative; 68 (tl) © yakovlev/Fotolia.com; 68 (tm) © Oran Tantapakul/Fotolia.com; 68 (tr) © Larisa Siverina/Fotolia.com; 68 (bl) © thongsee/Fotolia.com; 68 (bm) © valery12283/Fotolia.com; 68 (br) © Natika/Fotolia.com; 69 (l, r) © Chris Porsz; 70 (tl, tr) © Nathalie Speliers Ufermann/Shutterstock.com; 70 (m) © Steve Stock/Alamy Stock Photo; 70 (b) © schankz/Shutterstock.com; 71 © Pigprox/Shutterstock.com; 72 (t, b) © Cory Richards/National Geographic Creative; 74 © Mike Theiss/National Geographic Creative; 75 (tl) Portrait of Samuel Pepys (1633–1703) 1666 (oil on canvas), National Portrait Gallery, London, UK. © John Hayls/Getty Images; 75 (b) © rzeszutko/Shutterstock.com; 77 © Cora Mueller/Shutterstock.com; 78 Carlos Mora/Alamy Stock Photo; 79 (all) © Tom, Dick & Debbie Productions Ltd/Cengage Learning; 80 (tl) © Nathalie Speliers Ufermann/Shutterstock.com; 80 (tm) © schankz/Shutterstock.com; 80 (tr) imageBROKER/Alamy Stock Photo; 80 (b) North Wind Picture Archives/Alamy Stock Photo; 81 © Manoj Chaudhary; 82 (tl) SPUTNIK/Alamy Stock Photo; 82 (tr) © Heiko Kiera/Shutterstock.com; 82 (b) © Brian J. Skerry/National Geographic Creative; 84 © Saul Loeb/AFP/Getty Images; 87 (t) Watchtheworld/Alamy Stock Photo; 87 (m) Bella Falk/Alamy Stock Photo; 87 (bl) Maxime Dube/Alamy Stock Photo; 87 (br) Yoram Lehmann/Getty Images; 88 Alex Segre/Alamy Stock Photo; 89 claudio zaccherini/Shutterstock.com; 90 © Michael Melford/National Geographic Creative; 92 © dedek/Shutterstock.com; 93 Mario Babiera/Alamy Stock Photo; 94 (1) © Dmitry Naumov/Shutterstock.com; 94 (2) © Hurst Photo/Shutterstock.com; 94 (3) © Tarzhanova/Shutterstock.com; 94 (4) © Africa Studio/Shutterstock.com; 94 (5) © elenovsky/Shutterstock.com; 94 (6) © alekleks/Shutterstock.com; 94 (7) © Dario Sabljak/Shutterstock.com; 94 (8) © SuperStock; 94 (9) © Alexlukin/Shutterstock.com; 94 (10, 18) © gogoiso/Shutterstock.com; 94 (11) © Olga Popova/Shutterstock.com; 94 (12) © zey/Shutterstock.com; 94 (13) © maewshooter/Shutterstock.com; 94 (14) © oksana2010/Shutterstock.com; 94 (15) © Tarzhanova/Shutterstock.com; 94 (16) © arka38/Shutterstock.com; 94 (17) Zoonar GmbH/Alamy Stock Photo; 95 © Rags2Riches, Inc.; 96 (t) © Carles Masó; 96 (inset) Wamodo/Alamy Stock Photo; 97 © Roy Toft/National Geographic Creative; 99 (l, r) © JeongMee Yoon; 100 © Reinier Gerritsen; 102 © Winfield Parks/National Geographic Creative; 104 (3) © Tarzhanova/Shutterstock.com; 104 (4) © Dario Sabljak/Shutterstock.com; 104 (7) © zey/Shutterstock.com; 104 (9) © Alexlukin/Shutterstock.com; 104 (b) Yavuz Sariyildiz/Alamy Stock Photo; 105 © Volkan Güney; 106 (tl) Moviestore collection Ltd/Alamy Stock Photo; 106 (tr) Everett Collection, Inc.; 106 (mtl) Collection Christophel/Alamy Stock Photo; 106 (mtr) AF archive/Alamy Stock Photo; 106 (mbl) © Ralph Lee Hopkins/National Geographic Creative; 106 (mbr) World History Archive/Alamy Stock Photo; 106 (bl) ScreenProd/Photononstop/Alamy Stock Photo; 106 (br) © Mary Evans/Ronald Grant/Everett Collection; 109 © Adrian Seymour; 111 (tl) © Art Directors & TRIP/Alamy Stock Photo; 111 (tr) The Blue Elephant; O Elefante Azul, 2002 (acrylic, metallic paint and ink on canvas), Milhazes, Beatriz (b.1960)/Private Collection/Photo © Christie's Images/Bridgeman Images; 111 (m) Hinczow Lakes in the Tatra Mountains, 1907 (oil on canvas), Witkiewicz, Stanislaw Ignacy (1885–1939)/Private Collection/Agra Art, Warsaw, Poland/Bridgeman Images; 111 (b) © V&A Images/Alamy Stock Photo; 112 © Kike Calvo/National Geographic Creative; 113 © Robert Harding Picture Library/National Geographic Creative; 116 (l) © Frans Lanting/National Geographic Creative; 116 (l) Zoonar GmbH/Alamy Stock Photo; 116 (m) © PhotoDisc/Getty Images; 116 (r) © Himanshu Saraf/Shutterstock.com; 117 © Shao Feng/Li Xiang/X+Living (www.xl-muse.com); 118 © NASA; 120–121 © Nelson Dellis; 122 Daniel Valla FRPS/Stockimo/Alamy Stock Photo; 123 © AP Photo/Michael Sohn/AP Images; 124 © Oliver Eltinger/Corbis; 126 Agencja FREE/Alamy Stock Photo; 129 © Gary Arndt; 130 (l) © Panoramic Stock Images/National Geographic Creative; 130 (r) Lazyllama/Alamy Stock Photo; 132 Glyn Thomas Photography/Alamy Stock Photo 134 © alysta/Shutterstock.com; 135 © Keenpress/National Geographic Creative; 136 © Edward Parker/Alamy Stock Photo; 138 Katie Garrod/Getty Images; 140 NG Images/Alamy Stock Photo; 141 © Ira Block/National Geographic Creative; 144 © Paula Bronstein/Getty Images; 145 World History Archive/Alamy Stock Photo; 147 (tl) © Photobank gallery/Shutterstock.com; 147 (tr) © Lee Prince/Shutterstock.com; 147 (b) © Stocktrek Images, Inc./Alamy Stock Photo; 148 © Todd Gipstein/National Geographic Creative; 149 © Didou/Shutterstock.com; 150 © Design Pics Inc/National Geographic Creative; 153 (t) © Geoff Hardy/Shutterstock.com; 153 (m) Eye-Stock/Alamy Stock Photo; 153 (b) imageBROKER/Alamy Stock Photo; 154 (t) © DarioZg/Shutterstock.com; 154 (b) Radius Images/Alamy Stock Photo; 155 (left col: t) Eye-Stock/Alamy Stock Photo; 155 (left col: b) imageBROKER/Alamy Stock Photo; 155 (right col: tl) © stocksolutions/Shutterstock.com; 155 (right col: tr) Bon Appetit/Alamy Stock Photo; 155 (right col: ml) © Robyn Mackenzie/Shutterstock.com; 155 (right col: mr) Simon Reddy/Alamy Stock Photo; 155 (right col: bl) © Barbara Dudzinska/Shutterstock.com; 155 (right col: br) © Joe Gough/Shutterstock.com; 156 (t) © fstockfoto/Shutterstock.com; 156 (m) © DarioZg/Shutterstock.com; 156 (b) Radius Images/Alamy Stock Photo; 157 © Reinier Gerritsen.

Illustrations: 6–7 © National Geographic Maps. DATA SOURCES: Shaded relief and bathymetry: GTOPO30, USGS EROS Data Center, 2000. ETOPO1/Amante and Eakins, 2009. Land cover: Natural Earth. naturalearthdata.com. Population Density: LandScan 2012 Global Population Database. Developed by Oak Ridge National Laboratory (ORNL), July 2013. Distributed by East View Geospatial: geospatial.com and East View Information Services: eastview.com/online/landscan. Original copyright year: 2015; 23, 25, 40 (r), 160, 161, 179 Matthew Hams; 32, 33, 96, 104 (5, 8, 10) James Gilleard/Folio Illustration; 40 (l), 141, 143 David Russell; 61, 103, 104 (1), 118 (l) Laszlo Veres/Beehive Illustration; 101, 104, (2, 6), 131 (4, 8) emc design; 118 (r), 146, 154 Bob Lea; 131 (1–3, 5–7) Martin Sanders/Beehive Illustration.

ACKNOWLEDGEMENTS

The *Life* publishing team would like to thank the following teachers and students who provided invaluable and detailed feedback on the first edition:

Armik Adamians, Colombo Americano, Cali; Carlos Alberto Aguirre, Universidad Madero, Puebla; Anabel Aikin, La Escuela Oficial de Idiomas de Coslada, Madrid, Spain; Pamela Alvarez, Colegio Eccleston, Lanús; Manuel Antonio, CEL – Unicamp, São Paolo; Bob Ashcroft, Shonan Koka University; Linda Azzopardi, Clubclass; Éricka Bauchwitz, Universidad Madero, Puebla, Mexico; Paola Biancolini, Università Cattolica del Sacro Cuore, Milan; Lisa Blazevic, Moraine Valley Community College; Laura Bottiglieri, Universidad Nacional de Salta; Richard Brookes, Brookes Talen, Aalsmeer; Alan Broomhead, Approach International Student Center; Maria Cante, Universidad Madero, Puebla; Carmín Castillo, Universidad Madero, Puebla; Ana Laura Chacón, Universidad Madero, Puebla; Somchao Chatnaridom, Suratthani Rajabhat University, Surat Thani; Adrian Cini, British Study Centres, London; Andrew Clarke, Centre of English Studies, Dublin; Mariano Cordoni, Centro Universitario de Idiomas, Buenos Aires; Kevin Coughlan, Westgate Corporation; Monica Cuellar, Universidad La Gran Colombia, Colombia; Jacqui Davis-Bowen, St Giles International; Maria del Vecchio, Nihon University; Nuria Mendoza Dominguez, Universidad Nebrija, Madrid; Robin Duncan, ITC London; Christine Eade, Libera Università Internazionale degli Studi Sociali Guido Carli, Rome; Colegios de Alto Rendimiento, Ministry of Education of Peru; Leopoldo Pinzon Escobar, Universidad Catolica; Joanne Evans, Linguarama, Berlin; Scott Ferry, UC San Diego ELI; Juan David Figueroa, Colombo Americano, Cali; Emmanuel Flores, Universidad del Valle de Puebla; Bridget Flynn, Centro Colombo Americano Medellin; Sally Fryer, University of Sheffield, Sheffield; Antonio David Berbel García, Escuela Oficial de Idiomas de Almería, Spain; Lia Gargioni, Feltrinelli Secondary School, Milan; Roberta Giugni, Galileo Galilei Secondary School, Legnano; Monica Gomez, Universidad Pontificia Bolivariana; Doctor Erwin Gonzales, Centro de Idiomas Universidad Nacional San Agustin, Peru; Ivonne Gonzalez, Universidad de La Sabana; J Gouman, Pieter Zandt Scholengemeenschap, Kampen; Cherryll Harrison, UNINT, Rome; Lottie Harrison, International House Recoleta; Marjo Heij, CSG Prins Maurits, Middelharnis; María del Pilar Hernández, Universidad Madero, Puebla; Luz Stella Hernandez, Universidad de La Sabana, Colombia; Rogelio Herrera, Colombo Americano, Cali; Amy Huang, Language Canada, Taipei; Huang Huei-Jiun, Pu Tai Senior High School; Carol Humme, Moraine Valley Community College; Nelson Jaramillo, Colombo Americano, Cali; Jacek Kaczmarek, Xiehe YouDe High School, Taipei; Thurgadevi Kalay, Kaplan, Singapore; Noreen Kane, Centre of English Studies, Dublin; Billy Kao, Jinwen University of Science and Technology; Shih-Fan Kao, Jinwen University of Science and Technology, Taipei; Youmay Kao, Mackay Junior College of Medicine, Nursing, and Management, Taipei; Fleur Kelder, Vechtstede College, Weesp; Waseem Khan, YBM; Dr Sarinya Khattiya, Chiang Mai University; Lucy Khoo, Kaplan; Karen Koh, Kaplan, Singapore; Susan Langerfeld, Liceo Scientifico Statale Augusto Righi, Rome; Hilary Lawler, Centre of English Studies, Dublin; Jon Leachtenauer, Ritsumeikan University; Eva Lendi, Kantonsschule Zürich Nord, Zürich; Michael Ryan Lesser, Busan University of Foreign Studies; Evon Lo, Jinwen University of Science and Technology; Peter Loftus, Centre of English Studies, Dublin; José Luiz, Inglês com Tecnologia, Cruzeiro; Christopher MacGuire, UC Language Center, Chile; Eric Maher, Centre of English Studies, Dublin; Nick Malewski, ITC London; Claudia Maribell Loo, Universidad Madero, Puebla; Malcolm Marr, ITC London; Graciela Martin, ICANA (Belgrano); Michael McCollister, Feng Chia University; Erik Meek, CS Vincent van Gogh, Assen; Marlene Merkt, Kantonsschule Zürich Nord, Zürich; Jason Montgomery, YBM; David Moran, Qatar University, Doha; Rosella Morini, Feltrinelli Secondary School, Milan; Christopher Mulligan, Ritsumeikan University; Judith Mundell, Quarenghi Adult Learning Centre, Milan; Cinthya Nestor, Universidad Madero, Puebla; Nguyen Dang Lang, Duong Minh Language School; Peter O'Connor, Musashino University, Tokyo; Cliona O'Neill, Trinity School, Rome; María José Colón Orellana, Escola Oficial d'Idiomes de Terrassa, Barcelona; Viviana Ortega, Universidad Mayor, Santiago; Luc Peeters, Kyoto Sangyo University, Kyoto; Sanja Brekalo Pelin, La Escuela Oficial de Idiomas de Coslada, Madrid; Itzel Carolina Pérez, Universidad Madero, Puebla, Mexico; Sutthima Peung, Rajamangala University of Technology Rattanakosin; Marina Pezzuoli, Liceo Scientifico Amedeo Avogadro, Rome; Andrew Pharis, Aichi Gakuin University, Nagoya; Hugh Podmore, St Giles International, UK; Carolina Porras, Universidad de la Sabana; Brigit Portilla, Colombo Americano, Cali; Soudaben Pradeep, Kaplan; Judith Puertas, Colombo Americano, Cali; Takako Ramsden, Kyoto Sangyo University, Kyoto; Sophie Rebel-Dijkstra, Aeres Hogeschool; Zita Reszler, Nottingham Language Academy, Nottingham; Sophia Rizzo, St Giles International; Gloria Stella Quintero Riveros, Universidad Catolica; Cecilia Rosas, Euroidiomas; Eleonora Salas, IICANA Centro, Córdoba; Victoria Samaniego, La Escuela Oficial de Idiomas de Pozuelo de Alarcón, Madrid; Jeanette Sandre, Universidad Madero, Puebla; Bruno Scafati, ARICANA; Anya Shaw, International House Belgrano, Argentina; Anne Smith, UNINT, Rome & University of Rome Tor Vergata, Italy; Courtney Smith, US Ling Institute; Suzannah Spencer-George, British Study Centres, Bournemouth; Students of Cultura Inglesa, São Paulo; Makiko Takeda, Aichi Gakuin University, Nagoya; Jilly Taylor, British Study Centres, London; Caroline S. Tornatore, Austin Community College; Juliana Trisno, Kaplan, Singapore; Ruey Miin Tsao, National Cheng Kung University, Tainan City; Michelle Uitterhoeve, Vechtstede College, Weesp; Anna Maria Usai, Liceo Spallanzani, Rome; Carolina Valdiri, Colombo Americano, Cali, Colombia; Keith Vargo, Westgate Corporation; Gina Vasquez, Colombo Americano, Cali; Andreas Vikran, NET School of English, Milan; Helen Ward, Oxford, UK; Mimi Watts, Università Cattolica del Sacro Cuore, Milan; Yvonne Wee, Kaplan Higher Education Academy; Christopher Wood, Meijo University; Kevin Wu, Hangzhou No.14 High School; Yanina Zagarrio, ARICANA.